Minimalist Syntax

Generative Syntax

General Editor: David Lightfoot

Recent work in generative syntax has viewed the language faculty as a system of principles and parameters, which permit children to acquire productive grammars triggered by normal childhood experiences. The books in this series serve as an introduction to particular aspects or modules of this theory. They presuppose some minimal background in generative syntax, but meet the tutorial needs of intermediate and advanced students. Written by leading figures in the field, the books also contain sufficient fresh material to appeal to the highest level.

Minimalist Syntax

Edited by

Randall Hendrick

Blackwell
Publishing

© 2003 by Blackwell Publishing Ltd

350 Main Street, Malden, MA 02148-5018, USA
108 Cowley Road, Oxford OX4 1JF, UK
550 Swanston Street, Carlton South, Melbourne, Victoria 3053, Australia
Kurfürstendamm 57, 10707 Berlin, Germany

First published 2003 by Blackwell Publishing Ltd

Library of Congress Cataloging-in-Publication Data

Minimalist syntax / edited by Randall Hendrick.
      p. cm. — (Generative syntax ; 7)
   Includes bibliographical references and index.
   ISBN 0-631-21940-4 (hard : alk. paper) — ISBN 0-631-21941-2 (pbk. : alk. paper)
      1. Grammar, Comparative and general—Syntax.   2. Minimalist theory
   (Linguistics).   I. Hendrick, Randall.   II. Series.

   P291 .M54 2003
   415—dc21   2002038483

A catalogue record for this title is available from the British Library.

Set in 10/12pt Palatino
by Graphicraft Ltd, Hong Kong
Printed and bound in the United Kingdom
by MPG Books Ltd, Bodmin, Cornwall

For further information on
Blackwell Publishing, visit our website:
http://www.blackwellpublishing.com

Contents

Acknowledgments

This work was supported in part by NSF grant no. 0112231 and by an award from the Arts and Sciences Foundation of the University of North Carolina at Chapel Hill.

List of Contributors

Robert A. Chametzky, 736 Wheaton Road, Iowa City, IA 52246, USA. Contact email address: ui0049@blue.weeg.uiowa.edu

Danny Fox, Department of Linguistics and Philosophy, E39–245, Massachusetts Institute of Technology, 77 Massachusetts Avenue, Cambridge, MA 02139, USA. Contact email address: fox@mit.edu

Randall Hendrick, Department of Linguistics, University of North Carolina, Chapel Hill, NC 27599-3155, USA. Contact email address: hendrick@unc.edu

Norbert Hornstein, Department of Linguistics, 1401 Marie Mount Hall, University of Maryland, College Park, MD 20742-7505, USA. Contact email address: nh10@umail.umd.edu

Howard Lasnik, Department of Linguistics, 1401 Marie Mount Hall, University of Maryland, College Park, MD 20742-7505, USA. Contact email address: lasnik@wam.umd.edu

Höskuldur Thráinsson, Department of Icelandic, University of Iceland, Arnagardi v. Sudurgoetu, 101 Reykjavik, Iceland. Contact email address: hoski@rhi.hi.is

Introduction

Randall Hendrick

Syntactic theories change over time because they, like all scientific theories, confront the twin selectional pressures of conceptual simplicity and empirical adequacy. These forces shape the historical trajectory of theories, and no theory that we currently know will survive these challenges unchanged. And in this context we should not be surprised that there is not just one theory with such an historical arc. Although the existence of competing theories suggests to some outside observers the presence of confusion in a field of inquiry, competition is in fact useful to practicing researchers for the simple reason that it highlights the selectional pressures that give theories life. It is in this spirit of theoretical evolution that syntacticians should greet the prospect of a minimalist syntax with enthusiasm.

There are admirable histories of modern phonological theory (e.g. Anderson, 1985). But no one has, as yet, produced a similar companion to syntactic theory, perhaps because of the epic proportions such a tale has. If it is ever written, I believe it will depict syntacticians caught in a struggle between the same two titans that have shaped the phonological world: the colossus of rules and the colossus of representations.

In the early 1960s researchers explored with initial confidence the hypothesis that grammars were collections of rules that expressed systematic patterns of a language. Work was done, of course, on how these rules should be formulated (e.g. whether recursion was a property of phrase structure rules), but much more work was done on issues of representations, for example whether the history of application of phrase structure rules should be encoded in a representation (the familiar trees), whether NPs that did not branch were to be "pruned," whether negatives were verbs, whether the level of deep structure existed, and the like. There were interesting questions about rule application, most notably the theory of the transformational cycle, but most of the work done in the extended standard theory and in its wake has been concerned with motivating representations. To see this point one needs only to look at the vast literature on whether the site of a movement carried some representational "trace" of the moved constituent. The conceptual gambit that was replayed in various contexts was to isolate distinct representational systems, say the lexicon and the transformational component, and to place limits on their representations that had some important empirical consequences. Such a strategy is at work in Chomsky's (1965) elimination of generalized transformations and in his (1970) analysis of derived and gerundive nominals. It is also at play in Bresnan's (2001) distinction between lexical functions responsible for relating active and passive verbs in terms of grammatical relations, and other operations that build constituent structures. The Government and Binding Theory of Chomsky (1981) is firmly situated in this representational tradition. It is a theory with a rich inventory of principles that perform a filtering function on highly articulated representations. Only the subjacency principle had a non-representation flavor, and there were strong attempts to recast it in representational terms.

G & B

A completely different strategy of theory construction would be to appeal to rules rather than representations to carry a dominant explanatory burden. Some strands of generative semantics explored this route, notably Postal (1974), but the general strategy encountered resistance based in part on doubts about the cognitive plausibility of such rules. The negative history of the derivational theory of complexity summarized in Tannenhaus (1988) and the more specific appraisal of the transformational rule of passivization in Bresnan (1978) illustrate well the contours of this debate. It remains possible that, while there may be no rules in the sense of Chomsky (1965), where transformations paired structural descriptions and structural changes, properties of derivations produced by very general, universal operations such as Move α might still be the locus of explanation for an important class of syntactic phenomena. It is in this line of research that the Minimalist Program situates itself.

Some of the basic conjectures of Minimalism may already be familiar to the reader. Among them is included the idea that intermediate levels of syntactic representation (such as d-structure or s-structure) are to be eliminated if at all possible for reasons of conceptual parsimony because only levels that interface with other cognitive systems, such as Phonological Form and Logical Form (LF), are necessarily required. Movements are unified with the composition of phrasal structure as one general computational operation (Merge), making it possible to intersperse movements and the insertion of lexical material. Movements apply obligatorily in the presence of a triggering condition, which is hypothesized to be a formal feature that cannot be interpreted at an interface level. Such movements are motivated to remove this uninterpretable feature and are subject to substantive conditions of economy. These conditions have at least the appearance of a least effort quality: they opt wherever possible for covert movements at LF rather than overt movements because LF movements affect single features rather than the complex feature sets that make up phrasal constituents. These and other tenets of Minimalism set out in Chomsky (1995) are neatly catalogued in Epstein and Hornstein (1999). Here it is worth trying to appreciate why such claims come to have the status of theoretical imperatives.

Minimalism is an attempt to rethink many syntactic phenomena in the hopes of extracting greater insight by questioning the explanatory role of representations. One approach to this project is that it is a therapeutic labor with the goal of eliminating unnecessary representational mechanics. On this view, Minimalism insists on a maximally elegant theory with the minimum of theoretical primitives and statements consistent with familiar goals of description and explanation. Thus, Minimalism is motivated by a priori commitments to simplicity, elegance, and theoretical parsimony. This is the corrosive applied to the intermediate levels of d-structure and s-structure. It is possible, though, to embrace Minimalism for substantive reasons. From this perspective it is an attempt to formalize a substantive concept of economy in syntax that will resolve a variety of empirical problems that have proven recalcitrant to previous theorizing in representations. This concept of economy itself is not purely formal but stands in a special relation to the interface with other cognitive (sub)systems such as the sound system and the semantic system, or with some quite general principle of limiting cognitive effort. Every bit of representation is to be cached out by interpretation at the interface of one of these (sub)systems, and some types of operations are identified as entailing greater cognitive effort. From this perspective Minimalism instantiates a kind of functionalism, though it has different commitments and caveats than other styles of functionalism, as has been pointed out in Pesetsky and Torrego (2000).

As he observed the inception of the Minimalist Program, Marantz (1995) announced the death of syntax, echoing Nietzsche's epigram about the deity. From that perspective, the very title of this book is something of an oxymoron. But Marantz's obituary was provocative and, in the eyes of some syntactic theorists, premature (see, for example, Lappin, Levine, and Johnson (2000), and the replies and rejoinders it engendered). Clearly, some syntactic gods struggle on. There are researchers who have advocated the inevitability of rules dependent on constructions, and still others who advocate decomposing syntax into a number of distinct representations. In contrast, as I noted above, the minimalist project limits the autonomy of syntax and places a significant explanatory burden on how syntax facilitates, and perhaps even optimizes, the interpretation of interfacing cognitive systems. It is the severity of this stricture that was the foundation of Marantz's assessment of the eclipse of syntax. Nevertheless, Lasnik (1999, p. 6) has observed that "we are very far from being able to confidently proclaim any Minimalist details of syntactic theory." Such an assessment is sobering, coming as it does from one of the major proponents of Minimalism. This book takes the challenge of Lasnik's cautionary note seriously. It brings together a group of studies that tries to pin down the specific details of a Minimalist explanation for such important syntactic phenomena as control, anaphora, scope of quantification, verb raising, and phrase structure. Its search for a substantive theory of syntactic economy and its re-evaluation of the advantages of derivational explanations lead to new perspectives and, in many cases, specific results which I hope can answer Lasnik's challenge.

This volume collects some reasons to think that a minimized syntax offers more explanatory value for those interested in understanding why natural languages have robust recurrent properties. It does this by contributing to our understanding of the specific effects of the substantive theory of syntactic economy that is at the heart of Minimalism. Throughout, it emphasizes empirical problems that can be given an insightful explanation when the correct substantive theory of syntactic economy is adopted. In Chapter 1, Hornstein takes on the complex and stipulative theory of control outlined by Government and Binding Theory and develops a competing theory that rethinks the phenomenon of obligatory control as another instance of movement. The idea that obligatory control is a species of raising is built on questioning the premise in early minimalist work that there is a fundamental difference between thematic roles and morphological features. Only morphological features such as Case can be the motive for movement, not thematic roles. If Hornstein is right, movement can be equally driven by thematic roles. It is also standardly assumed in minimalist syntax that principles of syntactic economy favor covert movement at the expense of overt movement.

Fox reviews, in Chapter 2, the syntactic treatment of quantified expressions that were raised after s-structure by a covert movement, Quantifier Raising (QR), to derive the level of Logical Form in Government and Binding Theory. He questions whether covert application of QR is needed given the copy theory of movement in a minimalist syntax where one of the copies typically is forced to delete before a structure is interpreted at Phonological Form. Fox makes a fascinating case that Quantifier Raising is an overt movement rather than a covert one as has been traditionally thought. His argument is based on a careful examination of the interaction of QR with the theory of anaphora and gives new importance to extraposition phenomena, which are assimilated to (overt) QR.

The interaction of covert movements and the theory of anaphora is central to Lasnik's and my own Chapter 3. We assemble a range of evidence to conclude that covert movement does not change anaphoric relations. The evidence also suggests that scope in raising constructions is determined by the surface position of a DP while other LF licensing restrictions on anaphora, bound pronouns, idioms, and negative polarity items are free to apply to any member of a movement chain. This means rather surprisingly that, contrary to what has been widely believed, there is no scope ambiguity in raising constructions and that there is a kind of "A reconstruction."

Thráinsson takes on the variation of ordering verbs and adverbs in Western Germanic languages that has been used to motivate verb raising in Chapter 4. Thráinsson argues that verb raising is subject to two economy considerations. First, raising never applies optionally and only applies to eliminate an uninterpretable agreement feature(s). Second, languages are forced to have such a feature(s) if there is overt evidence of an agreement element independent of tense. The four chapters I have just mentioned are principally concerned with minimalism as a substantive claim about syntactic economy.

The facet of minimalism that requires economy of conceptual apparatus predominates in the fifth chapter. There Chametzky applies this conceptual corrosive to the familiar concept of phrase structure. Chametzky deploys several conceptual arguments that lead to the conclusion that Minimalism is incompatible with phrase structure. In the process of exploring clausal organization he identifies adjuncts as potentially forming a limit to minimalist analysis.

References

Anderson, S. (1985). *Phonology in the twentieth century: theories of rules and theories of representations*. Chicago: Chicago University Press.

Bresnan, J. (1978). A realistic transformational grammar. In M. Halle, J. Bresnan, & G. A. Miller (eds.), *Linguistic theory and psychological reality* (pp. 1–59). Cambridge, MA: MIT Press.

Bresnan, J. (2001). *Lexical functional grammar*. Oxford & Malden, MA: Blackwell.

Chomsky, N. (1965). *Aspects of the theory of syntax*. Cambridge, MA: MIT Press.

Chomsky, N. (1970). Remarks on Nominalizations. In R. Jacobs & P. Rosenbaum (eds.), *Readings in English Transformational Grammar* (pp. 184–221). Waltham, MA: Ginn.

Chomsky, N. (1981). *Lectures on government and binding*. Dordrecht: Foris.

Chomsky, N. (1995). *The minimalist program*. Cambridge, MA: MIT Press.

Epstein, S. D., & Hornstein, N. (1999). Introduction. In S. D. Epstein, & N. Hornstein (eds.), *Working minimalism* (pp. ix–xviii). Cambridge, MA: MIT Press.

Lappin, S., Levine, R. D., & Johnson, D. E. (2000). Topic . . . Comment. *Natural language and linguistic theory*, 18, 665–71.

Lasnik, H. (1999). *Minimalist analysis*. Oxford & Malden, MA: Blackwell.

Marantz, A. (1995). The minimalist program. In G. Webelhuth (ed.), *Government and binding theory and the minimalist program: principles and parameters in syntactic theory*. Oxford & Malden, MA: Blackwell.

Pesetsky, D., & Torrego, E. (2000). T to C movement. Causes and consequences. In M. Kenstowicz (ed.), *Ken Hale: a life in language* (pp. 355–426). Cambridge, MA: MIT Press.

Postal, P. (1974). The best theory. In S. Peters (ed.), *Goals of linguistic theory* (pp. 13–70). Englewood Cliffs, NJ: Prentice-Hall.

Tannenhaus, M. (1988). *Psycholinguistics: an overview*. In F. Newmeyer (ed.), *Language: psychological and biological aspects. Linguistics, the Cambridge survey, volume 3* (pp. 1–37). Cambridge: Cambridge University Press.

Chapter one

On Control

Norbert Hornstein

1.1 Introduction

Recently, control has become a hot topic, largely for Minimalist reasons.[1] In particular, the current passion for reexamining the conceptual foundations of Universal Grammar (UG) has prompted grammarians to reconsider whether, and how much, the grammatical processes underlying control configurations differ from the movement operations that lie behind raising constructions. The idea that the grammatical processes responsible for these two types of structures are less different than generally believed is *not* novel.[2] What is different is the conceptual setting afforded by Minimalist commitments, most importantly the premium now placed on "simpler" theories that eschew both theory internal levels (like d-structure) or formatives (like PRO) and multiple ways of establishing grammatical dependencies (by either movement or construal). The venerable dualism between control and raising offers a tempting target for those impressed with the razor sharp Ockhamism of the Minimalist program.

Before reviewing the issues in detail, it is worth pausing to slightly expand on the cursory comments above as they provide some of the methodological motivations for reconsidering the distinction between raising and control. The main motivation comes from two sources.

First, the observation that control brings with it considerable grammatical baggage, for example a whole additional module of the grammar (the Control module whose function it is to determine the controllers of PRO and the interpretation that a particular control structure carries), a theory internal formative – PRO – with its own idiosyncratic distributional requirements (it occurs in the subject positions of non-finite clauses and this prompts otherwise conceptually and empirically problematic technology, for example null case, to track this fact), and a set of grammatical processes (construal rules) *added to the movement processes already assumed to be available*, whose function it is to establish dependencies quite similar to those that movement already affords.

Second, the observation that the whole distinction conceptually rests on assuming properties of UG that are currently considered problematic from an MP perspective. Two such problematic conditions are d-structure and that part of the theta criterion that stipulates that theta roles and chains be biuniquely related (viz. be in a one to one relation). Both properties are methodologically suspect given minimalist commitments. Given Chomsky's (1993) objections to postulating levels like d-structure, it is natural to see if it is possible to eliminate d-structure and its various requirements entirely from the grammar. Moreover, from a purely conceptual point of view it is quite unclear why chains should be barred from bearing more than one theta role. Eliminating both d-structure and the biuniqueness condition on theta roles has obvious conceptual attractions. Interestingly, neither assumption fits comfortably with the assumption that control, like raising, is derived via movement. Thus rethinking the relation between movement and control immediately bears on these methodological issues and thereby on questions of optimal grammatical design.

This chapter reviews some of the recent hubbub surrounding these issues. Before proceeding, however, one last caveat is in order. Like all reviews, this one will suffer from the limited knowledge, perspective, interests and prejudices of the reviewer. The route taken here is but one of many. I hope that the trip proves interesting. However, I am sure that it is not the only worthwhile itinerary, nor the least contentious. Caveat lector!

1.2   Raising versus control

From the earliest work in Generative Grammar, Raising (1a) has been contrasted with Control (1b).

(1)a.   John seems/appears/is likely to like Mary
   b.   John tried/hoped/expected to like Mary

The contrast has been drawn along several dimensions.

First, there are various empirical differences between the two kinds of constructions despite the obvious surface similarity. These include the following.

In (1a) John is understood as discharging a single thematic function. He is the *liker of Mary*. This is coded by assigning a single theta role to *John*, that of the external argument of the embedded verb *like*. In contrast to this, John in (1b) is perceived as bearing two roles. He is at once Mary's *liker* and also a *trier/hoper/expector*. More, theoretically, *John* is related to a pair of thematic positions, the external argument of the matrix predicate and that of the embedded one.

This difference in the thematic properties of raising versus control brings with it a host of others. Two are noteworthy.

First, the subject position of raising predicates can be filled with expletives and idioms (all the while retaining the idiomatic interpretation) while those of control predicates cannot be.

(2)a.   There seemed/appeared/was likely to be a man here
   b.   *There tried/hoped/expected to be a man here

(3)a.   The fat seemed/appeared/was likely to be in the fire
   b.   *The fat tried/hoped/expected to be in the fire

Second, passivizing the embedded clause in raising constructions leaves the original meaning of the sentence largely intact. (4a,b) illustrate this property of "voice transparency"; the two sentences being virtual paraphrases of one another.

(4)a.   The doctor seemed to examine Mary
   b.   Mary seemed to be examined by the doctor

This contrasts sharply with what happens if we passivize in a control structure. (5a,b) are not voice transparent, not being even remote paraphrases.

(5)a.   The doctor tried to examine Mary
   b.   Mary tried to be examined by the doctor

These two facts can be directly tied to the thematic differences between raising and control verbs. One can explain the contrast between (2) and (3) by observing that expletives like *there* and idioms cannot bear theta roles. However, this is what they must do in examples like (2b) and (3b), on the further assumption that all theta roles of a predicate must be assigned. The trouble with (2b) and (3b) is that the theta roles that must be assigned cannot be assigned to any appropriate element given the resistance it is natural to assume that expletives and idioms have to bearing such roles. In (2a) and (3a) there is only one theta role to assign and as such no similar problem arises.

Analogous considerations account for (4) and (5). In control structures like those in (1b), the matrix subject fulfills two thematic requirements; that of the matrix verb and that of the embedded one. Thus, in (5a) the doctor is both *trier* and *examiner*, while Mary is merely the *examinee*. However, by passivizing the embedded clause, Mary becomes the matrix subject and thereby assumes two thematic functions, *trier* and *examinee*, while the doctor has just one thematic role, the *examiner*. This accounts for the clear difference in meaning between (5a,b). In contrast, the subject position of raising predicates is not associated with any thematic role. Consequently, similar manipulation of the embedded clause in (4) has no thematic repercussions. The thematic status of the doctor in both (4a,b) is that of *examiner* and that of Mary is that of *examinee*. As the thematic properties of the two constructions are undisturbed, the sentences remain essentially paraphrases.

These empirical differences between raising and control structures have generally been traced to an underlying difference in grammatical etiology. Specifically, the operations underlying raising configurations are distinct from those that generate control structures. The former are the province of movement rules. In contrast, control structures are either formed by applications of the non-movement rule Equi NP deletion (in the Standard Theory) or, in more recent Government Binding (GB) analyses, control is the result of construal rules that relate a phonetically null DP, "PRO," to its antecedent. Structurally, then, raising structures differ from control configurations as in (6).

(6)a.   John$_1$ seems [t$_1$ to like Mary]
   b.   John$_1$ seems [PRO$_1$ to like Mary]

(6a) indicates that *John* has moved from the embedded subject position, leaving a co-indexed trace in its movement site. In (6b) *John* controls a base generated null expression *PRO*. The indicated indexations, therefore, arise from two different processes: movement for raising and construal for control. Similarly, the empty categories arise from two different processes: movement in the case of raising and lexical insertion in the case of control. The empirical differences noted above trace back to these different derivational histories that invoke different types of grammatical operations and employ different formatives.

It is worth considering the details. Specifically: what forces movement in (6a) and requires construal in (6b)? The answer, in a GB (and also an *Aspects*) style theory, is d-structure. The theoretical basis within GB for distinguishing the two constructions relies on contrasting traces and PROs: PROs head chains, traces do not; d-structure implements this difference. In fact, the classical distinction between raising and control follows seamlessly from the assumption that d-structure exists. Consider the reasoning.

D-structure has two distinctive properties: it is input to the transformational component and the locus of all thematic discharge; a representation of "pure GF-θ."[3] Thus, prior to "displacement" operations (i.e. transformations) that rearrange phrase markers, words/morphemes are assembled into d-structure phrase markers by being lexically inserted into the available theta-positions. After lexical insertion, transformations apply to map d-structure phrase markers into others.

Given the requirements of d-structure, transformations cannot relate theta-positions (via movement) as all theta-positions have been filled by lexical insertion in forming the d-structure phrase marker. In particular, d-structure prohibits the movement in (7) from the embedded subject to the matrix subject position as the matrix subject is a theta position and so must be filled at d-structure. Consequently, it is unavailable for occupancy via movement.

(7)   John$_1$ tried [t$_1$ to like Mary]

In this way, d-structure thematic requirements make movement between θ-positions impossible and thus prohibit control relations (which involve multiple theta-roles) from being the observed manifestations of movement operations.

Furthermore, if d-structure has *only* θ-positions filled (in addition to all such positions being filled), then raising structures must be products of movement. In particular, a structure like (8), a non-movement version of a raising construction, is ill-formed at d-structure given that the matrix non-theta subject position is filled by *John*. Given d-structure thematic requirements, this position must be vacant at d-structure, that is it cannot be filled by lexical insertion. The only remaining option is to fill it at some later phase of the derivation, that is by movement.

(8)   John$_1$ seemed [PRO$_1$ to like Mary]

In sum, the classical vision of d-structure as the representation of pure GF-θ, that is the phrase marker where all and only thematic information is grammatically rendered, theoretically forces the empirical distinction between raising and control. Raising is required where d-structure thematic conditions prohibit the insertion of lexical material (e.g. the subject position of a raising verb as in (6a)) while it is prohibited where d-structure thematic conditions require the presence of lexical insertion (e.g. the subject positions of the control complement and matrix subjects in (6b)).

The Theta-Criterion further buttresses this view of d-structure, in particular the idea that all thematic information is discharged via lexical insertion. The relevant feature of the Theta-Criterion is the requirement that there be a biunique relation between θ-roles and chains, in particular, that every chain bear *at most* one θ-role. This effectively prohibits all movement from one θ-position to another. But if movement into θ-positions is forbidden, yet all θ-roles must be discharged, then the only alternative is to fill each θ-position via lexical insertion. The step from the Theta-Criterion to the postulation of PRO and construal rules that relate PROs to their antecedents is a short one.[4]

In sum, given the canonical view about d-structure and the Theta-Criterion, we theoretically derive the fact that raising is due to movement while control is due to construal. From this, the observed empirical differences follow. It's a nice story and it has had a lot of staying power. Nonetheless, there are problems given minimalist scruples. Here are three.

First, it requires the postulation of a theory internal formative PRO. PRO is similar to, but different from a trace. In a GB style theory, at LF, both traces and PROs are categories without phonetic contents. They are of the form "$[_{NP} e]_1$." PROs have the same structure at LF. However, whereas traces are the residues of movement, PROs are lexical expressions which receive their indices not in the course of the overt derivation but at LF via construal operations. That a lexical item (PRO) and a grammatical formative (trace) should be essentially identical at LF is quite unexpected. Indeed, identity of structure suggests that either both are lexical items or both are grammatical formatives.

Within a minimalist setting, things get worse. Nunes (1995) and Chomsky (1998) have noted that traces are theory internal constructs which are best avoided on conceptual grounds if possible. In place of traces, copies have been pressed into service.[5] This leaves the proposed structure of (6a) as (9).

(9)   John seemed [John to like Mary]

However, (9) now raises a question for PRO. What is its structure? What kind of *lexical* item do we have here? It cannot simply be a null pronoun, as in many environments, for example (6b), it requires an antecedent. It might simply be a null reflexive, but if so why *must* it be phonetically null? Recall that minimalism resists the postulation of theory internal entities. Thus, the more the features of PRO are idiosyncratic (i.e. the more PRO is distinguished from more run of the mill lexical items) the less explanatory weight PRO has in a minimalist setting. Humdrum is best. However, within GB, PRO is hardly run of the mill given that it brings in its train a whole module of grammar, the Control module, whose job it is to find its antecedent and provide an interpretation depending on its grammatical setting. We shall see that PRO continues to enjoy a special status in some recent reanalyses.

A second worry arises from the fact that control requires construal rules. Recall that Minimalism places a premium on simple theories. In the present context, it favors theories of UG that minimize rule types. A theory that has *both* movement rules and construal rules has two ways of establishing inter-nominal dependencies in the grammar. Ockham dictates that a theory with just one set of operations is preferred. On the assumption that movement is independently required (e.g. for feature checking), this suggests that construal processes should be eliminated, including those that underlie control.[6]

A third problem with the standard GB approach to control lies with its reliance on d-structure. As outlined above, the distinction between raising and control relies on the thematic requirements d-structure places on derivations. However, d-structure is a theory internal level (see Chomsky, 1993) and should be avoided if possible. If DS-centered accounts of control are suspect given standard minimalist assumptions then this casts doubt on GB approaches to control given their reliance on d-structure requirements for their explanatory punch.

There are other more technical problems with the GB approach to control, some of which we review below. However, even this brief discussion hope-fully indicates that control theory as earlier conceived fits ill with the main methodological emphases of the Minimalist Program. The question is how radical a departure from traditional approaches is warranted empirically and is desirable theoretically. Various answers to this question have been offered and we review some below.

In sum, from a minimalist perspective, the standard approach to control presents various difficulties and motivates a search for alternatives to the stand-ard GB accounts. In what follows, I will assume that these problems are suffi-cient reason to re-examine control phenomena.

1.3   Some basic properties of control

The theory of control must address two issues: (i) where PRO appears, and (ii) how it is interpreted. Let us consider these in turn.

1.3.1   *The distribution of PRO*

PRO most conspicuously appears in the subject position of non-finite clauses. (10a–e) are thus fully acceptable, while (10f–i) are not.

(10)a.   John tried/hoped PRO to eat a bagel
    b.   John tried/preferred PRO eating a bagel

c.   John thinks that [PRO eating/to eat a bagel] would be fun
d.   John saw Mary before PRO leaving the party
e.   John told Mary where PRO to eat a bagel
f.   *John hoped that PRO eat a bagel
g.   *John preferred for Bill to meet PRO
h.   *John hated Bill meeting PRO
i.   *John talked to PRO

What unifies the first four cases is that PRO sits in the subject position of a non-finite clause, in contrast to the four examples that follow.

It is reasonable to assume that in (10f–i) PRO is governed by various lexical heads. In (10f) it is the finite morpheme in Infl, in (10g,h) the verb *meet* and in (10i) the preposition *to*. If one further assumes that non-finite clauses do not contain lexical heads (at least of the relevant sort), then the presence of PRO in (10a–e) correlates with the absence of (head) government of these Spec IP positions.[7] Thus, the distribution of PRO conforms to the descriptive generalization (11).

(11)   PRO can only appear in ungoverned positions

Note that (11) does not prohibit generating PRO in a governed position. This is fortunate as PRO can be base generated in object position so long as it moves to an ungoverned position by s-structure (SS). (11) is a generalization that holds at s-structure or later.

(12) $John_1$ tried [PRO_1 to be recognized t_1]

As is well known, there were several attempts within GB to reduce (11) to more basic principles. This is not the place to review these efforts.[8] Suffice it to say, that these analyses do not currently enjoy much support. In section 1.4, we review two kinds of minimalist approaches to the distribution of PRO.

1.3.2   The interpretation of PRO

Control structures come in two varieties: local and long distance.

(13)a.   John hopes [PRO to eat a bagel]
   b.   John hopes that [[PRO eating a bagel] will be fun]

In the earliest treatments, two distinct rules were involved in the derivations of (13a,b). Equi NP deletion applied to yield (13a) while Super Equi was involved in the derivation of (13b). Equi interacted closely with the Principle of Minimal Distance in determining the antecedent of PRO in (13a) while this principle did not regulate applications of Super Equi.[9] GB has honored essentially this same analysis by endorsing a distinction between structures of Obligatory versus Non-obligatory control (OC vs. NOC).[10]

OC and NOC differ in several important ways. Consider the following paradigm illustrating the interpretive properties of obligatory control structures.[11]

(14)a. *It was expected PRO to shave himself
   b. *John thinks that it was expected PRO to shave himself
   c. *John's campaign expects PRO to shave himself
   d. John expects PRO to win and Bill does too (= Bill win)
   e. *John$_i$ told Mary$_j$ PRO$_{i+j}$ to leave together/each other
   f. The unfortunate expects PRO to get a medal
   g. Only Churchill remembers PRO giving the BST speech

(14a) shows that an obligatory control PRO requires an antecedent. (14b) indicates that this antecedent must be local and (14c) indicates that it must c-command the PRO.[12] (14d) shows that this PRO cannot have split antecedents.[13] PRO in (14f) only has the "de se" interpretation in that the unfortunate believes *of himself* that he will be a medal recipient. (14g) has the paraphrase (15a), not (15b). On this reading only Churchill could have this memory for Churchill was the sole person to give the speech. The two different readings follow on the assumption that obligatory control PRO must have a c-commanding antecedent. This requires "only Churchill" to be the binder. The unavailable reading has "Churchill" as the antecedent. This is possible in (15b) where the pronoun can have a non-c-commanding antecedent.

(15)a. Only Churchill remembers himself giving the BST speech
   b. Only Churchill remembers that he gave the BST speech

PRO in non-obligatory control environments contrasts in every respect with the obligatory control cases.

(16)a. It was believed that PRO shaving was important
   b. John$_i$ thinks that it is believed that PRO$_i$ shaving himself is important
   c. Clinton's$_i$ campaign believes that PRO$_i$ keeping his sex life under control is necessary for electoral success
   d. John thinks that PRO getting his résumé in order is crucial and Bill does too
   e. John$_1$ told Mary$_2$ that PRO$_{1+2}$ leaving together/each other was important to Bill
   f. The unfortunate believes that PRO getting a medal would be boring
   g. Only Churchill remembers that PRO giving the BST speech was momentous

(16a) indicates that non-obligatory control PRO does not require an antecedent. (16b) demonstrates that if it does have an antecedent it need not be local. (16c) shows that the antecedent need not c-command this PRO. (16d) contrasts with (14d) in permitting a strict reading of the elided VP, that is the reading in which it is John's resume which is at issue. (16e) can support split antecedents,

(16f) can have a non "de se" interpretation and (16f) is consistent with many people other than Churchill recalling that the BST speech was a big deal. Note that each non-obligatory control reading contrasts with those available in the obligatory control examples in (14). The cases in (14) and (16) contrast in one further interesting way; the former can be paraphrased with PRO replaced by a reflexive while the interpretive doubles of (16) replace PRO with pronouns. (17) illustrates this with the counterparts of (14c) and (16c).

(17)a.   *John's$_i$ campaign expects himself$_i$ to shave himself
     b.   Clinton's$_i$ campaign believes that his$_i$ keeping his sex life under control is crucial for electoral success

In short, the differences in obligatory and non-obligatory control structures duplicate, where applicable, what one finds with locally bound anaphors versus pronouns. This makes sense if PRO is actually ambiguous – an anaphoric expression in obligatory control configurations and pronominal in NOC structures. The question facing the theoretician is to explain, first, why PRO should display these two sets of properties and why we find the OC properties in "Equi" configurations while we find the NOC cluster in "Super Equi" structures. In other words, why do the properties cluster as they do and why do they distribute as they do.

1.4   Two approaches to the distribution of PRO

1.4.1   *Null case*

Chomsky and Lasnik (1993) argue that the standard GB analysis of control in terms of government (see (11) above) cannot be reconciled with the last resort motivation for movement within Minimalism.[14] The empirical difficulty is illustrated in (18).

(18)a.   We never [PRO$_1$ expected to be found t$_1$]
     b.   *We never expected [PRO$_1$ to appear to t$_1$ [that Bill left]]

If movement is last resort and PRO must be ungoverned then the threat of being governed should suffice to license PRO's movement in (18a). But if it suffices in (18a) why is it insufficient in (18b)? Chomsky and Lasnik argue that the two cases fall together if we assume that PRO has a case that must be checked.[15] To get this to work technically, they assume that PRO has its own (idiosyncratic) case, dubbed "null case," that can only be checked by the T^0 of non-finite control clauses. PRO (and PRO alone) can and must check null case. Given these assumptions, (18b) violates greed in that PRO moves from one case position to another thereby violating last resort.

This same set of assumptions suffices to account for the facts in (10) repeated here.

(10)a.   John tried/hoped PRO to eat a bagel
    b.   John tried/preferred PRO eating a bagel
    c.   John thinks that [PRO eating/to eat a bagel] would be fun
    d.   John saw Mary before PRO leaving the party
    e.   John told Mary where PRO to eat a bagel
    f.   *John hoped that PRO eat a bagel
    g.   *John preferred for Bill to meet PRO
    h.   *John hated Bill meeting PRO
    i.   *John talked to PRO

In (10a–e), it is assumed that PRO is in the Spec of a T^0 able to check null case. Hence their acceptability. In contrast to this, PRO is in a nominative case position in (10f), and accusative position in (10g–i). These are not positions in which null case can be checked and so the structures underlying these sentences are ungrammatical.

The most fully worked out version of this null case approach to obligatory control is Martin (1996).[16] Following Stowell (1982), he argues that control infinitives differ from raising infinitives in that the former have tensed Infls. In effect, Martin provides motivation for the assumption that some infinitives can check case by assimilating them to the class of clauses that uncontroversially do so: finite clauses. Both finite IPs and control infinitives are +Tense and so it is not surprising that their respective Spec IPs are case positions. Given the further assumption that only PRO bears null case, only it can appear in the Spec IP position of tensed infinitives.

As mentioned, Martin follows Stowell in observing that some embedded clauses appear to have tense specifications. Stowell distinguishes between control clauses and raising clauses in that the latter always share the tense specifications of the clause they are embedded under while the former do not. The examples in (19) illustrate the point.

(19)a.   John decided/remembered [PRO to go to the party]
    b.   John believed [Mary to be the best player]

In (19a) the embedded event of going to the party takes place in the future with respect to John's decision (or recollection). In contrast, in (19b) Mary being the best player temporally coincides with John's belief. Stowell (1982) accounts for this by assuming that the embedded clause in (19a) has a T^0 specified for tense and so the embedded event can be temporally located independently of the main clause event. In contrast, the embedded T^0 of raising clauses is not specified for tense and so its temporal specification cannot be independent of the one in the main clause. Martin assumes that it is the presence of a temporal operator in control clauses that allows them to check (null) case.[17]

Martin (1996) provides further interesting evidence for the assumption that null case is a property of +tensed non-finite clauses. Here is one more bit. Martin claims that event denoting predicates cannot occur under raising predicates.[18]

(20)a.   *Everyone believed Rebecca to win the game right then
   b.   *The defendant seemed to the DA to conspire against the govern-
        ment at that exact time

Following Enç (1990), Martin assumes that event denoting predicates contain event-variables which must be bound by "tense or some other (temporal)
operator in order to denote an individuated event" (Martin, 1996, p. 59). Without such an operator only a stative predicate is possible. The absence of a
tensed T^0 in raising predicates accounts for the oddity of the examples in (20).
   With this in hand, Martin (following Boskovic, 1997) observes the following
contrast between Romance *croire* and its English counterpart *believe*. The latter
is a raising predicate with the exceptionally case marked subject of the embedded clause residing in its Spec VP.[19] For example, (21a) has the structure (21b).

(21)a.   John believes Mary to be tall
   b.   John$_1$ [$_{VP}$ Mary$_2$ [$_{VP}$ t$_1$ v [believes [t$_2$ to be tall]]]]

The former, however, shows the characteristics of a control predicate, as the
following French example indicates.

(22)   Je crois [PRO avoir   fait   une erreur]
       I believe   to have made a   mistake

Interestingly, in Romance, the restriction to statives/habituals noted on embedded clausal complements of *believe* does not hold for *croire*. Contrast (23a)
and (23b), its English counterpart.

(23)a.   Jean croit   rêver
         John believes to dream
   b.   John believes himself to dream

(23a) has the interpretation *John believes himself to be dreaming*. Note that this
reading is unavailable for (23b). (23b) is unacceptable in English because *believe*
is an ECM verb and so cannot take a control complement. What the data here
appear to indicate are two things: first, that in French *croire* is not an ECM verb
but a control verb and second, that when it is a control verb it allows eventive
predicates. Martin concludes from this that control infinitives have tensed T^0s
and that raising predicates do not.
   One last interesting bit of corroborating evidence for this comes from a
further observation. Boskovic observes the following interesting fact. There
are cases of apparent ECM – like uses of *croire*, as in (24).[20]

(24)   Qui$_1$ Ana croyait-elle [t$_1$ plaire à Pierre]
       "Who did Ana believe to please Pierre"

In these cases, moreover, the eventive reading noted in (23) is unavailable.
Only a habitual interpretation is available.

(25) *Qui crois-tu rêver
"Who do you believe to be dreaming"

In sum, Martin provides interesting evidence that null case correlates with the presence of temporally active T⁰s. In effect, he argues that null case can be checked by a T^0 if and only if the T^0 is +tense and −finite. If one further assumes that PRO can *only* bear null case, then a full account for the distribution of PRO follows.

1.4.2   Some problems for null case

Before discussing other approaches to the distribution of PRO, let me voice some skepticism regarding the proposed correlation between tense/eventive properties and the nature of T^0 in raising and control structures. Consider first the claim regarding eventive predicates under raising versus control verbs.

The noted unacceptability of eventive predicates under raising verbs is most pronounced for the ECM predicate *believe* (see (20a)). There are perfectly acceptable raising constructions with embedded eventive predicates. So contrast the examples in (26) with (27).

(26)a.   Rebecca seemed to win the game right then
   b.   John appeared to take the wrong medicine
   c.   John is likely/certain/sure to eat a bagel

(27)a.   *John believed Rebecca to win the game right then
   b.   * John showed Bill to take the wrong medicine
   c.   * John believed Bill to eat a bagel

This contrast suggests that the tense property of relevance relates to ECM verbs, rather than to raising predicates in general. But if so, then the conclusions Martin draws are too broad. The distinction of theoretical interest is raising versus control complements. Given this broad contrast, the cases in (26) and (27) should be entirely parallel.

Note, incidentally, that (26c) above has one other curious property. The complement clause is most naturally interpreted as in the future with respect to the tense of the matrix. Thus, it means, more or less, that it is *currently* likely/certain/sure that John *will* eat a bagel. This temporal ordering is unexpected given Stowell's claim that raising predicates do not contain independent tense specification.

Martin (1996, pp. 80–105) observes similar facts and concludes from this that such cases involve control rather than raising. In fact, if one uses these temporal diagnostics, it appears that all the standard (non-ECM) raising predicates are actually ambiguous, with both a raising and a control structure. This assumption runs into problems. Consider how.

Assume that whenever one sees an eventive embedded predicate then the clause has a control structure. The sentences in (28) have embedded eventive predicates.

(28)a.   The shit appeared to hit the fan then
   b.   It seemed to start to rain exactly then
   c.   ?There appeared to enter several men at that very moment

(28a) means, roughly, *it appeared that pandemonium erupted then*. The presence of the punctual adverb reinforces this point. Given this, by assumption these sentences all have control structures, with the matrix subject controlling an embedded PRO. The problem is that were this so, we would expect idioms and expletives to be barred from the subject matrix position. (28) indicates that this is incorrect.

Observe that we also would expect to find no voice transparency in raising constructions where the embedded predicate had an eventive interpretation. This also appears to be incorrect.

(29)a.   The doctor seemed to then examine Mary
   b.   Mary seemed to then be examined by the doctor

In both (29a,b) the embedded clause is interpreted eventively. Nonetheless, voice transparency seems to hold. Recall that the absence of voice transparency and the limited distribution of expletives and idioms are the classical hallmarks of control. The absence of these thematic diagnostics in (28) and (29) suggests that they are standard raising, not control, constructions. If so, it can be argued that tense diagnostics do not correlate well with the standard thematic diagnostics that distinguish raising from control and this, in turn, argues against seeing some T^0s as assigners of null case.[21]

The data that Martin provides (following Boskovic, 1997) is also restricted to a contrast between ECM predicates in Romance and English. It does not contrast non-ECM raising predicates (such as *seem*) with control predicates. This is noteworthy for it is the latter contrast that is of obvious theoretical interest, not the former.

It is unclear what makes ECM predicates exceptionally able to assign case. However, it would not be remarkable if ECM verbs imposed semantic restrictions on their complements, selecting, for example, non-eventive clausal complements. Were this the case, then one would expect the correlations noted by Boskovic *even in the absence of case assignment in the embedded clause in control complements*. In other words, if Boskovic's observations pertain exclusively to ECM verbs then their peculiarities tell us nothing about the thematic contrasts between control and raising verbs. It is only if the properties that Boskovic noted are properties of raising predicates in general that his observations suggest that control predicates are null case markers.

A few last points. There are ECM verbs that do not display the diagnostics noted in the text. For example, *expect* takes eventive predicates and requires a temporal specification of the embedded event later than the matrix.

(30)   John expected Mary to leave the party

This implies that in such a case the embedded clause has a +tense T^0. This then further implies either that (i) the structure of (30) is similar to what one finds with a *persuade* verb or (ii) that *Mary* is case marked by some element in C^0 as is the case, arguably, for *want*.

There are problems for assumption (ii). Were this so, we would expect passivization to be blocked and *for* to appear overtly (in some configurations) parallel to what we witness with *want*. Both expectations are unrealized.

(31)a. *John was wanted to leave
 b. John was expected to leave
 c. John wants very much for Bill to leave
 d. *John expects strongly for Bill to leave

This leaves the (i)-option that what we have is a *persuade*-like configuration. However, this suggestion also has its problems. Recall the standard thematic differences between *persuade* and *expect* verbs. These are not suspended when we find the embedded clause with an eventive/future interpretation. For example, we find idioms and expletives with eventive/future readings (32a,b) and we find voice transparency (32c,d) are paraphrases.

(32)a. John expected the shit to hit the fan at exactly 6
 b. John expected there to erupt a riot
 c. John expected the doctor to examine Mary then
 d. John expected Mary to be examined by the doctor then

This is unexpected if these are control structures.

Finally, consider one last set of empirical difficulties.[22] Stowell (1982) observes that gerunds, in contrast to infinitives, vary their tense specifications according to the properties of the matrix verb.

(33)a. Jenny remembered [PRO bringing the wine] (Stowell, 1982, (8b))
  (J remembered a past event of bringing the wine)

 b. Jim (yesterday) counted on [PRO watching a new movie (tonight)]
  (J counted on a future event of movie watching)

In light of this, Stowell (1982) proposed that gerunds are generally marked −tense.

If correct, this constitutes a problem for the view that only +tense T^0s can assign null case and thereby license PRO given the presence of PRO in (33a,b).[23]

In fact, other gerunds provide potentially more serious problems. Pires (2001) identifies a class of TP defective gerunds which with respect to their tense properties are very similar to ECM infinitives in that their time interval must coincide with the event time of the matrix.

(34) *Bill last night avoided [PRO driving on the freeway this morning]

In such cases the argument against postulating a +tensed T^0 on Stowell-like grounds is stronger still.

I have briefly reviewed some problems for the null case theory as proposed by Chomsky and Lasnik (1993) and most fully elaborated and developed in Martin (1996). Before moving on to consider another approach to the distribution of PRO (one that I personally prefer, I must confess), it is worth recalling the virtues of the null case account. It directly addresses one of the main characteristics of control phenomena; namely that it is *subjects* that are controlled. Once one gives up government as a core concept of grammar (and with it the generalization (11) that PRO only occurs in ungoverned positions) it becomes a challenge to identify the subject position of non-finite clauses in any sort of unified principled manner. Chomsky and Lasnik (1993) provide one way of doing this: via a case marking property unique to non-finite clauses. Martin's (1996) suggestion that null case is a property of some +tense T^0s is a reasonable attempt to provide a principled foundation for this idea and thereby account for the limited distribution of PRO.

1.4.3   (OC) PROs as traces

Consider now a second approach to the distribution of PRO.[24] It starts from one observation and one methodological qualm. The observation is that control, like raising, affects subjects of non-finite clauses. The qualm is that the theory of null case is stipulative and, hence, methodologically suspect. In fact, null case singles out PRO for special treatment in two distinct ways. First, it is the *only* lexical item able to check it or bear it. No other DP can bear null case, not even phonetically null expressions like WH-traces.[25]

(35)a.   John asked Bill *Mary/PRO to eat a bagel
    b.   *The man$_1$ (who) John asked Bill t_1 to eat a bagel

(35a) with *Mary* as the embedded subject is ungrammatical as *Mary* cannot check nor carry null case. PRO is fine in this position because it can. Note that (35b) is also unacceptable, presumably because t_1 cannot check/carry null case either. Thus, the only phonetically non-overt element able to bear null case is PRO.

Second, to my knowledge, it is the *only* lexical item whose case properties are grammatically specified. There are no other DPs, to my knowledge, that can bear but a single case.

Null case does not pattern with other structural cases in other ways. For example, it contrasts with WH-traces in not blocking *wanna* contraction. (36a) cannot be contracted as in (36c) while contraction for (36b) as in (36d) is fine.[26]

(36)a.   Who$_1$ do you t_1 want to visit Mary
    b.   I$_1$ want PRO$_1$ to visit Mary
    c.   *Who do you wanna visit Mary
    d.   I wanna visit Mary

It thus seems that an accusative case marked non-phonetic WH-trace suffices to block sandhi effects like *wanna* contraction while a null case marked non-phonetic PRO does not.

In sum, whatever the other virtues null case may have, its peculiar characteristics are evident. With this as prologomena, consider a movement based approach to control.[27]

The core of such a theory is that OC PRO is identical to an NP-trace. It is the residue of overt A-movement. Thus, the overt structure of (37a) is (37b).[28]

(37)a.   John tried to win
   b. $[_{TP}$ John [past $[_{VP}$ (John) $[_{VP}$ try [(John) to [(John) win]]]]]]

Note that this is entirely analogous to what one finds in raising constructions with one caveat. In a raising construction, movement is from the embedded clause to a matrix non-theta position while in control structures, movement is via a matrix theta position. Note the trace in the spec of the matrix VP in (37b).

This proposal accounts for the distribution of PRO as follows. Assume that the subject positions of all non-finite clauses are not case marking positions (clearly the null hypothesis given the unacceptability of cases like (38a)). Then A-movement from this position is permitted. Further, as A-movement from case positions is prohibited (see 38b) and if (OC) PRO is the residue of A-movement, then we should never find PROs in case positions (see (10f–i), repeated here).

(38)a.   *John hopes [Frank to leave]
   b.   *John seems [t is nice]

(10)a.   John tried/hoped PRO to eat a bagel
   b.   John tried/preferred PRO eating a bagel
   c.   John thinks that [PRO eating/to eat a bagel] would be fun
   d.   John saw Mary before PRO leaving the party
   e.   John told Mary where PRO to eat a bagel
   f.   *John hoped that PRO eat a bagel
   g.   *John preferred for Bill to meet PRO
   h.   *John hated Bill meeting PRO
   i.   *John talked to PRO

(10f–i) are underivable as they all involve movement from a case position. (10a–e) are all acceptable as each involves movement from a non-finite clause via a matrix theta position ending in a matrix case position. If we assume that non-finite clauses do *not* assign case to their subjects, then movement from the embedded IP to the matrix IP will not be prohibited by last resort (i.e. Greed) as it is in (10f–i).

In addition, note that the null phonetic value of PRO (here just an NP-t) correlates with the fact that traces of A-movement are all phonetically null.[29] In other words, whatever it is that renders copies due to A-movement phonetically null will extend to explain the null status of PRO. We need invoke no special null case properties and need invoke no special lexical item that is only able to carry such a case. This grouping of PRO with NP-t also accounts for why both behave similarly in *wanna* contraction contexts.

(39)a. I seemta (seem+to) eat bagels every morning
   b. I wanna (want+to) eat bagels every morning

Thus, the fact that (OC) PRO is typically a subject of non-finite clauses, follows from the basic premise that it is the residue of overt A-movement. This is merely a descriptive generalization. The proposal here is that control, like raising, is due to movement motivated by case concerns. It is not necessarily restricted to non-finite subject positions. If some non-subject position is not a case position, it can also be occupied by PRO. Lasnik (1995a,b), following a proposal by Munn, suggests that examples like (i) involve control.

(i)   John washed/shaved/dressed

Note that these do have the expected properties of control verbs. Thus, for example, *John* is related to two theta-roles in the case of these reflexive predicates. If one assumes that such verbs need not assign case to their objects, then one can treat these as cases of A-movement (and so, control). Note that were this a case of control, it would argue against the null case theory as here we would have a PRO unrelated to a T^0.

One other point. Were this a case of control, then we would need to explain why it is that sentences like (ii) are unacceptable.

(ii)   John$_1$ hoped Bill washed PRO$_1$

This movement would not be blocked by case as the object position of *wash* need not be case marked. However, minimality (shortest Move) would be violated by moving over the intervening DP *Bill*. (40) lists the assumptions required to permit the sort of movement advocated here.

(40)a. Theta roles are features
   b. There is no upper bound on the number of theta features that a DP can have
   c. Movement is Greedy
   d. Greed is understood as "enlightened self interest"

Of these four assumptions, (40a,b) are the most contentious. They amount to rejection of the two basic ideas behind the standard theory of control: (i) that DS (or any analog) regulates the possibilities of movement and (ii) that there is any requirement limiting DPs to at most one theta-role. Both assumptions seem natural enough in a minimalist setting. Consider why.

Chomsky (1993) argues that grammar internal (non-interface) levels have no place in an optimal theory of grammar. DS, he observes, is such a level. As such, it is methodologically suspect and should be eliminated. Chomsky (1993) provides some empirical arguments to this same conclusion. Assume that these considerations are decisive. Then one might expect the restrictions that DS placed on grammatical operations to also disappear. Recall, that it was the thematic restrictions that DS imposes that forced the distinction between raising and control in earlier theory. Without DS, however, we might expect the two types of operations to fall together, as proposed in a movement approach to control. Put more baldly, a movement theory of control is a natural consequence of the minimalist elimination of DS.

This conclusion has been resisted. Chomsky's proposed elimination of DS does not entail that the thematic restrictions found in earlier DS based theories play no role in the grammar. Chomsky (1995) achieves the functional equivalent of DS by assuming that theta-roles are *not* features. Coupled with the idea that all legitimate movement must check a feature, that is be greedy, the claim that theta-roles are not features results in a system where control cannot be reduced to movement as movement into theta positions is unmotivated and so blocked by Greed. (40a) amounts to a rejection of this way of re-introducing DS conditions once DS is abandoned. The assumption that theta-roles are features is aimed at allowing movement between theta positions.[30]

(40b) has a similar motivation. The prohibition against a DP's bearing at most one theta-role has no conceptual justification (in contrast to the idea that a DP bear at least one, which plausibly follows from a principle of Full Interpretation). The restriction, however, would follow were movement into theta positions prohibited. Given that control always involves the relation of a DP to at least two theta positions, a movement approach to control must countenance a DP's having more than one theta-role.

(40c,d) are standard minimalist assumptions. I here adopt the enlightened self-interest interpretion of Greed as I take theta roles to be features of predicates that DPs obtain by merging with them (via either pure merge or copy plus merge viz. Move). Theta features, then, are primarily properties of predicates and only derivationally properties of arguments. If so, checking a feature of one's target must suffice to license movement. Greed as enlightened self-interest permits this.

Given these four assumptions, then, a movement theory of control is viable. I have argued that they are conceptually natural (if pressed, I might say optimal) given a minimalist setting. I now want to consider empirical support for (40a,b) that arises outside the domain of control phenomena.

1.4.4 *Movement into theta positions*

If control is movement then movement into theta positions must be possible. There is independent evidence that such movement obtains. I here review two cases in the literature.

Boskovic (1994, pp. 268 ff.) discusses the following examples from Chilean Spanish.[31]

(41)a. Marta le   quiere gustar   a Juan
        Martha clitic wants to please to Juan
        "Marta wants Juan to like her"

   b.   A Juan le quiere gustar Marta
        "Juan wants to like Marta"

Three facts regarding examples like (41) are of present interest.

First, *a* case marks *Juan*. That *Juan* bears this case is a lexical property of the verb *gustar* which assigns a quirky/inherent case to its thematic external argument much as Belletti and Rizzi (1988) argue with respect to similar verbs in Italian.

Second, (41a) differs from (41b), as the glosses indicate, in that *Marta* has two thematic functions in the first sentence while *Juan* has two in the second. This suggests that both are control structures with the matrix subject controlling the external argument in the embedded clause. Third, note that in (41b) the matrix subject bears the inherent case marker *a*. Given that *a* is an inherent case assigned by the embedded verb *gustar*, this implies that *a Juan* has moved to the matrix subject position in (41b) from the embedded position in which *a* and its corresponding theta-role were assigned to *Juan*. Such movement is also observed in raising constructions with inherent case marked subjects (*al* is the case marker).[32]

(42)   Al professor le empezaron a gustar los estudiantes
       "The professor began to like the students"

These three facts together implicate movement from one theta position to another. The *a* case on *Juan* in (41b) indicates movement from the domain of *gustar*, whence the inherent case marking was effected. However, in contrast to (42), *quiere* has an external thematic argument to assign and in (41b) *Juan* clearly bears it as the gloss indicates. The obvious implication is that *Juan* has moved from the thematic position of *gustar* to a thematic position of *quiere* and thereby obtained a second theta-role, as Boskovic (1994) concludes.[33]

Boskovic and Takahashi (1998) provides a second argument that movement into theta positions is possible. The phenomenon analyzed is long distance scrambling in Japanese.

As Boskovic and Takahashi note, long-distance scrambling – (43b) – is odd given minimalist assumptions that it seems unmotivated. The base form from which it is derived is well formed (43a).

(43)a. John-ga [Mary-ga   sono hon-o   katta   to] ommotteiru (koto)
             -nom   -nom that book-acc bought to] that thinks fact
        "John thinks that Mary bought that book"

   b.   Sono hon-o$_1$ John-ga [Mary-ga t$_1$ katta to] ommotteiru (koto) .
        "That book, John thinks that Mary bought"

The lack of semantic motivation for the movement is supported by the fact that unlike Wh-movement and topicalization, scrambling does not seem to establish an operator-variable relation at LF.[34] In particular, it seems that the long scrambling *must* be undone at LF. (44) illustrates this.[35] Boskovic and Takahashi note that a (long) scrambled QP cannot take scope over a matrix QP subject.

(44)   Daremo₁-ni   dareka-ga   [Mary-ga t₁ atta to] omotteiru (koto)
       everyone-dat someone-nom   Mary-nom met that thinks (fact)
       "Everyone someone thinks that Mary met"

(44) must be interpreted with *dareka* (someone) scoping over *daremo* (everyone) despite the fact that the latter c-commands the former in overt syntax. This follows if the scrambled *daremo* must reconstruct at LF.

Where does the scrambled expression move to at LF? According to Boskovic and Takahashi, it moves to its theta position. This movement is obligatory for were it not to so move, it would violate full interpretation. In fact, as Boskovic and Takahashi argue, virtually all of the characteristics commonly associated with long scrambling follow if it is assumed that the scrambled expression is Merged in overt syntax in its scrambled position and then moved covertly to its theta position at LF. However, for this analysis to be viable, it must be possible to *move* to a theta position and this movement must have some sort of feature checking motivation given standard assumptions. Both desiderata are met if it is assumed that theta roles are sufficiently like features to license greedy movement, assumption (40a) above.[36]

To sum up, there is independent evidence for movement into theta positions. The existence of this movement indirectly enhances the proposal that control is the overt manifestation of movement via multiple theta positions. Why, after all, should UG have recourse to a specialized theory internal expression like PRO if movement can independently forge the requisite relations? The redundancy inherent in such an approach speaks against its adoption on purely methodological grounds.[37]

1.4.5   Conclusion

This section has discussed the two dominant current minimalist approaches to the distribution of PRO. Both attempt to respond to the fact that minimalist assumptions leave little room for the standard GB approach to this issue. The basic descriptive generalization is that PROs are subjects and are found in non-finite sentences.[38] How to account for this without theoretically alluding to government is the basic challenge that both approaches try to meet.

1.5   The interpretation of PRO

There are two broad approaches to the interpretive properties of control in the current literature. The first is a structural approach. Abstracting from many interesting differences, structuralists generally see the interpretive properties of control as reflecting structural facts concerning the syntax of control configurations.[39] These properties, then, are analyzed as reflecting the internal workings of the grammar. The second approach is more eclectic. Eclectics see the interpretive properties of control as being due to the complex interaction of various modules, some of which are external to the syntax properly speaking. Chomsky sums up the view well:

> the theory of control involves a number of different factors: structural configurations, intrinsic properties of verbs, other semantic and pragmatic considerations. (Chomsky, 1981, pp. 78–9)

This section concentrates on the first approach. The next reviews objections lodged against it from the more eclectically inclined. The main reason for this is methodological; all things being equal, structuralism is preferable to eclecticism. The reason is that all agree that grammatical structure is *part* of any adequate approach to control. What distinguishes structuralists from eclectics is whether this information exhausts what is needed. All things being equal then, structuralism is preferable if attainable. The main arguments in favor of eclecticism are the purported empirical inadequacies of structuralism. As such, starting from the former position and considering possible empirical problems that beset it should reveal the virtues and vices of both views.

As noted in section 1.3.2, not all PROs are interpreted in the same way. A contrast exists between PROs in Obligatory Control configurations (OC PRO) and those in non-obligatory structures (NOC PRO). The former have properties roughly equivalent to those of reflexives while the latter pattern interpretively largely like pronouns.[40] For illustration consider the two paradigms first outlined in section 1.3 and repeated here.

Recall that (14) and (16) differ completely. The OC PROs in (14) require local, c-commanding antecedents, require sloppy readings under ellipsis, forbid split antecedents, only have *de se* readings and require bound readings with *only* antecedents. The latter need no antecedents, need not be c-commanded locally by an antecedent if one is present, allow a strict reading under ellipsis, permit split antecedents, can have a non *de se* reading and can have a referential reading with *only* antecedents.

(14)a.   *It was expected PRO to shave himself
    b.   *John thinks that it was expected PRO to shave himself
    c.   *John's campaign expects PRO to shave himself
    d.   John expects PRO to win and Bill does too (= Bill win)
    e.   *John$_i$ told Mary$_j$ PRO$_{i+j}$ to leave together/each other
    f.   The unfortunate expects PRO to get a medal
    g.   Only Churchill remembers PRO giving the BST speech

(16)a.   It was believed that PRO shaving was important
    b.   John$_i$ thinks that it is believed that PRO$_i$ shaving himself is important
    c.   Clinton's$_i$ campaign believes that PRO$_i$ keeping his sex life under control is necessary for electoral success

   d. John thinks that PRO getting his resumé in order is crucial and Bill does too

   e. John$_1$ told Mary$_2$ that PRO$_{1+2}$ leaving together/each other was important to Bill

   f. The unfortunate believes that PRO getting a medal would be boring

   g. Only Churchill remembers that PRO giving the BST speech was momentous

There is an important fact worth bearing in mind in what follows. The data illustrated in (14) and (16) illustrate that OC PRO has a proper subset of the properties of NOC PRO. Thus, (16d) differs from (14d) in allowing a strict reading which the latter forbids. (16d) can support a sloppy reading. This holds for (most of) the other properties as well. This means that OC PRO and NOC PRO *cannot* be in free variation. In particular, positions inhabited by OC PRO must exclude NOC PRO. Were this not so, we would never be able to observe OC PRO as its signature properties would never emerge, being, as they are, a proper subset of NOC PRO. What this means theoretically is that we need some way of excluding NOC PRO when OC PRO is present. This has implications for any general theory of control and we return to it at the end.

1.5.1   Some properties of a structural theory

Assume for the nonce that OC PRO is the residue of NP movement. If so, the structure of a subject control verb is roughly as (45a) and an object control verb looks like (45b).

(45)a. DP$_1$ V [$_{IP}$ t$_1$ [$_I$ –finite] [$_{VP}$ t$_1$ V. . . .]^{41}

    b. DP$_1$ V DP$_2$ [$_{IP}$ t$_2$ [–finite] [$_{VP}$ t$_2$ V. . . .] ^{42}

Several features of these configurations are of interest in relation to the paradigm in (14).

First, the fact that OC configurations require local c-commanding antecedents follows directly from their being residues of movement. In fact, it is the same as the reason why A-traces require local, c-commanding, antecedents.

Second, the facts concerning sloppy readings under ellipsis, the prohibition against split antecedents, the required *de se* reading for (14f) and the bound reading in (14g) also follow given a movement analysis. The required sloppy reading parallels what one finds in raising constructions.[43]

(46) Bill was expected t to win and Harry was too

Split antecedents are barred on a movement analysis. For an OC PRO to have DP as its antecedent implies that PRO is the trace left by the movement of DP from PRO's position. Split antecedents would require having two distinct DPs move from the very same position. This contemplated derivation is theoretically impossible and so split antecedents are ruled out.

It is worth noting that there is nothing that would rule out the possibility of OC PRO taking split antecedents were PRO a base generated expression any more than there is an explanation for why, given standard assumptions, locally bound reflexives cannot have split antecedents. Rather, the impossibility of split antecedents for reflexives and OC PRO is a stipulation motivated entirely on empirical grounds. The fact is tracked by an axiom explicitly forbidding split antecedents for reflexives and controlled PROs.[44]

Within a theory of control in which antecedents to PRO are functions of idiosyncratic lexical features of particular verbs the problem is perhaps worse. Why do control predicates designate only a single antecedent for PRO in OC configurations? Why not two (or more) antecedents? Were this possible then split antecedence would follow naturally. Thus, the impossibility of split antecedents and the fact that control predicates "choose" but a single controller are closely related facts. Both are immediately accounted for on a movement theory of OC.

The *de se* interpretation found in (14f) also follows. As a result of movement via multiple theta positions one ends up with a chain with multiple theta-roles. The natural semantic interpretation of such a syntactic object is of one expression, a chain, "saturating" several distinct argument positions. Semantically, this yields a complex monadic predicate, roughly of the form (47).

(47)   DP[$\lambda x\ (Px,x)$]

Such complex monadic predicates contrast with configurations of binding in forcing *de se* readings.[45] Thus, as movement via multiple thematic positions leads to the formation of complex monadic predicates and given that these only permit *de se* readings, it follows that if OC PRO is a residue of movement that it will require a *de se* interpretation. It is, once again, worth noting that this interpretive fact, though consistent with a base generation of a PRO approach, does not follow from it.

The facts concerning (14g) also follow. On the movement theory, the PRO is actually the residue of overt movement and so must have a c-commanding antecedent. *Only Churchill* is a possible antecedent. *Churchill* alone is not. Thus, the relevant structure must be one in which *only Churchill* is the antecedent of PRO. The logical form of (14g) is (48).

(48)   Only Churchill λx (x remembers x giving the BST speech)

In sum, *if* OC is formed via movement, then the interpretive properties illustrated in (14) follow rather directly.

One technical point is worthy of note before considering further facts friendly to the movement analysis. The above account relies on there being an LF chain relating controller to OC PRO at LF. This structural property is compatible with many different views of movement. Thus, Hornstein (2000), Manzini and Roussou (2000), Martin (1996), and O'Neill (1995) implement a movement analysis in rather different ways. Nonetheless, one common feature of all four is that at LF PRO and its controller are links of a single common chain. This suffices to derive the facts above.[46]

1.5.2 The Minimal Distance Principle

There are other characteristics of OC PRO constructions that follow naturally if movement is involved. Rosenbaum (1967, 1970) observed that the controller/ PRO relation generally obeys the Minimal Distance Principle (MDP). Thus examples like (49) must be controlled by the object, not the subject.

(49) John$_1$ persuaded Mary$_2$ PRO$_{*1/2}$ to go home

The vast majority of control structures with matrix transitive verbs like *persuade* require object control.[47]

Furthermore, when verbs can optionally alter their argument structures Rosenbaum (1967) noted shift in the potential controllers.

(50)a. John$_1$ asked/begged/got Mary$_2$ PRO$_{*1/2}$ to leave
    b. John$_1$ asked/begged/got PRO$_1$ to leave

In (50a), *John*, the subject, cannot control PRO. In (50b), when the object is not generated (at least in overt syntax), the subject can be (and must be) the controller.

These sorts of cases can be accounted for in terms of the MDP. Assume for the moment that the MDP is a descriptively adequate generalization. Why does it hold? Note that it follows on a movement theory of control if one assumes that movement is governed by minimality, a standard assumption. To see this, consider what the derivation of (49) would have to be like were *John* the antecedent of PRO.

(51)a. John [$_{VP}$ John persuaded Mary [$_{IP}$ John to [John go home]]]

The copies of *John* mark the history of derivation. Note that in moving from the embedded Spec IP to the matrix Spec VP *John* crosses the intervening DP *Mary*. This move violates minimality and is so barred. The only derivation not prohibited by minimality is one in which the DP in Spec IP raises to the next highest potential DP position, in this case the object. The derivation is illustrated in (51b).

(51)b. John [$_{VP}$ John persuaded Mary [$_{IP}$ Mary to [Mary go home]]]

So, if OC PRO is the residue of A-movement, the MDP follows.

1.5.3   *Adjunct control and movement*

Rosenbaum (1970) extends the MDP to cases of adjunct control.

(52)   John saw Mary after/before/while PRO eating a bagel

In (52) only *John* can control the PRO in adjunct position. Control from the object position is forbidden. This falls under the MDP on the assumption that *John* but not *Mary* c-commands the adjunct.

Unfortunately, this assumption is not obviously correct. For example, it is possible for objects to bind pronouns found within adjuncts, as Orson Wells taught us.

(53)   John will drink no wine$_1$ before it$_1$ is ready for drinking

If we assume that to be interpreted as a bound variable a pronoun must be c-commanded by its antecedent, this implies that *it* in (53) is c-commanded by *no wine* at least at LF. But then objects should be able to control into adjuncts, contrary to fact.

Note that one might get around this difficulty if one assumed that the generalization described by the MDP holds for overt syntax. Were this so, then one could argue that at LF, the object might c-command the adjunct but in overt syntax it does not. The problem, given a minimalist grammatical architecture, is how to state this generalization. Hornstein (2000) offers a solution along the following lines.[48]

Minimalism has generally taken movement to be a complex operation made up of two simpler ones, copy and merge. Assume that this is so. Nunes (1995) observes that if this is correct, then it should be possible to copy an expression from one sub-tree and merge it into another.[49] Call this sequence of operations "sidewards movement." It is possible to analyze adjunct control as involving this sort of operation. In particular let us assume the following:[50]

(54)a.   Sidewards movement is a species of movement and it is possible
     b.   Adjuncts headed by *after, before, while*, etc. are adjoined to VP (or higher)

(54a) makes two claims: that sidewards movement is a grammatically viable operation *and* that it falls under the same general restrictions that govern more conventional kinds of movement. (54b) says where the adjuncts of interest are merged. It assumes, contra Larson (1988) for example, that the adjuncts in (52) are basically adjoined to VP and are not generated within the VP shell. Assuming (54), consider a derivation of adjunct control structure like (55).

(55)   John saw Mary after PRO eating lunch

The derivation proceeds as follows. First construct the adjunct; merge *eating* and *lunch* then merge *John* to *eating lunch* then merge *after*. This yields (56).

(56)   after [John eating lunch]

Next construct the matrix. Merge *saw* and *Mary*. This yields a derivation with two unmerged sub-trees as in (57).

(57)   [saw Mary] [after [John eating lunch]]

At this point, we have exhausted the numeration but the external argument position of *saw* is still unfilled. To fill it we copy *John* and merge it into the Spec VP position, as in (58).

(58)   [John [saw Mary]] [after [John eating lunch]]

We then merge the two sub-trees and finish the derivation in the conventional manner yielding (59).[51]

(59)   [John T^0 [[John [saw Mary]] [after [John eating lunch]]]]

There are several things to note about this derivation. First, *John*'s sidewards movement is what allows its case to be checked. Were it not to move from the adjunct, the derivation would crash as *John* would have an unchecked case. Second, the movement only occurs after *Mary* has merged into the complement of *saw*. Why could *John* not move into this position? Were it to do so then we could have object control so we need to discover what prevents this. I assume that economy restricts sidewards movement and so one cannot move if the derivation can proceed without movement. In this case, we can merge *Mary* into this position so movement is blocked. This then forces *John* to move only after *Mary* has merged into the object position. This is why the controller of a PRO inside an adjunct cannot be an object.[52]

Thus, the spirit of the MDP can be captured in cases of adjunct control as well, if we see movement as the composite of Copy and Merge and thereby permit sidewards movement.

This is actually a very positive result. The reason is that adjunct control displays all of the diagnostic properties of OC PRO.

PRO headed adjuncts require local, c-commanding antecedents.

(60)a.   *John$_i$ said [that Mary left after PRO$_i$ dressing himself][53]
   b.   *John's$_i$ picture appeared after PRO$_i$ shaving himself
   c.   *[that Bill left] seemed true before PRO$_{arb}$ noticing

The PRO in these adjuncts do not tolerate split antecedents:

(61)a.   *John$_i$ said that Mary$_j$ left after PRO$_{i+j}$ washing themselves
   b.   *John$_i$ told Mary$_j$ a story after PRO$_{i+j}$ washing themselves

PRO headed adjuncts only have sloppy readings under ellipsis.

(62)   John left before PRO singing and Bill did too

Thus, (62) only has the reading paraphrased in (63a). It cannot be understood as (63b).

(63)a.   . . . and Bill left before Bill sang
    b.   . . . and Bill left before John sang

In "Churchill" sentences – (64a) – they cannot take "Churchill" as antecedent. In other words, (64b) is not an adequate paraphrase of (64a).

(64)a.   Only Churchill left after PRO giving the speech

    b.   Only Churchill left after Churchill gave the speech

And within adjuncts of the appropriate type (e.g. purposives), they display the obligatory *de se* interpretation.[54]

(65)   The unfortunate sent his report (in order to) PRO to get a medal

All in all then, cases of adjunct control display both MDP effects as well as the standard interpretive properties associated with OC structures. This is what we expect if they are indeed formed by movement.

It is quite interesting that cases of adjunct control can be analyzed in terms of movement. The reason is that such control is unlikely to be reducible to the thematic requirements of an embedding control predicate. In other words, the control one finds in such cases is *not* a function of the properties of the matrix predicate. Hence the controller cannot be some designated argument of the control predicate as has been proposed for cases of complement control. Nonetheless, these cases of control display all the diagnostic properties of OC. This suggests that, in at least some cases of obligatory control, the controller is structurally specified. Moreover, if the properties of OC PROs within adjuncts are structurally determined then it would be odd to treat cases of complement control (where the very same properties appear) as derived by entirely different operations and in entirely different ways.

This section has shown how movement accounts for some central features of obligatory control configurations. The account covers standard cases of complement control as well as adjunct control. The general characteristics of OC PRO make sense once OC PRO is seen as the residue of overt A-movement. In the next section, we consider some possible empirical problems for this sort of approach.

1.6   Problems for movement

Several authors have noted empirical difficulties for the movement analysis of control. This section reviews empirical challenges to the approach.

1.6.1   Promise: *and markedness*

One prominent argument rests on denying the general validity of Rosenbaum's MDP.[55] The form of the argument is as follows: movement is subject to minimality. Minimality is an inviolable condition on movement. Thus, we should find no cases of subject control in transitive control predicates. However, it is well known that there are a class of predicates that appear to violate the MDP, for example verbs like *promise* require subject control.

(66) $John_1$ promised $Mary_2$ $PRO_{1/*2}$ to leave

Thus, a movement based approach to control cannot be correct as it is incompatible with violations of minimality.

There is something curious about this argument. It appears to concede Rosenbaum's observation that *in general* one finds object control in transitive control predicates. However, the existence of a semantically coherent class of exceptions (the *promise* class which includes *vow* and *commit* among others), is taken to indicate that the reduction of the MDP to minimality cannot be correct. Here is Landau's version of the argument.

> Hornstein (1999) is aware of the exceptions to the MDP, but rather than attributing them to some hidden (double object) structure, he proposes to view the MDP as [a, sic] markedness condition.   (Landau, 1999, pp. 231–2)

The problem is that the MDP is not a primitive in Hornstein's system: "the MDP reduces to the MLC [Minimal Link Condition/i.e. Minimality NH]." This reduction is taken to be a strong argument in favor of the whole approach. But then any properties of the MDP should follow from properties of the MLC. In particular, if the MDP is a markedness condition, so should the MLC be. This is clearly not the case, however; the MLC is exceptionless, and its violations are sharply ungrammatical, whereas the "marked" violations of the MDP (i.e. subject control) are perfect.

There are several replies that one can make to this argument. First, let us be clear what it would mean to say that the minimality should be understood as a "markedness condition." One way to interpret this is that verbs that fail to respect minimality are marked in the sense that environments that appear to allow it will necessarily be hard to acquire. What "hard" means is that its acquisition will be data-driven with the language acquisition device requiring considerable evidence before it abandons the view that the witnessed operations are actually permitted in the observed environment. That is all that "marked" means.[56] In this sense, then, a movement theory treats control verbs like *promise* as marked in that they should be harder to acquire than the normal run of transitive control verbs like *persuade*. As Hornstein (1999) observed (and Landau, 1999 recognizes), there is acquisition data from C. Chomsky (1969) indicating that it is indeed the case that *promise* predicates are acquired late.[57]

Note, the MDP and the minimality approach to control provides the beginnings of an *explanation* for *promise*'s odd acquisition profile. Contrary to Landau (1999), it makes little difference whether the MDP is itself part of UG or is reduced to more fundamental properties of UG. In either case, if interpreted according to the logic of markedness, the relevant UG condition simply states that derivations that deviate from the condition, be it the MDP or minimality, will require substantial data to acquire. This, to repeat, seems to be true for *promise* verbs.

Moreover, any view that "regularizes" the properties of *promise*, for example by claiming that it falls under a broader generalization in terms of which its behavior is grammatically impeccable, *cannot* account for why it is acquired late. If indeed there is nothing grammatically (be it syntactic or semantic) untoward about *promise* then it should be learned as smoothly as any other transitive control predicate.[58]

This does not yet settle the matter however. It is still behooves us to find out in what way *promise* is marked. There are several ways of stating this. Most baldly, one can state that *promise* type verbs are exceptional in allowing their objects to be ignored for purposes of minimality. This is not pretty, but it is not impossible to state.[59]

A second more interesting possibility is that *promise* has a null preposition in its structure similar to the one found in other *promise*-like verbs such as *vow* and *commit*.

(67) I_1 vowed/committed *(to) Bill PRO_1 to leave[60]

In (67), there is no obvious problem for a movement analysis in that the object of the preposition does not c-command the position PRO occupies, at least in overt syntax. In this respect, the examples in (67) would be analogous to those one finds with the raising constructions in (68).

(68)   John seemed/appeared to Mary t to be nice

As is well known, English is somewhat exceptional in allowing movement across the indirect object in a raising construction (see Chomsky, 1995). Even the movement in English might seem problematic given that the indirect object is known to induce principle C effects in its complement. In this regard, (67) and (68) are similar.

(69)a.   *John seemed to $them_1$ to like the men_1
      b.   *John vowed to $them_1$ to hit the men_1

Let us assume that *promise* is similar to these other control verbs in having an indirect object in overt syntax and that this preposition becomes null (perhaps by incorporating into the verb) in the course of the derivation.[61] In many other languages *promise* is an overt indirect object and in its nominal form the *to* surfaces, so this may not be an unreasonable assumption.

(70)   John's promise *of/to Mary

If this were so, then the prepositional complement structure of *promise* would be opaque to the child and its late acquisition would be expected.

Observe that this is just one way of implementing the idea that *promise* is odd. It retains the view that it is marked and proposes a specification of how it is marked. However, to repeat, the movement analysis could survive if this specific proposal were incorrect and it was simply asserted as a lexical fact (similar to what one has with ECM verbs) that *promise* allows movement across its object.

One further point is worth making. Landau (1999) suggests that minimality violations are not found in other kinds of A-movement. This is not quite accurate. The problems with raising across the prepositional arguments of *seem* and *appear* have been touched on above. These are quite parallel to what we find with *vow* and *commit*. There are also raising analogs of *promise* in English.[62]

(71)a.   John$_1$ strikes Bill as t$_1$ dumb
   b.   It strikes Bill that John is dumb
   c.   It$_1$ strikes Bill as t$_1$ likely that Bill is dumb
   d.   John$_1$ strikes Bill as t$_1$ likely t$_1$ to be dumb

The raising verb *strikes* seems to violate minimality in allowing movement across its object in (71a,c,d). Here too, it is plausible to think that the apparent object is actually an indirect object. Whether this is so or not, it appears that contrary to what Landau (1999) asserts, there are apparent cases of A-raising that violate minimality.

In short, the existence of a limited number of counter examples to the MDP do not, I believe, invalidate either Rosenbaum's initial generalization or attempts to reduce the MDP to more basic properties of UG. In fact, the marked nature of *promise*, displayed in its tardy acquisition profile, argues in favor of a theory that treats *promise* as an exception and speaks against regularizing its grammatical status.

1.6.2   *Control shift*[63]

There is a second phenomenon that suggests that what one sees in *promise*-like cases is sensitive to semantic conditions. Consider cases like (72).

(72)a.   John$_1$ asked/persuaded/begged/petitioned Mary$_2$ [PRO$_{1/*2}$ to be allowed to leave early]
   b.   ?John$_1$ promised Mary$_2$ PRO$_{1/2}$ to be allowed to leave

As Landau (1999, pp. 212–14) notes, the examples above vary in acceptability from speaker to speaker and are subject to a variety of pragmatic influences in determining acceptability.[64] To my ear, the results are best when the embedded context is actually of the form *be allowed* ... At any rate, the contexts where this is acceptable are rather subtle.[65] What implications does this have for the notion that OC is parasitic on movement? So far as I can gather, none whatsoever. Let me explain.

The dominant view concerning these cases of control is that they are due to "special mechanisms" (this is Landau's term). Various proposals exist but they all seem to involve some specialized mechanism designed to obtain the relevant control facts. There is little reason to think that such a special mechanism could not also be grafted onto the movement theory.

Moreover, these phenomena are problematic for a movement account only if they involve obligatory control, for only then does a movement approach to PRO propose that movement is involved in the derivation of the control structure.[66] Non-obligatory control involves the binding of a null pronominal expression (see below).

So the question arises whether in control shift contexts we have a case of OC or NOC. The data suggest that the latter is the case. Consider the following data.

(73)a.   John was asked/begged PRO to be allowed to leave early
   b.   John's mother asked/begged Mary PRO to be allowed to shave himself before dinner
   c.   John petitioned/begged/asked Mary PRO to be allowed to leave early and Frank did too (OK with John's leaving early)
   d.   John asked/begged Mary PRO to be allowed to shave each other
   e.   The unfortunate petitioned congress PRO to be allowed to get a medal

In each of these cases, it appears that the PRO allows NOC readings. In (73a) it has no antecedent. In (73b) the antecedent can be the non-c-commanding *John*. (73c) allows a strict reading under ellipsis. (73d) permits split antecedents and (73e) allows a non *de se* reading. As these are standard characteristics of NOC structures, it leads to the conclusion that control shift involves a change from an OC to a non-OC structure.

If this is correct, it leaves several questions open. For example, it does not address the issue of why in these cases we get a shift from OC to NOC. One possible reason for this comes from considering sentences like (74).

(74)a.   John asked/begged/petitioned Mary that Peter be allowed to leave
   b.   *John asked/begged/petitioned Mary$_1$ that she$_1$ be allowed to leave

The indicated binding of a pronoun in cases like (74) leads to unacceptability. If so, we have an explanation for why the analogous obligatory control reading should be unavailable. Perhaps the unavailability of the required reading allows the emergence of the other NOC structure. We note below that NOC only arises if OC is blocked. (74b) indicates that identifying the embedded subject with the matrix object in environments analogous to those in control shift leads to unacceptability. This plausibly allows the NOC structure to emerge and permit the otherwise blocked binding relations. Why, however, this holds largely with *be allowed to* and not more widely remains a mystery.

To sum up, the movement theory of control is not obviously put at risk by control shift.[67] This does not mean to say that the above sketch is a sufficient account of all the subtleties of this phenomenon (see especially note 67). However, it seems possible to account for a number of the properties of the phenomenon without abandoning the basic movement approach to OC.

1.6.3   Partial control

Consider next another characteristic of some control structures that has been taken to be problematic for a movement based theory of control. Landau (1999) notes that control predicates differ as to whether or not they are able to sustain a "partial" reading. This reading is illustrated in the contrast in (75).

(75)a.   *The chair$_1$ managed PRO$_1$ to meet/gather at 6
   b.   The chair$_1$ preferred PRO$_{1+}$ to meet/gather at 6

Meet and *gather* are verbs that require semantically plural subjects to be well-formed. Other such verbs are *assemble* and *congregate*. Some control configurations license a reading in which the controller is part of a larger group denoted by PRO. This is designated by the suffix 1+ in (75b). In such cases, the PRO's reference is determined as follows: the controller is included in a set possibly supplemented by other individuals pragmatically determined in the discourse situation. The question to be addressed here is whether partial control is incompatible with a movement based approach to control.

Landau (1999, p. 69) notes that partial control (PC) has the same properties as exhaustive control (EC) save the partial versus exhaustive reading.[68] Let us assume that Landau's description of the phenomenon is correct and see what implications it has for the movement theory of control. One possibility is that it sinks it; unless a formative like PRO exists how could one obtain a partial reading? This is the question addressed here. But before coming to it, let us consider Landau's analysis of the PC versus EC effect.

Landau (1999) hangs the distinction on a difference we have encountered previously; the difference between tensed and non-tensed infinitives. The proposal is that only tensed infinitives manifest partial control. The idea is that PC occurs when T^0 moves to C^0 thereby blocking AGREE from taking place between PRO and a higher functional category F (either T^0 for subject control or v^0 for object control) that also agrees with the matrix controller. (76a) represents the EC and (76b) the PC structures.

(76)a.   [. . . [$_{FP}$ [F^0 [$_{VP}$ DP [$_{v'}$ V [$_{CP}$ C [$_{TP}$PRO [$_{T'}$ T-Agr [$_{VP}$ t$_{PRO}$ . . .]]]]]]]]]

   b.   [. . . [$_{FP}$ [F^0 [$_{VP}$ DP [$_{v'}$ V [$_{CP}$ T-Agr+C [$_{TP}$PRO [$_{T'}$ t$_{T-Agr}$ [$_{VP}$ t$_{PRO}$ . . .]]]]]]]]]

AGREE operates in (76a) to match the features of F^0 and DP and PRO in (76a). This licenses the EC reading. In (76b), the T-Agr moves to C^0 and this blocks the matrix F^0 form directly agreeing with the embedded PRO. Rather, here agreement is indirect with PRO first agreeing with the embedded T-Agr and this complex then agreeing with the matrix F^0. This is the configuration of PC. The important feature of the analysis is that finite T^0 must move to C thereby inducing a blocking effect on agreement and thus licensing the PC interpretation.

1.6.4   Some problems for Landau (1999)

It is unclear (at least to me) how the blocking effect in (76b) is meant to work technically. The idea is reported as follows (Landau, 1999, pp. 80 ff.). Following Chomsky (1999, pp. 4 ff.), the F feature in (76a) is a probe with DP and PRO as goals. PRO is unspecified for the number feature in non-finite clauses. The matrix F has number features. AGREE is a "maximizing operation, matching as many features of the probe it can with the goal. Since semantic number is one of F's features, PRO inherits it" (Landau, 1999, pp. 81). (76b) involves a different set of AGREE operations. First AGREE holds between the lower T-Agr and PRO.[69] Neither is specified for semantic number. Then the T-Agr raises to C. It then enters a second AGREE operation with the matrix F as probe. It is assumed that this raising blocks F from agreeing with PRO directly.

   This proposal is not without some problems, I believe. First, it is assumed that both EC and PC constructions are CPs. This would appear to put PRO outside the reach of the matrix probe on a phase based theory by the Phase Impenetrability Condition (PIC).[70] The proposal must assume that this C is porous unless T-Agr adjoins to it. It is theoretically unclear why adjunction should so function. What is clear is that this assumption is empirically vital. Note that were this not assumed then F would be able to reach PRO in both structures in (76), nullifying the difference between the two.

   Second, it is unclear how the probe F can "see" PRO in (76a) given that the matrix DP intervenes. It is generally assumed that AGREE is sensitive to minimality in that the Probe cannot see through the first accessible goal where feature Match applies (see Chomsky, 1998, p. 38, (40iii)). The minimality restriction is important to the probe/goal/AGREE based theory of feature checking. Chomsky, for example, accounts for the absence of nominative agreement in Icelandic constructions such as (77) on this basis (1998, p. 47, (51ii)). He notes that the nominative/Agr probe in the matrix cannot target the embedded object as goal as the *John* intervenes.

   (77)   me(DAT) seem (pl) [t_{me} [John(DAT) to like horses(pl, NOM)]]

   The structures proposed in (76) should prevent F from targeting PRO if minimality were in effect. The matrix DP intervenes between F and PRO in (76a) and F and T-Agr in (76b) and so should block any AGREE relation between F and these expressions. It appears, therefore, that minimality is irrelevant in these cases, and so the AGREE operation assumed here must be different from standard instances of AGREE. In other words, the AGREE operation underlying control is a special case of AGREE with properties specially suited to the phenomenon at hand. Clearly, this negatively affects the explanatory force of the proposed analysis.

Third, it is unclear how AGREE is understood in this proposal. In Chomsky (1998, 1999) it is taken to be an operation that compares features of two expressions and checks those that need checking. The match is either under strict identity or non-distinctness. In the current proposal, it is neither of these operations. Rather it is both a checking and a copying rule. The probe checks to see if the goal's features match and *if* the feature sets do not conflict then the probe can transfer to the goal those that it has, but which the goal does not. This way, PRO acquires semantic features contextually (Chomsky, 1999, pp. 76–7 and esp. (99d)). Note that this is a different conception of AGREE in that the operation involves both checking and copying.

Furthermore, the copy operation appears to violate the Inclusiveness Condition. Landau (1999, p. 76) accepts that semantic number is "determined by the lexical entry" as opposed to purely formal phi-features that are appended to expressions prior to their entering the derivation. What of PRO? Landau proposes that PRO acquires its *semantic* number contextually. As noted, this violates Inclusiveness and so needs strong independent motivation in a minimalist context. Moreover, PRO is unique among lexical items in having its number specification contextually specified. Other lexical items, Landau (1999, p. 76) assumes, are inherently specified for semantic number "in the lexical entry." This, then, makes PRO special in two ways: its null case is special and its semantic number features are special. As noted at the outset, the more the PRO's properties are special or unique the less its properties are explained.

Fourth, it is not clear how the mechanism proposed actually codes the basic control property. In fact, it is unclear whether the proposed AGREE operations suffice to determine the antecedent of PRO. Consider why. What AGREE does is check features. It is clear that having the same features as some other expression cannot be sufficient to establish antecedence or control. One might reply that it is not *having* the same features that is crucial but having one's features established by being checked against a common probe that results in the control relation. This would suffice to establish control between DP and PRO in (76a) as they are both taken as goals of the same F probe (issues of minimality aside). However, why should DP be taken as controller of PRO in (76b)? All they have in common is that they share some features as they have agreed with two heads that themselves agree. It seems that what is being assumed here is that if B agrees with A, C agrees with A, and D agrees with C then B and D agree as well. In (76b) this reasoning is as follows: If DP agrees with F and T-Agr agrees with F and PRO agrees with T-Agr then PRO agrees with DP. The assumption seems to be that DP controls PRO *in virtue of* PRO's agreement with DP. However, it is not clear how it is that PRO does so agree. Let me explain.

AGREE establishes a relation between two expressions. To see if the chain of specific agreements above implies control requires seeing what kind of relation AGREE is. The minimal assumption here must be that it is transitive. However, this is not enough. Landau must also be assuming that AGREE is symmetric. However, this is hardly self-evident and seems counter to the view advocated by Chomsky (1998, 1999) where AGREE seems to be an asymmetric relation. It is not that A and B agree but that the Probe A agrees with the goal A and this introduces an asymmetry into the relation: so Probes AGREE with goals not vice versa as Probes c-command and seek out goals and have their features checked by goals rather than the reverse. If this is correct, that is if AGREE is not symmetric, then we cannot establish a control relation through the series of AGREE operations noted above even if we assume that AGREE is transitive. The reason is that we cannot deduce that DP agrees with PRO from the fact that the other agreement operations took place. But if we cannot do that we cannot derive the fact from the proposed set of operations that in (76b) PRO is controlled by DP as they have not been related by AGREE. Only if we assume that AGREE is symmetric (and thereby cancel the inherent asymmetry in a probe/goal system) and transitive can we get DP and PRO in any sort of relation able to undergird control.

It should be observed that similar difficulties underlie the standard case of EC as outlined above. In (76a), F agrees with both PRO and DP. But from this it does not *follow* that DP AGREEs with PRO or vice versa. From aRc and aRb it does not follow that cRb or bRc even if we assume R is transitive. But if not, how does AGREE code the antecedence relation?[71]

There is another conceptual point I would like to briefly make. Say that AGREE is symmetric and transitive. Why should multiple agreement code control? In particular why should the fact that two DPs (one a *PRO*) both agreeing with the same functional head or both agreeing with different functional heads that agree with each other lead to control? Note, the question is not *could this be the case*? We can stipulate anything we want. The question is why it *should* be so. Why should multiple agreement operations set up control relations especially when the agreement is quite indirect? Clearly this is not so for other cases of multiple agreement. There is no conceptual reason that I can see why it should be so here. Let me put this another way. Landau (1999) seems to tacitly hold the following in order to get the relevant antecedence relation from AGREE: A and B agree iff A is the antecedent of B or B is the antecedent of A. In other words, it is not enough to observe that antecedence implies agreement, the converse must hold as well. There is little reason to think that anything like this is well motivated either empirically or conceptually.

Let me say this one more way. On a movement theory, control is the reflex of chain membership. In particular, it is the reflex of a chain's spanning multiple thematic positions. Control holds because of the COPY operation and is defined over identical instances of the same expression. On Landau's (1999) proposal, control is a reflex of AGREE but it is not clear why AGREE should have the power to establish antecedence, especially when it is as round about as in (76b) where the DPs only agree with each other in virtue of agreeing with a common functional head (in EC) or distinct heads (in PC).[72]

There are further problems with the proposed analysis. I briefly mention a few of them here. Section 1.4.2 reviewed some problems for theories of null case that used the standard diagnostics for the tense of non-finite clauses following the original work of Stowell (1982). These problems are compounded in Landau's proposal. He assumes that both EC and PC control structures have PRO subjects. However, this defeats at most a principled version of the null case theory, one like Martin (1996) that tries to assimilate null case to nominative by having it be the property of +tense non-finite clauses. Landau must reject this version of the null case theory and leave it simply as a stipulation that control T⁰s assign case regardless of their feature composition. He codes this by assuming that control infinitives all contain anaphoric Agr projections regardless of their tense specifications. This use of Agr works but has no apparent motivation beyond coding the fact that both environments can host PRO. It is presumably this anaphoric Agr feature that licenses PRO via some sort of null case. This makes evident the stipulative nature of the null case theory and leaves us without any principled explanation for the distribution of PRO. In effect, Landau's theory appears to sacrifice a principled account for the distribution of PRO in order to accommodate the PC property of some control configurations.

Note incidentally, that this approach requires some version of the EPP. The reason is that in (83a) the PRO must raise to get outside the domain of the lower T-Agr and get close enough to the higher matrix F projection. There is currently considerable skepticism regarding the status of the EPP.[73] This proposal appears to require it.

There is also a problem with the generalization that Landau proposes. It ties PC to +tensed non-finite clauses. However, we have evidence that gerunds too can have PC readings.

(78) John prefers meeting/to meet at 6

If this is correct, then these gerunds must have +tensed T⁰s and have movement of this T⁰ to C. Section 1.4.2 reviewed evidence that gerunds did not have +tense T⁰s yet these can display PC. Recall that Stowell (1982) argued against treating gerunds as +tense. Moreover, there is very little evidence that gerunds ever have a CP layer. There are no gerundive indirect questions for example, nor do they come with overt complementizers. If they are bare TPs, a common assumption (see Pires, 2001 for discussion), then they should never be able to host PROs at all, nor should they be able to manifest PC readings, contrary to fact.

There is one more curious feature of Landau's analysis. He argues that there is movement of T-Agr when the latter is tensed, but not when it is untensed. What is curious is that the latter set of cases manifest a strong aspectual dependency between the matrix and the embedded clause. Thus, for example, the event referred to in the embedded clause in (79) is cotemporaneous with respect to the matrix event. In (79a) John's finishing drinking the wine terminates an event of drinking while in (79b) the starting point initiates the drinking and in (79c) the trying spans the drinking.

(79) a. John finished PRO drinking the wine
     b. John started PRO drinking the wine
     c. John tried drinking the wine

How should one code this dependency? Note that it cannot be via selection given the intervening C between the matrix verb and the embedded T-AGREE. One way of finessing this problem is to raise T-Agr to C (if there is one). However, by assumption, this T-Agr does not raise or it would permit PC readings. Thus there are dependencies that would naturally be coded by raising to C that cannot be so handled on this analysis. On the other hand, Landau does not say what one gains by raising +tensed T-Agr to C. It is against the spirit of the minimalist program to simply assume that such raising occurs without any other interface requirement being furthered. One can force such movement by placing a feature in C. However, this does not explain *why* there should be such movement and is thus, on methodological grounds, without explanatory foundation.

One last point. The movement required to track the PC data must be overt given the motivation behind AGREE as an operation able to dispense with LF like operations. There is, to my knowledge, little evidence that such overt T to C movement takes place, at least in English. Thus, in embedded questions, there is little evidence of T to C movement in overt syntax for full finite clauses, hence the absence of Aux inversion in embedded clauses. One could treat this movement as covert. However, here too there is a problem. It is unclear that covert movement suffices to block the AGREE operation licensing partial control from applying *prior* to this movement. But then the structure of EC should be met and the structural distinction between EC and PC will be idle.

The above remarks have concentrated on technical aspects of Landau (1999). They could surely be finessed. However, I would conclude from the above that Landau (1999) is more a description of partial control than an explanation of it. The question still lingers, however, whether the existence of partial control is incompatible with a movement theory or whether the latter can be supplemented to accommodate the EC/PC distinction.

1.6.5   Movement and partial control

If there is no element like PRO how is partial control to be accommodated? There are several brute form approaches that could be pressed into service which, though not particularly elegant, are no worse than the other approaches in the literature. The least interesting (yet adequate) approach would be to treat PC as the result of an optionally applicable meaning postulate licensed by certain matrix verbs when taking control complements. If Landau's (1999) description is correct, the relevant class of verbs are those that take non-finite +tense complements.

What would the meaning postulate look like? It would have roughly the content of (80).

(80)   If "DP Vs [$_{TP}$ to VP]" then "DP Vs [$_{TP}$ DP and some contextually specified others to VP]"

With regard to an example like (81a), (80) would license the inference (81b).

(81)a. John wants to meet at 6
　　b. John wants John and some contextually specified others to meet at 6
　　c. John wants [John to meet at 6]

The PC interpretation is then provided by (81b) or, redundantly, the conjunction of (81c) and (81b). (81c) alone is what the syntax licenses. It licenses the interpretation that John wants himself to meet at 6. As it is a property of verbs like *meet* that they require that the class of "meeters" be semantically plural, (80) applies, licensing the inference (81b). But now John wants both himself and some contextually specified other(s) to meet at 6 and this suffices to give the predicate the requisite semantic plurality and the indicated partial reading. In cases involving verbs like *meet* the application of (80) is forced, otherwise unacceptability results. In other cases, it may or may not apply (recall (80) is optional) yielding either a PC or EC reading as the case may be.[74]

This is clearly a *very* uninteresting account of the PC phenomenon as it is specifically crafted to cover the partial reading data. Despite this, the approach has more or less the correct empirical requirements for the purpose at hand. For example, if we assume that anaphors such as *themselves* and *each other* require syntactic licensing (a standard assumption), the meaning postulate approach implies that structures that license PC readings will not be able to license reciprocals and plural reflexives. This is correct (as Landau (1999) observes). Note that (81a) only has the syntactic phrase marker (81c) in which *John* (and only *John*) is the subject of the embedded clause. Being singular, it cannot license a plural anaphor (cf. (82)) and so the sentence is unacceptable.

(82)a. *John wants to meet each other
　　b. *John wants to wash themselves

A second virtue of this approach relates to the fact that PC is a property of control *complements*. It is absent from adjuncts.

(83)a. *John saw Mary after/without meeting/gathering at 6
　　b. *John saw Mary early (in order) PRO to meet/gather at Max's at 6

This too is expected if PC is due to a meaning postulate tied to a higher predicate. Predicates exercise their lexical powers over their arguments, not over adjuncts. As such, we might expect to find PC absent within control adjuncts.[75]

(83b) offers a possible contrast between this approach and Landau's (1999) proposal. The latter, recall, ties partial readings to the presence of +tense nonfinite inflections. The purpose clause in (83b) shows some of the hallmarks of being +tense. For example, we can have contrasting adverbs in the main and the adjunct clauses.

(84) John saw Mary yesterday (in order) to leave early tomorrow

If this is a diagnostic of +tense non-finite inflections, then the purpose clause must be tensed (see Landau, 1999, p. 71). But then we would expect to see PC in such structures, contrary to fact. Observe that these purpose adjuncts have all of the characteristic properties of obligatory (adjunct) control.[76] For example, it is subject oriented, (85a); requires a prominent antecedent, (85b); and a local one ((85c) is only acceptable with the purpose clause modifying the matrix); requires sloppy readings under ellipsis, (85d); forbids split antecedents, requires a *de se* reading, (85a); and gets the bound reading with *only* DP antecedents, (85f).

(85)a. John$_1$ saw Mary$_2$ in order PRO$_{1/*2}$ to get a medal
   b. John$_1$'s mother saw Mary in order PRO$_{*1}$ to get a medal
   c. Bill$_1$ said John saw Mary in order PRO$_1$ to get a medal
   d. John$_1$ saw Mary in order PRO$_1$ to get a medal and Bill did too
   e. *John$_1$ saw Mary$_2$ in order PRO$_{1+2}$ to shave each other
   f. Only John saw Mary in order PRO to get a medal

Thus, PROs in these contexts act like OC PROs, lodge in non-finite sentences that appear +tense, and also forbid PC readings. Were PC a property of +tense non-finite inflections we would expect PC to arise here as well, contrary to fact. This is compatible with a meaning postulate approach on the assumption that PC is due to lexical powers exercised by predicates over their embedded complements.

Consider one further interesting case.

(86) John wants/prefers to talk about himself all together at dinner tonight

(86) can have a PC reading, as *all together* indicates. If so, what binds the reflexive? If the embedded subject has a plural or unspecified number specification then why does the reflexive appear in the singular? It is generally the case that reflexives agree in syntactic number with their antecedent.

(87)a. The committee congratulated itself/*themselves
   b. The pants were folded over themselves/*itself

If so, this should indicate that the syntactic antecedent of *himself* in (86) has singular formal number features. In short, it appears that in PC cases, there is evidence both that the PRO is semantically plural and that it is syntactically singular. This is a problem for Landau's (1999) proposal.

However, the meaning postulate approach predicts that a singular reflexive should be licensed here as, *in the syntax*, the embedded subject is a copy of *John*.

(88) John wants/prefers John to talk about himself . . .

On Landau's (1999) account, the embedded subject is not singular but is either plural or unspecified for number. Neither assumption is consistent with the fact that a *singular* reflexive is licensed here.[77]

I conclude that it is *possible* to combine a movement account with some other mechanism to obtain the PC facts. The meaning postulate approach, though very crude, has the desired properties: it is tied to specific lexical predicates and so allows a distinction between EC and PC complements, being a meaning postulate it is not expected to interact with the syntax and so not license plural anaphors, and being a lexical property it is not expected to affect adjuncts.

This section has sketched an approach to partial control consistent with the movement theory of control. This suffices to demonstrate that the simple existence of partial control does not *in and of itself* argue against the possibility of a movement approach to obligatory control. This said, the existence of PC readings does raise a challenge for the approach to control phenomena outlined here. One of the charms of the movement approach is that it derives the basic distributive and interpretive facts concerning control without further assumptions. Once it is seen as an instance of movement, all the details follow. Partial control phenomena do *not* follow from the movement theory. What I have argued is that they are compatible with movement, not that they follow from it. Thus the EC versus PC distinction as well as why PC holds at all remains as a puzzle for the minimalist ambition of entirely eliminating any specific mention of control within UG.[78]

1.6.6   Control in nominals

Finally, let us turn to what (in my view) is the greatest challenge to the movement theory of control. We have, to this point, restricted attention to control within verbal complements. However, there is also quite a bit of (at least) apparent control inside nominals, as in (89).

   (89)   John's attempt/plan/desire PRO to leave

The question is how this is to be handled given a movement theory.

The problem for a movement account is quite complex as the data are very intricate.[79] The aim here is *not* to handle all of the data that have been put forward. Rather it is to suggest one way of construing the facts so that their properties are compatible with a movement account. The form of the argument that I present is not very novel. The suggestion is that what we find in nominals is not obligatory control. This suggestion goes back at least to Williams (1980) who argued that PRO within nominals did not require syntactic antecedents and so were different in kind from verbal cases of control. Thus, alongside (89) we find (90) where there is no overt syntactic controller.

   (90)   any attempt/plan/desire PRO to leave

Moreover, the contexts in (90) are ones that support arbitrary readings, as Williams (1980) also observed.

   (91)   Any attempt/plan/desire to conceal oneself

In verbal settings, obligatory control contexts do not permit the arbitrary interpretation of PRO.

> (92)   *It was attempted/planned/desired to conceal oneself

There are other indicators that what one has in such contexts is not obligatory control. For example, nominals can support split antecedents, in contrast to their verbal counterparts.

> (93)a.   John approved Bill's attempt/plan PRO to sneak each other/ themselves into the party
> b.   John distrusted Bill's desire PRO to promote each other/themselves
> c.   *John said that Bill attempted to sneak each other/themselves into the party
> d.   *John said that Bill desired to promote each other/themselves

Note too that in the case of (93a,b) one of the antecedents is non-local in the sense of being across an intervening subject. This is forbidden in the verbal cases in (93c,d) where *John* cannot be an antecedent of PRO.

It is also possible to get strict readings under ellipsis.

> (94)a.   John's plan to sneak himself into the convention was not as clever as Mary's
> b.   John's attempt to sneak himself into the convention failed though Mary's succeeded

In both (94a,b) it is possible to read the ellided portion strictly, for example (94a) can be understood as Mary's plan for John to sneak himself in.

There is one further contrast of interest. It seems that verbs and their nominal counterparts differ with respect to partial control. Verbs like *try/attempt* resist PC interpretations. However, their nominal counterparts are quite felicitous with the PC reading.

> (95)a.   *John said that the chair attempted to meet together at 6
> b.   John criticized the chair's attempt to meet together at 6

Thus, on a range of diagnostics for OC it appears that verbs and their nominal counterparts differ. This suggests that Williams (1980) was largely correct in assuming that what we have in nominals is non-obligatory control.[80]

Consider what this means if correct: the movement theory is not put at risk by the control facts within nominals. The reason is that the movement theory of control only applies to obligatory control structures. Non-obligatory control is *not* due to movement. Rather, as we will see below, it rests on the assumption that NOC's properties are due to the presence of a null pronominal (akin to *pro*) in NOC contexts. If this is correct, then we do not expect to see the marks of OC in nominal structures.[81]

This is, of course, a negative result. It does not say what is going on within nominals. Rather it says that whatever it is, it is not the province of the theory of movement. For present purposes this is enough. If correct, it insulates the movement theory of control from the nominal data.

However, it still leaves the question of how to explain the fact that in examples like (89) there is a very strong preference for understanding John to be both the attempter/planner and the leaver. Why so? What follows are some very speculative remarks aimed at this question.

DPs with genitive "subjects" have one general interpretive feature. The genitive is interpreted as in some contextually specified way related to the rest of the DP.[82] This holds even where there is no apparent control going on at all.

(96)a. John's book
    b. John's claim that Frank kissed Mary
    c. John's rumor that Frank kissed Mary

In each of these cases, *John* is interpreted as related *in some way* to the book, claim or rumor. These specifications can be very lax. For example, (96a) allows John to be the owner, author, subject, caretaker, etc. For (96b,c) more obvious relations are salient. Thus, one natural way for a claim to be John's is that he made it. But another can be that he defends it, moots it, discovers it, publicizes it, or publishes it. Similarly for rumors. Thus, (96b,c) can be used with the understanding that John is the claimer or originator of the rumor but they need not be so understood. What is required is that there be a contextually specified relation between the genitive and the following nominal.

With this in mind, consider another instance of a similar restriction within sentences.

(97)a. As for John, Mary likes him a lot
    b. Concerning John, Mary said that he was great
    c. As for the Canadiens, I like Toe Blake
    d. Concerning Toe Blake, the Habs knew how to win

Sentences with left positioned "hanging" topics like those in (97) require that the topic be related in some way to the proposition that follows. One rather easy way to accomplish this is by having a pronoun interpreted as anchored to the topic. Thus, the most salient reading of (97a,b) is the one in which *John* is the antecedent of *him/he*. This sort of binding, however, is not required. The relation can be quite a bit looser, as illustrated by (97c,d). Here, the sentences are felicitous if one knows, for example, that Toe Blake coached the great Montreal hockey teams of the late 1950s and early 1960s. The relation can be quite loose. But a relationship there must be. And if one is salient, it is often the one adopted.

With this in mind, consider cases like (89), repeated here, one more time.

(89) John's attempt/plan/desire PRO to leave

John needs to be related to the nominal that follows in some way. Clearly, one very salient way to relate to the following is to be the leaver and the attempter/planner/desirer. However, given the right context, it seems to me that this is not at all forced. So, for example, John need not be the planner in (89) if he is related to the plan in some other way, say as the backer of the plan, or expositor. Nor need he be the leaver. So for example, imagine a plan John is backing in which he gets hidden by being buried in a pit. Then, one can use a phrase like (98) to refer to this plan where *him* refers to *John*.

(98)   John's plan to bury him in the pit just won't work

Here John is not the planner, nor is he a burier under the intended interpretation. However, *John* is related in the roundabout way described and so all is well. I believe that similar ingenuity leads to acceptable readings in the other cases as well. If this is characteristic of control within nominals, then it suggests that what has been interpreted as control, is not due to mechanisms of control at all, but is the reflex of a restriction imposed by the aboutness relation that genitive's impose on DP phrases.

Two more points before leaving this very complex topic. First, once the problem is finding an aboutness relation then many factors may come into play. For example, consider the sentence in (99).

(99)   John's attempt to leave was amusing

One plausible paraphrase of (99) is (100).

(100)   John attempted to leave and it was amusing

Note that under the paraphrase (100) of (99) John is necessarily understood as both attempter and leaver. Note that the paraphrase involves verbal control, not control within nominals. (100) is not the only paraphrase of (99) but it is a plausible one and maybe even a salient one. To the degree it is salient, to that degree *John* will be understood as "controlling" the PRO. Not because it does so in (99) but because it does so in (100) and (100) is thought to be *in the context* a good paraphrase of (99). In this way, the properties of verbal control can "leak" into those of nominal control. However, it is worth bearing in mind that there might well be cases in which this sort of paraphrase is not particularly felicitous and in those cases the indicated (control) inference will be blocked.[83]

Second, the discussion here is much too cursory to be compelling. However, my aim has been more modest. Though the facts regarding control in nominals are very complex and though I have barely scratched the surface, I hope to have shown that the control facts as generally described, at least in some central cases, are more elusive than generally thought. Furthermore, there are reasons for thinking that the control seen here is not obligatory control at all. If this is correct, it cannot be understood as undermining the movement approach to OC.

1.6.7 Conclusion

This section has reviewed a variety of objections to a movement theory of OC. I have argued that none of the proposed objections are fatal. This said, the facts discussed are complex and the conclusions reached here should be considered very tentative. What I would like to emphasize, however, is that given the theoretical virtues of the movement theory, it behooves us to have compelling empirical reasons against it before we abandon it. The objections reviewed above, though provocative, do not yet meet this higher standard, in my view.

1.7 Non-obligatory control (NOC): a short note

For the movement theory, NOC[84] is the elsewhere case. What this means to say is the following: if the movement theory is on the right track, then OC and its attendant properties receive a principled grammatical account in terms of movement via multiple theta positions. When such movement can occur, it must. When it cannot occur, NOC results. Several questions arise assuming this story to be correct.

First, are NOC structures all of a piece? In other words, do they all embody identical structures or are there various kinds of NOC configurations?

Second, what underlies the NOC properties noted in (16) above? Is there some structural reason for the fact that NOC configurations do not require local c-commanding antecedents, license strict readings under ellipsis, etc.?

Third, why is it that OC and NOC structures are in complementary distribution? More exactly, why is it that NOC cannot occur precisely where OC does? Note that we empirically know that this is *not* possible. Were it so we would have little evidence for the existence of OC given that the properties of OC configurations are a proper subset of those displayed by NOC structures. However, we would like a theoretical reason for why it is that NOC is possible just in case OC is not.

Let us now consider NOC PRO in light of these questions. There is one particularly interesting fact about NOC structures, at least in a core set of cases. They occur within islands. Thus, the examples in (16), repeated here, all find NOC PRO inside a subject of a finite clause.

(16)a. It was believed that PRO shaving was important
   b. John$_i$ thinks that it is believed that PRO$_i$ shaving himself is important
   c. Clinton's$_i$ campaign believes that PRO$_i$ keeping his sex life under control is necessary for electoral success
   d. John thinks that PRO getting his résumé in order is crucial and Bill does too
   e. John$_1$ told Mary$_2$ that PRO$_{1+2}$ leaving each other was important to Bill
   f. The unfortunate believes that PRO getting a medal would be boring
   g. Only Churchill remembers that PRO giving the BST speech was momentous

What makes this observation interesting is that if OC is the reflex of movement, then we would expect OC to be exempt from subjects as these are
islands.[85] This seems to be correct.[86]

If movement prohibits relating the PROs in (16) to their antecedents what
grammatically underpins them? The only realistic option is some sort of binding operation. Thus, the relation between *John* and *Mary* and *PRO* in (16e)
must be some sort of binding or co-reference.[87] And if this is so, then it is likely
that PRO is (more or less) some sort of pronominal in these configurations. To
state things baldly, NOC PRO is (roughly) akin to *pro*, a null pronoun. It is
interesting to note the sentences in (16b–g) all have paraphrases with overt
pronouns in place of PRO.

> (101)b.   John$_i$ thinks that it was believed that his/him$_i$ shaving himself was
>   important
>   c.   Clinton's$_i$ campaign believes that his/him$_i$ keeping his sex life
>   under control is necessary for electoral success
>   d.   John thinks that his/him getting his résumé in order is crucial and
>   Bill does too
>   e.   John$_1$ told Mary$_2$ that their/them$_{1+2}$ leaving each other was import-
>   ant to Bill
>   f.   The unfortunate believes that his/him getting a medal would be
>   boring
>   g.   Only Churchill remembers that his/him giving the BST speech
>   was momentous

Were NOC PRO (more or less) equivalent to *pro* then the pattern observed in
(16) is what we would expect to find given the facts in (101).[88] It is also what
we would expect theoretically. Pronouns are not subject to the locality and
prominence conditions characteristic of A-traces. Thus if NOC PROs are akin
to pronouns while OC PROs are A-traces we would expect to find the attested
differences in their distribution and interpretation.

This said, it is not actually crucial for the movement theory of control that
NOC PRO be *pro*. What is crucial is that it *not* be the residue of movement. I
mention this, for some have argued that what we find in cases of NOC PRO
are logophors rather than pronouns.[89] Landau (1999, pp. 138–9; (66)–(68)) cites
the following data from Kuno (1975).

> (102)a.   John said about Mary that it would be easy *(for her) to prepare
>   herself for the exam
>   b.   John sued Mary for divorce because it was no longer possible *(for
>   her) to support him

Kuno analyzes such cases as involving logophors, rather than mere pronouns,
to account for the contrast with overt pronouns.[90]

As said, the movement theory is compatible with the idea that some NOC
PROs are logophors rather than pronouns. However, whether this is a significant difference awaits further specification of the basic licensing properties of

logophors: Do they require c-commanding antecedents? Do they support split antecedents? Do they allow strict readings under ellipsis? Can they be interpreted as bound variables? I do not know. One element that is commonly assumed to be a logophor, Japanese *zibun*, is interpretable as a bound pronoun but is not able to support split antecedents – (103a) – nor license a strict reading under ellipsis – (103b) only has a sloppy reading.[91]

(103)a. Takahashi$_1$-ga   Mariko$_2$-ni [Kenji$_3$-ga   zibun$_{1/3/*1+2/*1+3}$-o
         -nom   -dat   -nom   SELF-acc
         suisenshita-to] tsugeta
         recommended reported
         "Takahashi reported to Mariko that Kenji recommended self"

   b. Takahashi$_1$-ga   zibun-o home, Kenji$_2$-mo soo-shita
      -nom self   praise   -too so did
      "Takahashi praised himself and Kenji did too"

If *zibun* is a typical logophor, it cannot be the case that all NOC PROs are logophors given the data presented in (16) above.

   Note too that whatever NOC PROs are they can be bound by quantificational antecedents and still display the same range of properties.[92] For example, split antecedents are permitted with NOC PROs. Contrast the examples in (104). (104a) requires OC PRO and prohibits split antecedents while (104b) has an NOC PRO and permits them. Note that the relevant reading is one in which the value of *someone* varies with that of the antecedent.

(104)a. *Everyone$_1$ persuaded someone$_2$ PRO$_{1+2}$ to wash each other
   b. Everyone$_1$ persuaded someone$_2$ that PRO$_{1+2}$ washing each other
      would amuse Mary

   What is descriptively important, then, is that whatever logophors are, their properties track those of pronouns with respect to the features noted in (16). If they do not, then *at least some* NOC PROs cannot be logophors.[93] If, however, logophors are essentially pronouns with other added complexities, then the story provided here, the one that treats NOC PRO as essentially *pro*, can be modified without much difficulty.[94]

   Consider now the second issue; the trading relation between OC and NOC PRO. Why are OC and NOC PRO in complementary distribution? In particular, why does NOC PRO not occur wherever OC PRO does?

   There are several possible approaches to this question. One can simply stipulate that *pro* must be licensed by specific features of T^0 and that these features are absent, for some reason, in OC configurations. However, this tack leaves us in ignorance as to why NOC configurations congregate within islands. Why, for example, isn't there a verb just like *hope* but which displays the NOC properties in (16) rather than the OC features of (14)?

   Consider another approach to this complementarity in terms of economy. Hornstein (2000) proposes that UG prefers movement operations to construal processes. Slightly more precisely, if an expression E can be related to a position P via movement, then it must be associated via movement. Only if movement cannot establish the liason can construal operate to link E to P. If we assume that something like this obtains within UG then the presence of OC removes the possibility of NOC as the former are more "economical" than the latter. Note, if this is correct, then we will expect to find NOCs within islands as these are configurations from which movement is barred.[95] Furthermore, where movement is licit we will expect that NOC is absent, the reason being that as movement (and so OC) suffices for derivational convergence, the more costly non-movement derivation, that brings NOC interpretations in its train, will be barred by economy.

This kind of story brings with it many additional questions. For example, why is construal more costly than movement? Is there any additional evidence that construal or binding operations are "last resort" in the relevant sense? How should one code the trading relation between movement and construal? All these are legitimate concerns, though we do not address them here.[96] However, what is of interest now is that so interpreting OC and NOC makes available a possible answer to a pressing question: why OC and NOC are in complementary distribution.

So, we answer the three questions above as follows. NOC has the properties in (16) because NOC PRO is *pro*, a null pronominal. NOC might involve logophors as well as pronouns without affecting the basics of the movement approach to OC. And, OC and NOC are in complementary distribution because movement is preferred to construal/binding. As such, we will find NOC where movement cannot apply, within islands, and expect to find NOC absent where movement is possible.[97] This cut seems roughly correct.[98]

1.8 Extensions

The earlier sections have defended a movement approach to control. It is movement-based in two senses. First, OC PRO is identified with A-traces, the residues of overt A-movement. Second, NOC *pro* is parasitic on A-movement in that it is available only if A-movement is prohibited. This section reviews analyses that develop the movement theory and thereby add to its empirical vivacity.

1.8.1 *Backwards control*

Polinsky and Potsdam (2000) analyze a case of "backwards" control in Tsez, a language of the Caucasus.[99] Backwards control describes cases in which the controlled PRO (asymmetrically) c-commands its antecedent. This sort of control configuration is unexpected in standard approaches to control as it should lead, among other difficulties, to a principle C violation once the control relation is established. However, as Polinsky and Potsdam observe, backwards control can be accounted for in a movement based theory in a rather straight-forward manner. Let us consider the facts and the argument.

Polinsky and Potsdam argue that backwards control (BC) occurs in clauses like (105).

(105) $\text{PRO}_{1/*2}$ [kidba$_1$ ziya   bisra] yoqsi
                   girl-erg cow-abs feed-inf began
       "The girl began to feed the cow"

Both *-oqa* (begin) and *-ica* (continue) occur in such syntactic configurations. Observe that the PRO in (105) necessarily takes *kidba* as its antecedent. The evidence for the proposed structure is the following.

First, these verbs are thematic in that they impose selectional restrictions on their subjects. They cannot host idiomatic subjects. The subject of the idiom in (106a) cannot move to the matrix clause in (106b).

(106)a. T'ont'oha   buq   bac'xo
         darkness-erg sun-abs eat-pres
         (lit.: Darkness ate the sun)
         "The sun eclipsed"

     b. *T'ont'oha   buq   bac'a baq
         darkness-erg sun-abs eat-inf begin-fut
         "The sun will begin to eclipse"

Moreover, the subject positions of these BC verbs impose animacy and voli-tionality restrictions on potential subjects, hence the unacceptability of (107b) and (108b).[100]

(107)a. Haca   nesis xot'o   zek'si
         door-erg his   foot-abs hit-past-evid
         "The door hit his foot"

     b. *Haca   nesis xot'o   zek'a yaq
         door-erg his   foot-abs hit-inf begin-fut
         "The door will begin to hit his foot"

(108)a. Kidber hazab   bukay-n
         girl-dat suffering see-past-nonevid
         "The girl suffered"

     b. *Kidber hazab   bukada y-oq-si
         girl-dat suffering see-inf II-begin-past-evid
         "The girl began to suffer"

Second, the case marking on the overt subject is always that which is found on subjects in the embedded clause. For example, *bic'zi boqa* (understand.inf) takes a dative subject regardless of whether it is embedded under *-oqa*.[101]

(109)   kidber   hisab   bic'zi   boqa y-oq-si[102]
        girl-dat math-abs understand-inf II-begin-past-evid
        "The girl began to understand math"

Third, In Tsez, scrambling is rather free both to the left and the right. However, it is also clause bounded. In particular, scrambling out of an infinitive is not permitted. With this in mind, scrambling can be used as a diagnostic of sentence structure. In *-oqa* constructions, the overt subject cannot scramble with matrix clause elements.

(110)a.   hul   [kidba ziya bisra] y-oq-si
          yesterday girl   cow feed   began
          "Yesterday, the girl began to feed the cow"

     b.   *kidba hul   [ziya bisra] y-oq-si
          Girl   yesterday cow feed   began

Moreover, it is possible to scramble the whole embedded clause and when one does the subject cannot be left behind but must scramble with the rest of the clause.

(111)a.   hul   [kidba ziya bisra] y-oq-si
          yesterday girl   cow feed   began
          "Yesterday, the girl began to feed the cow"

     b.   hul   y-oq-si [kidba ziya bisra]
          Yesterday began   girl   cow feed

     c.   *hul   kidba y-oq-si [ziya bisra]
          Yesterday girl   began   cow feed

This is what we expect if the overt subject *kidba* is part of the complement clause.

Event quantification data further support the proposed BC phrase structure. Consider (112a). It is ambiguous with *uyrax* (four times) modifying the embedded verb (four feedings, (112b)) or the matrix verb (four beginnings, (112c)). (112d), in contrast, only has the reading in which the embedded clause is modified (four feedings). This is what we would expect if the overt subject were in the embedded clause.

(112)a.   Uyrax   kidba ziya bisra y-oq-si
          four times girl   cow feed began
          "The girl began to feed the cow four times"

     b.   Uyrax [kidba ziya bisra] y-oq-si

     c.   [Uyrax kidba ziya bisra] y-oq-si

    d.   [kidba uyrax   ziya bisra] y-oq-si
          girl   four times cow feed begin

Polinsky and Potsdam present other evidence all pointing to the same conclusions; namely that in Tsez BC constructions the subject position of the matrix is obligatorily null, thematic, and obligatorily bound by the embedded overt subject. They account for these facts by proposing that BC constructions involve covert movement of the embedded subject to the matrix theta position at LF. Thus, examples like (113a) have LF structures like (113b).

(113)a.   EC [kidba ziya bisra] yoqsi
         EC girl   cow feed begin

    b.   Kidba [kidba ziya bisra] yoqsi

At LF, *kidba* moves to the matrix theta position of *-oqa* and thereby assumes the matrix theta role.

Polinsky and Potsdam provide independent evidence for the proposed LF A-movement. Tsez reflexives are clause bound (114a). However, a reflexive in the matrix of a BC construction can be bound by a DP in a lower clause (114b). This makes perfect sense if the lower DP raises to the matrix clause at LF and from there binds the reflexive.

(114)a. Babir_1 nesa $\text{nesir}_{1/*2}$ etin   [uza_2 yutku roda]
         Father refl   wanted boy house make
         "The father wanted for himself that the boy build the house"

    b.   Nesa nesir_1 oqsi [yesi zek'a_1 yutku roda]
         refl   begin this man   house make
         "Then the man began for himself to build a house"

Polinsky and Potsdam offer further elaborations of the proposal sketched here and they discuss various technical issues related to its implementation. However, their main point is twofold. First, that the standard theories of control that involve PRO and binding cannot easily account for BC constructions. In fact, in most versions of the standard approach, BC should simply be impossible. Second, they show that it is possible to explain the properties of BC phenomena if one adopts a movement approach to control. In fact, Polinsky and Potsdam note that if theta-roles are syntactic features (as they must be in a movement theory) then "the theory leads us to expect that theta-role features could . . . be weak and thus checked covertly. In the case of Control, a weak theta-role would yield a Backward Obligatory Control configuration in which the lower argument is overt and the higher one is unpronounced" (p. 2).[103]

In sum, Polinsky and Potsdam (2000) offers a plausible account of backward control phenomena in terms of a movement approach to control. The properties of these constructions resist explanation in terms of more standard PRO based accounts.

Polinksy and Potsdam's analysis of backwards control in Tsez extends to other cases in Brazilian Portuguese (BP) described in Farrell (1995). Farrell (1995) discusses the "periphrastic causative construction" illustrated in (115).[104]

(115)a.   A   mulher fez   o   nenê dormir
          The woman made the baby to sleep
          "The woman put the baby to sleep"

     b.   Eu mandei o   sapateiro concertar esse sapato
          I   had   the cobbler fix   these shoes

Farrell (1995) presents evidence that these constructions have the thematic structure of control complements but the surface syntax of ECM constructions. Thus, in overt syntax, in a GB style analysis, (126a) would have the structure (116) and so display backwards control.

(116)   A mulher [fez [PRO₁ [o nenê₁ dormir]]]

Farrell (1995) offers several kinds of evidence for the conclusion that *fazer* (make) and *mandar* (have) have empty thematic objects. Let us review some of these.

First, some evidence that these verbs have a *persuade*-like thematic structure. They do not display voice transparency, that is (117a) is not a paraphrase of (117b).

(117)a.   Eu mandei/fiz o   médico examinar   a minha filha
          I   had/made the doctor to examine to my   daughter
          "I had/made the Dr examine my daughter"

     b.   Eu mandei/fiz a minha filha   examinanda pelo médico
          I   had/made to my   daughter examined   by   the doctor

Expletives are barred from these constructions.

(118)a.   Pro_expl é óbvio que eu sou forte
          it is   obvious that I am strong
     b.   *Aquilo faria Pro_expl ser óbvio   que eu sou forte
          That would make it   obvious that I   am strong

They also impose selectional restrictions on the subject of the embedded clause. Thus, *mandar* does not allow inanimate DPs.

(119)   *Ele mandou a minha temperatura aumentar
        He had   to my   temperature to-rise
        "He had my temperature rise"

These facts all follow if the subject of the embedded clause is also the thematic complement of the matrix *fazer*/*mandar*.

However, there is also evidence that the thematic complement is not a syntactic object of the matrix in overt syntax. For example, in contrast to standard object control verbs, these cannot be passivized. Compare (120a) and (120b).

(120)a.   Os alunos   foram forçados a estudarem mais
          The students were   forced   to study   more

     b.   *O   nenê foi feito dormir
          The baby was made to sleep

These two constructions also differ with respect to being able to use a subject pronoun for the thematic object. Compare (121a,b).

(121)a.   A professor mandou/fez eu apagar o quadro
          The teacher had/made me   erase the board

     b.   *A professor prohibiude eu apagar   o   quadro
          The teacher prohibited me from erasing the board

(121b) prohibits the *eu* form as expected given that this is not allowed in object positions quite generally (122b). However, it is allowed in (121a), suggesting that in overt syntax *eu* is in the embedded subject position, a position that permits *eu* (122a).

(122)a.   Eu falei com ela
          I spoke with her

     b.   *Ela viu eu
          She saw me

The above illustrates the arguments that Farrell (1995) presents to support the conclusion that thematically *fazer/mandar* are *persuade*-like though in their overt syntax they are more like *expect*.[105] Farrell (1995) treats these constructions as instances of backwards control. The movement analysis of control can treat these analogously to the Tsez cases via a process of movement of the embedded subject to the internal theta position of the matrix verb at LF. It is less clear how these data are to be accommodated given a PRO based approach to control.

1.8.2   Brazilian Portuguese null subjects

Consider now a second kind of control, one that appears in sentences that look a lot like finite clauses.[106]

Brazilian Portugese (BP) is in the process of losing pro-drop. It is still possible to find *pro* headed matrix clauses but only if the subject is non-referential. Thus we observe the contrast in (123).

(123)a.   Esta chovendo
          is   raining
          "it is raining"

   b.   Mataram o   presidente
        killed   the president
        "Someone killed the president"

   c.   *Comprou   um carro novo
        bought-3sg a   car   new
        "He bought a new car"

As shown, weather and impersonal constructions permit pro-drop. However, referential use of *pro* is no longer available in matrix clauses.

   Apparent cases of referential null subjects, however, are found in embedded clauses.

   (124)   O Joao$_i$ disse [que ec$_i$ comprou um carro novo]
           John$_i$ said that he$_i$ bought   a   car   new

How is the asymmetry between main and embedded clauses to be accounted for? Ferreira (2000) and Rodrigues (2000) propose that what we find in (124) is not *pro* but control. In particular, they assume, that in cases like (124) the embedded clause need not case mark the subject; this optional case marking being related to the fact that the verbal paradigm is undergoing simplification, which in turn is related to the loss of referential null subjects. In support of this proposal they observe that the empty category in embedded subject position in (124) displays the diagnostic properties of OC. Thus, this empty category requires a local c-commanding antecedent (125a–c), forbids split antecedents (125d), requires a sloppy reading under ellipsis (125e), has to have the bound reading with *only* DPs (125f), and requires *de se* readings (125g).

   (125)a.   *pro$_{expl}$ parece que ec tinha telefonado
             "It seems that he had telephoned"

   b.   *o Joao$_i$ disse [que a Maria acha [que ec$_i$ e esperto]]
        "John said that Mary thinks that he is smart"

   c.   *A Mae do Joao$_i$ acha [que ec$_i$ e esperto]
        "John's mother thinks that he is smart"

   d.   *O Joao$_i$ disse [que Maria$_j$ acha [que ec$_{i+j}$ sao espertos]]
        "John said that Maria thinks that they are smart"

   e.   O Joao acha que ec vai ganhar a corrida e a Maria tambem
        "John thinks that he will win the race and Mary thinks that she
        will too"

f. So o João acha que ec vai ganhar a corrida
    "Only John thinks that he himself will win the race"

g. O Reagan esta convencido de que ec foi um dos nelhores presidentes dos EUA
    "Only Reagan is convinced that he himself was one of the best presidents of the USA"

Further evidence that the empty categories in (125) are not null pronouns comes from the fact that they cannot act as resumptive pronouns, in contrast to *pro* in other Romance languages. Consider the contrast between (126a) and (126b).

(126)a. Ese el tipo que$_1$ Maria conoce a la mujer [con quien ec$_1$ se casó]
         "That is the guy that Maria knows the woman he married"

b. Esse é o rapaz que$_1$ a Maria conhece a garota que ele$_1$/*ec$_1$ gosta
    "This is the guy that Maria knows the girl that he likes"

The *ec* in (126a) is a null pronoun that can act as a resumptive expression. Overt pronouns in BP can play a similar role as (126b) indicates. However, there is no null pronoun in BP as there is in Spanish.

In sum, the empty expression in these constructions looks very much like an OC PRO.

Both Ferreira (2000) and Rodrigues (2000) propose that these empty categories are residues of overt movement. The possibility of such movement is related to the idea that the agreement system in finite clauses is undergoing radical simplification and this is related to the progressive loss of pro-drop in BP. As Ferreira and Rodrigues note, if we assume that in BP the embedded clauses optionally bear case features, we can permit movement from the embedded clause just as we do in standard control complements. We can further relate this quirk in BP to Chomsky's (1999) idea that only a full complement of phi-features must assign case.[107]

There are two more interesting set of facts. First, it appears that BP allows raising from finite clauses.

(127)a. O João parece que ec comprou um carro novo
         John   seems that he bought   a   car   new

b. O João disse que ec comprou um carro novo
    John   said that he bought   a   car   new

As Ferrira (2000) observes, the acceptability of cases like (127a) is not surprising given the proposal that the *ec* in (127b) is due to movement.

Lastly, it appears that one sees similar phenomena inside adjuncts. Most interestingly, the same requirement found in English adjunct control structures (viz. that the subject be the antecedent) extends to these cases.

(128)a.   O João$_1$ foi embora depoi que ec$_1$ brigou   com a Maria
       John$_1$ left   after   he quarreled with   Mary

    b.   *O João conheceau a Maria$_1$ depois que ec$_1$ ficou   rica
       John   knew   Mary after   that she became rich-fem

Rodrigues (2000) notes that these adjunct cases display the diagnostics characteristic of OC. (129a) indicates that the *ec* requires an antecedent. (129b)
shows that the antecedent must be local and (129c) that it c-command the *ec*.
(129d) indicates that split antecedents are prohibited, (129e) that only sloppy
readings are allowed, and (129f) that bound readings are required with *so*
(= only).

(129)a.   *ec$_{expl}$ chove toda vez que ec fala   com o Paulo
       It   rains every time that she speaks with   Paulo

    b.   A Ana$_1$ disse que a Maria$_2$ olha para o   chão   toda
       Ana   said that   Maria looks at   the ground every
       vez que ec$_{*1/2}$ fala   com Paulo
       time that she   speaks with Paulo

    c.   [A Mãe   da Maria$_1$]$_2$ olha para o   chão   toda vez
       The mother of Mary   looks at   the ground every time
       que ec$_{*1/2}$ fala   com Paulo
       that she   speaks with Paulo

    d.   *O Luca$_1$ disse que a Ana$_2$ chorou pra caramba depois que ec$_{1+2}$
       Luca   said that   Ana cried   a lot   after   that they
       deixaram o Brasil
       left   Brazil

    e.   A Ana$_1$ voltou   o Rio depois que ec$_1$ ficou gràvida   e
       Ana   returned to Rio after   that she got   pregnant and
       o Luca também
       Luca   too
       (= after Luca got pregnanat, NOT after Ana did)

    f.   Só o Maluf$_1$ ficou triste depois que ec$_1$ perdeu as eleições
       (= Only M is an x such that x got upset after x lost the elections)

In sum, Ferreira (2000) and Rodrigues (2000) show that certain empty categories in finite complements and adjuncts behave just like OC PRO. They
show how to extend the analysis of control as movement in non-finite clauses
to control in these "finite" configurations. These facts are compatible with
a non-movement approach to control. However, it is interesting that these
BP clauses tolerate both control and super-raising, suggesting that both raising and control are reflexes of the same kind of operation, as a movement

approach to control would lead us to expect. Second, instances of both complement control and adjunct control are possible from these "finite" configurations supporting the idea that both are generated by the same grammatical operations, viz. movement on the present proposal.

1.8.3   PRO gate effects

Consider the following contrast noted in Higginbotham (1980).[108]

(130)a.   *Mary's/his$_1$/him$_1$ kissing his$_1$ mother made everyone$_1$ late
     b.   *Who did Mary's/his$_1$/him$_1$ kissing his$_1$ mother upset t$_1$
     c.   PRO$_1$ kissing his$_1$ mother made everyone$_1$ late
     d.   Who did PRO$_1$ kissing his$_1$ mother upset t$_1$

(130a,b) exemplify weak cross over (WCO) effects which Higginbotham analyzed as barring the binding of a pronoun by an antecedent to the right of the pronoun. In (130a) the antecedent is *everyone* (or its LF trace); in (130b) it is the WH-t left by movement of *Who*. What is interesting is that (130c,d) seem to allow the binding prohibited in (130a,b). The PRO in the gerund acts as a "gate" permitting the indicated binding. Higginbotham dubbed this amelioration effect with respect to WCO PRO gate effects. A natural question that arises is why PROs act as gates. Kiguchi (2000) provides an explanation in terms of the movement theory of control. The account proceeds roughly as follows.

Kiguchi (2000) observes that A-movement circumvents the WCO condition. (131) illustrates this.

(131)a.   *Who$_1$ did it seem to his$_1$ mother t$_1$ liked Bill
     b.   Who$_1$ t$_1$ seemed to his$_1$ mother t$_1$ to like Bill

A'-moving *who* in (131a) does not allow pronominal binding as it violates WCO. However, raising *who* to the matrix subject and then A'-moving to Spec CP does not similarly induce a WCO violation, as the acceptability of (131b) shows. Kiguchi's (2000) idea is to generalize this to cases like (130c,d). In particular, if OC PRO is simply an A-trace, then OC PRO should obviate WCO effects. If the PROs in (130c,d) are OC PROs then we can account for their gate-like status.

There is evidence that these PROs are indeed OC PROs. Thus, such PROs require antecedents.

(132)a.   *PRO shaving himself impressed Mary
     b.   *PRO shaving himself made it seem cold outside

Second, they resist split antecedents.

(133)   *John$_1$ said that PRO$_{1+2}$ shaving themselves upset everyone$_2$

Third, they require *de se* readings and only permit bound readings in *only* sentences. Contrast the sentences in (134) with those in (135) where we have an overt pronoun. (135a) is ambiguous with both a *de se* and non-*de se* reading. (134a) only has the *de se* interpretation. (135b) only has a strict reading with the pronoun coreferential with Churchill. This is the reading missing in (134b) where the PRO is interpreted as bound by *only Churchill*.

(134) a.   PRO receiving the medal unnerved the unfortunate
      b.   PRO giving the speech upset only Churchill.

(135) a.   His/him receiving the medal unnerved the unfortunate
      b.   His/him giving the speech upset only Churchill.

Last of all, there are locality and prominence conditions on the antecedent. Thus, the antecedent of PRO must be the most prominent of a series of DPs and cannot be buried inside another DP.

(136)   *PRO_1 shaving himself made Mary believe $John_1$

(137)   *PRO_1 shaving himself upset $John's_1$ mother

Kiguchi (2000) shows that these data all follow if we assume that the PRO in PRO gate constructions are all the residue of sidewards A-movement, the same movement operative in adjunct control.

In sum, the relevant PROs display the diagnostics of obligatory control, which is what we would expect if they were the residues of A-movement, in this case, sidewards A-movement. As such, we can account for their gate-like properties along the lines sketched above.

This approach to PRO gate effects makes a second interesting prediction. Those PROs that cannot be the residue of movement should not act as gates and should not ameliorate WCO violations. This too seems to be correct. Consider sentences like (138).

(138) a.   *Who_1 did the fact that PRO_1 cooking his_1 lunch took all afternoon annoy t_1
      b.   *The fact that PRO_1 cooking his_1 mother lunch took 30 minutes kept no one_1 in the kitchen

The PROs here are OC PROs as they occur within complex NP islands. As such, they cannot be the residues of movement but must be null pronominals like *pro*. As such, they should not aid in ameliorating WCO effects.

Moreover, we expect these PROs to function like pronouns in other ways. As (139) indicates, this expectation is born out.

(139) a.   The fact that PRO cooking for oneself takes time annoys John
      b.   The fact that PRO_1 cooking herself lunch took 30 minutes made John angry at $Mary_1$

c. The fact that PRO_1 cooking himself lunch took 30 minutes made John's mother angry

d. The fact that PRO_{1+2} cooking themselves lunch took 30 minutes made $John_1$ angry at $Mary_2$

e. The fact that PRO_1 receiving the medal took 30 minutes annoyed the $unfortunate_1$

f. The fact that PRO_1 giving the speech took 30 minutes annoyed only $[Churchill]_1$

These PROs do not require proximate prominent antecedents (139a–c). They allow split antecedents (139d), non-*de se* readings (139e) and strict readings with *only* (139f). These are the hallmarks of a pronoun. It is thus not surprising that like other pronouns they are subject to WCO conditions and do not function like OC PROs in ameliorating WCO effects.

In sum, Kiguchi (2000) provides an independent argument that OC PROs are residues of A-movement and that NOC PROs are pronoun like. The former act like gates with respect to WCO just like A-traces do in more familiar raising constructions. The latter, being pronominal, do not. This account of PRO gate effects constitutes independent evidence for the supposition that OC PROs are formed by movement.

1.9   Conclusion

Recently there has been a resurgence of interest in control phenomena prompted by the theoretical turn to minimalism. Like all actions in some theoretical direction, this one has prompted a reaction against movement based approaches. This review has had three aims: to re-advertise the virtues of a movement approach, to parry some of the principal arguments against its viability and to present some more recent evidence that supports it. It is for the reader to judge how successful this effort has been. However, before closing, let me reiterate two points made at the outset. First, there are many versions of the movement approach. I am most familiar with one of these and so I have illustrated the virtues of the movement theory using it. However, much of what was advanced here in one technical garb could have been equally well promoted exploiting other details of implementation. Second, it is worth bearing in mind that these movement based analyses are of relatively recent vintage. We should thus expect empirical problems to beset them. What I find interesting is not that they indeed have empirical weaknesses, but that there are not more of them.[109] Movement theories can only get off the ground by rejecting long-held core assumptions about the principles that regulate grammatical structure and derivations. It must reject the theta criterion and the idea that thematic roles can only be saturated by merge/lexical insertion (i.e. cannot be saturated by movement). It is surprising, I believe, that setting these assumptions aside does not result in theoretical chaos. If nothing else, putting these assumptions to one side has allowed us to explore our earlier theoretical assumptions more closely. It has also opened up, or, more accurately perhaps, revived, novel ways of thinking about control phenomena. Even if these should prove to be incorrect, I hope that they will serve as useful foils for future more theoretically principled and empirically richer proposals.

Notes

1   Various people have commented on earlier drafts of this chapter. I would like to thank David Lightfoot, Juan Uriagereka, Acrisio Pires, Klea Grohmann, and Martin Hackl for their kind indulgence. I would also like to thank Randy Hendrick for detailed comments on an earlier draft. This work was supported by NSF grant SBR-9817569.

2   Bowers (1973) is the earliest proposal that I know of in the generative literature for treating raising and control as essentially the same. Others have made similar proposals since, including Bresnan (1982).

3   This concept goes back to the earliest models of generative grammar. The thematic properties of d-structure are roughly identical to those enjoyed by kernel sentences in a *Syntactic Structures* style theory. Kernel sentences were input to transformational processes and were the locus of (what we now call) theta-roles. *Aspects* substitutes the base for kernel sentences. The base is a pre-transformational phrase marker generated by phrase structure rules. Like kernel sentences, it is the input to the transformational component and the locus of thematic information. This role for the base has been retained in some form in all subsequent theories.

4   Having both d-structure and the theta criterion as parts of UG is redundant and so, undesirable. Note that there is little to methodologically recommend the idea that DPs (or chains) can bear but single theta-roles. There is nothing odd about the idea that a single expression should saturate several variable positions and hence bear several theta-roles. Thus structures like (i) are perfectly coherent and plausibly represent a situation on which one expression, *John* bears two theta-roles, viz. the washer and washee.

    (i)   John λx (x wash x)

If so, on its own, the biuniqueness assumption stipulated in the theta criterion is methodologically as interesting as all stipulations are. This does not imply, however, that the stipulation is empirically without merit, only that it has no conceptually independent motivation.

5   Move is resolved into two more basic operations, Copy and Merge. In place of traces, therefore, we find copies. There are other ways of implementing the idea that traces be replaced by copies (e.g. via a re-merge operation) but which technical implementation is adopted is of no relevance here.

6   I do not mean to say that movement *is* independently motivated. Only that a theory with both kinds of processes is to be avoided *ceteris paribus*. I assume that the preferred reduction is construal to movement but the methodological point remains even if the other tack is taken.

7   One needs to further assume that in examples like (10e) the +WH C^0 does not govern across IP.

8   See Bouchard (1984) where there is an attempted account of (11) in terms of case theory and Chomsky (1981) where the distribution of PRO is accounted for in binding theoretic terms on the assumption that PRO is at once +pronominal and

+anaphoric. For a brief review of these issues against a minimalist backdrop see Hornstein (1997).

9   See Rosenbaum (1970).

10   See Williams (1980), Koster (1984), Lebeaux (1984–5) and Manzini (1983).

11   This paradigm derives from Williams (1980), Lebeaux (1984–5), Higginbotham (1992) and Fodor (1975).

12   At least in the standard cases. We return to this below in the discussion of sidewards movement.

13   The split antecedent diagnostic has been challenged by Landau (1999, p. 136). He claims that OC PRO can support split antecedents "in most environments." I believe that this is simply incorrect. There is a very clear contrast between cases like (14e) and (16e). The latter easily permits the binding of a reciprocal while the former strongly resists this.

The counterexample offered by Landau are sentences like (i).

(i)   John$_1$ persuaded/suggested to Mary$_2$ [PRO$_{1+2}$ to get themselves a new car]

However, these sorts of examples show very little. First, many native speakers of English find examples like (i) simply unacceptable. Second, even for those who accept these marginally, they reject the sentences when the anaphor is replaced with a reciprocal.

(ii)a.   *John persuaded Mary to get each other a car
    b.   *Did you suggest to Mary to get each other a new car?

Third, for some of these same speakers, examples like (iii) where the reflexive is replaced by a pronoun are also marginally acceptable. Thus, there may not be a complementary distribution between anaphors and pronouns in this context.

(iii)   ?*John$_1$ persuaded Mary$_2$ [PRO$_{1+2}$ to get them$_{1+2}$ a new car]

Fourth, myriad other examples are uniformly rejected.

(iv)a.   *John persuaded Mary PRO to wash/shave themselves/each other
    b.   *John persuaded Mary PRO to drive each other/themselves around

Fifth, for those who accept examples like (i), there is no clear contrast between them and (v), these latter not being control contexts at all.

(v)   John$_1$ expected Mary$_2$ to get themselves$_{1+2}$ a new car

It is worth noting that none of this affects the NOC examples in (16) where the analogous examples are all perfectly fine. For example, contrast (iv) and (vi).

(vi)   John persuaded Mary that [PRO washing/shaving each other/themselves] would amuse Sam

Cases like (vi) are uniformly acceptable.

I conclude that the claim that OC PRO resists split antecedents is well grounded and that OC and NOC PRO contrast significantly along this dimension.

14   Minimalist reasoning also casts suspicion on government as a primitive grammatical relation. To the degree that government cannot be exploited as a descriptive predicate, the standard GB analysis fails. See Chomsky (1993, 1995) for discussion.

15   This, in effect, returns us to a version of Bouchard's proposal that reduced the distribution of PRO to case theory. The details of the Chomsky and Lasnik proposal, however, are rather different.

16 See also Landau (1999) and Wurmbrand (1998) for further refinements.
17 For some criticism of Stowell's assumption that raising clauses have different tense properties from control clauses see Brugger (1997). Martin (1996) also notes that some raising clauses have independent tense specifications.
18 These examples are from Martin (1996, p. 59, n. 82). Event denoting predicates are meant to contrast with stative predicates like (i).

    (i)   John believes Mary to be tall

    I do not fully agree with Martin's specification of the facts presented here. See the following note for a brief discussion.
19 I assume that case is checked in the outer spec of *v* rather than AgrO, though nothing hangs on this. I also assume for expository purposes that the raising is overt and that further V-movement provides the requisite linear order.
20 ECM only appears to be acceptable with subjects that are WH-traces, not full DPs; why is unclear.
21 Observe that this does not argue against treating some T^{0}s as tensed and others as untensed, as suggested in Stowell (1982). Rather, it argues against correlating this property of T^0 with any null case assignment properties. For a sophisticated consideration of related issues and possible answers to the objections raised here see Martin (1996, ch. 2).
22 This section is based on the discussion in Pires (2001). See this paper for a detailed discussion of the points briefly made here. For related observations based on Japanese control configurations, see Aoshima (2001).
23 Virtually all current theories of control would require a PRO in such configurations, including those like Wurmbrand (1998) that treat some control structures as PRO-less. The reason is that these gerunds alternate with those that can have overt accusative subjects.

    (i)   John remembered Bill bringing the wine

24 This section focuses on OC PRO. NOC PRO is discussed in section 7. The details of this proposal exploit the ideas outlined in Hornstein (1999, 2000). However, there are other proposals that adhere to the logic outlined here though they differ in technical implementation. See, for example, Manzini and Roussou (2000) and O'Neill (1995). Both these proposals involve the assumption that the same grammatical operations underlie control and raising, though they differ as to how this difference is to be characterized.
25 Note that *who* is deletable in (26b) so that the problem is not with some case that the WH element must bear.
26 These data are discussed in Boeckx (2000) and Hornstein (2000).
27 Before proceeding, however, one point is worth making: these problems for null case do *not* imply that this approach to the distribution of PRO is wrong. Perhaps it is empirically superior to the movement based account outlined below. However, it is clear that the null case theory has *methodological* problems which should prompt a minimalist to hope to do better.
28 I assume here the copy theory of movement. A deleted copy is represented in brackets, e.g. (John). I also assume that the predicate internal subject hypothesis is correct. Thus, all subjects are theta marked within the immediate projection of a thematic head. For present purposes, I adopt the idea that the EPP holds for all clauses, including non-finite clauses.
29 Why this is so is an interesting question. See Nunes (1995) for a possible answer.

30 It is not clear what makes a feature a feature. What is relevant here is the assumption that theta-roles are feature-like in the following way: checking one suffices to allow greedy movement.

31 His discussion is based on earlier work by González (1988, 1990).

32 These cases parallel certain examples in Tsez, a caucasian language, discussed below in section 1.8. These data also contrast in an interesting manner with what occurs in Icelandic control structures. Here raising and control structures contrast in that one cannot get DPs that bear the quirky case of an embedded predicate surfacing as the subject of a control predicate though this is common in raising constructions (Thráinsson, 1986). It remains unclear why it is that Icelandic differs in this regard from Tsez and Spanish. However, Icelandic control clauses are quite problematic for most current minimalist accounts. For example, it appears that control clauses bear regular case, not simply null case (Sigursson, 1991). Moreover, control clauses contrast with raising clauses in requiring V to I(nflection) movement for some reason (see Sigurssson, 1989; Hornstein, 1990). It is unclear how (or whether) these differences relate to the facts noted above. However, it is clear that the Icelandic facts and the Tsez, Spanish facts are pulling in opposite directions.

33 Boskovic provides numerous other examples that lead to this same conclusion, viz. that movement between thematic positions is possible. He (1994, p. 273) notes a rather interesting case from Italian first discussed in Burzio (1986). It concerns sentences like (i).

> (i) (expletive) ne vorrebbero arrivare molti all festa prima di Mario
>   of them would want to arrive many to the party before Mario
>   "Many of them would want to arrive at the party before Mario"

As noted, *molti* is clearly located in the embedded clause in overt syntax. However, it is also interpreted as the matrix clause subject (in conjunction with the cliticized *ne*). Burzio notes that these examples are a problem for theta theory as the matrix subject theta-role is unsaturated in both DS and SS. Note that these structures pose no serious problem for a movement theory if we assume that movement through theta positions is licit at LF. For other cases that can be analyzed similarly, cases of "backwards control," see the discussion in section 1.8 below.

34 Saito (1992) provides a lot of evidence establishing this fact.

35 Boskovic and Takahashi review other evidence pointing to this conclusion. The interested reader is referred to their paper and the references cited there.

36 Boskovic and Takahashi (1998) rely on the assumption that long scrambling must be base generation as movement is greedy while Merge need not be. This relies on an assumption in a vintage form of minimalism in which Move differed from Merge in being subject to Greed (see Chomsky, 1995). However, recent versions of minimalism have assumed that Merge too is subject to Greed (see Chomsky, 1998). If so, the theory internal motivation for having the long scrambled expression merged into its surface position is weakened, though the empirical reasons offered still stand.

37 Which, of course, does not mean that it is false. Boskovic (1994) offers a way of doing this. However, what is clear is that adopting this sort of view requires a methodological compromise that, *ceteris paribus*, is best avoided.

38 However, recall that this is only the *typical* case. If inherent reflexives like *wash*, *dress*, *comb*, *shave*, etc. also involve movement, then this constitutes a further problem for a case theoretic approach to control that ties null case to the properties of certain T^0s.

39   This is the standard view within generative grammar starting with Rosenbaum (1970). It assumes that the core properties of control can be largely traced to the structural properties of control configurations.

40   As observed in section 3, the distinction between OC and NOC PRO goes back to the earliest days of generative grammar where the rule of Equi NP Deletion was contrasted with Super Equi. It survived in various forms into the EST era. For discussion, see Chomsky and Lasnik (1977), Fodor (1975), Koster (1984), Lebeaux (1984–5), Manzini (1983), and Williams (1980). Though not every author endorsed exactly the same distinction, the opposition between the two cases of control has been widely recognized.

   For present purposes, I do not distinguish between types of pronouns: logophoric versus bound versus referential, etc. There may well be further differences that this crude distinction glosses over. For the nonce, we abstract away from these differences.

41   This derivation assumes that the EPP holds in non-finite clauses. This assumption has been challenged in Castillo, Drury, and Grohmann (1999) Epstein and Seely (2000), and Hornstein (2000). There are good theory internal reasons to suppose that a movement approach to OC fits poorly with the idea that the EPP holds in non-finite clauses. However, for present purposes, I abstract away from these issues. See the work noted above for discussion.

42   (46) has an underlying small clause structure. I ignore these details here.

43   Furthermore, the strict reading is not derivable if we adopt the approach to NOC PRO outlined in section 1.7 below. In particular, to get a strict reading requires having a pronoun-like expression in cases like (14d). So the LF must be like (i) for ellipsis to be licensed (see Merchant, 1999 for discussion of the semantic equivalence conditions required for ellipsis).

   (i)   John$_1$ wants pro$_1$ to win and Bill$_2$ wants pro$_1$ to win

   However, we assume below that *pro* can be used in control structures only if movement is barred. This is not the case in these configurations. As such, the "pronominal" PRO required here to license the strict reading is prohibited. As such, only the sloppy reading is available. The semantic form of the sentence is (ii).

   (ii)   John $\lambda x\{x$ wants x to win$\}$ and Bill $\lambda x\{x$ wants x to win$\}$

   This yields the sloppy reading. Ellipsis is possible because the two VPs mutually entail one another.

44   See Lasnik and Uriagereka (1988, ch. 5) for a review of Higginbotham's original discussion of this. See Hornstein (2000, ch. 5) and Lidz and Idsardi (1997) for proposals that local anaphors are also the residues of overt A-movement.

45   See Salmon (1986) for discussion. He points out that there is an important semantic difference between an expression saturating two argument positions and two distinct expressions that are in a binding relation but with each saturating its own argument position. The former has a *de se* reading that the latter lacks. (ia) illustrates a case in which a pronoun bound by a quantificational antecedent allows a non *de se* reading. This contrasts with (ib) where only a *de se* reading is possible.

   (i)a.   No unfortunate$_1$ expected that he$_1$ would receive a medal
      b.   No unfortunate expected PRO to receive a medal

   The contrast shows that binding is insufficient to force a *de se* reading. See Hornstein (2000, ch. 2) for further discussion of this point.

46 Martin (1996) offers a hybrid theory in which PRO is base generated but there is a kind of clitic raising that results in a chain being formed between the PRO and its antecedent at LF. Roussou and Manzini (1997) develop a theory based on feature attraction rather than movement but they too end up with a chain at LF. O'Neill (1995) and Hornstein (1999) implement the movement theory using a standard overt A-movement analysis. They too end up with a single chain at LF mediating the controller and controllee.

47 We return to some exceptions to this generalization in a moment.

48 This solution is based on earlier work by Nunes (1995) on parasitic gaps where sidewards movement operations are advocated.

49 See Nunes (1995) where parasitic gaps are analyzed in this way. The idea is also explored by Bobaljik and Brown (1997) and Uriagereka (1998) for head movement.

50 Several other assumptions are required for the following proposal to be viable. As the details have been discussed in Hornstein (2000), I do not review them here. However, one important additional assumption is (i)

(i) The Extension Condition holds for all grammatical operations including the merger of adjuncts

(i) is needed to account for CED effects. Note that the present proposal allows apparent movement from an adjunct. However, this is mere appearance. At the time that movement occurs, what will *become* the adjunct has not yet adjoined. Once adjoined it triggers CED effects. Assumption (i) is required to derive this result. (i) treats adjunction like any other kind of merge operation in requiring it to obey extension. Thus, adjuncts cannot be counter cyclically merged. This differs from Chomsky (1993) where adjunction is treated as an exception to the Extension Condition. For discussion, see Hornstein (2000).

51 The derivation abstracts away from whether accusative case is checked by overt movement.

52 What drives this conclusion then is an economy assumption. In Hornstein (2000) I assumed that the economy assumption was similar to the one underlying the preference for Merge over Move as in Chomsky (1995). However, this may be incorrect. There is evidence that sidewards movement may be inherently more "expensive" than movement within a single sub-tree. In other words, structural descriptions involving two sub-trees are less preferable than those involving but one. If so, sidewards movement will be delayed as long as possible. This too will derive the fact that adjuncts are controlled by subjects, not objects (at least in transitive constructions).

53 This sentence is acceptable with the indicated reading if the adjunct is interpreted as modifying the matrix verb. This is, however, an irrelevant reading for the point being made. Note that if one preposes the adjunct, the preferred reading is modification of the matrix verb.

54 These cases were pointed out to me by John Nissenbaum (private communication).

55 See Culicover and Jackendoff (2001) and Landau (1999).

56 I suspect that this is not how Landau understands the notion "marked." I suspect that for him it means something like "OK, but not perfectly acceptable." This is a non-technical use of the term which has no theoretical standing so far as I can tell. Marked constructions can be perfectly acceptable (e.g. Verb raising in Romance) and unmarked constructions rather unacceptable (e.g. center-embedded sentences). There exists no theoretical relationship between being marginally acceptable and grammatically marked, so far as I know.

57   Gary Milsark (p.c.) believes that the data in C. Chomsky (1969) contains an even more powerful argument for the markedness of *promise* than the one noted here. Chomsky (1969) claimed late acquisition for the *promise* structures. However, Milsark observes that her data make a different argument: the acquisition data are all over the place with some 9-year-olds never getting it right and some 6- and 7-year-olds doing just fine. It appears that some speakers never quite get the hang of sentences like "Fred promised Bill to leave." If this is correct, as Milsark notes, it provides an even more direct argument for the markedness of *promise*. It appears that it really is very difficult to finally converge on subject control readings in sentences like this, so difficult that some never do manage. This is precisely what the MDP (and the movement based account that subsumes it) would lead one to expect.

58   Let me beat this horse dead with an example. Farkas (1988) proposes that control is sensitive to the RESP(ONSIBILITY) relation in that controllers are intentional initiators of situations that they bring into effect. This is intended to cover both *persuade* and *promise* verbs. Say that this is so. We now have a problem. Why is it that the two verbs are learned at different rates? Why is *promise* more marked? It must be because it and *persuade* are not the same with respect to the RESP relation in some way. Indeed Farkas' proposal is intended to be understood in terms of markedness. But then we are back where we started. How do we code this? In the verb type. But whether the verb is marked with respect to RESP or minimality seems of little moment logically.

59   In fact, Lakoff (1970) explores various ways of lexically marking exceptions to grammatical processes.

60   Note that (i) *without* the preposition displays object control.

   (i)   John committed Bill PRO to leave early

   This suggests that what allows subject control in the *commit to* construction is the presence of the preposition.

61   Kitihara (1996) has a proposal to this effect. There are various ways to implement this. One might argue that *to* incorporates into *promise* or that it is null to begin with. What is important is that where overt movement applies a preposition is present so minimality is irrelevant and at LF the presence of the preposition can be ignored. This can be implemented in a derivational theory in various ways.

62   I owe this point to discussion with Jacek Witkós.

63   For a good review of the various approaches to this effect see Landau (1999, ch. 5.3).

64   Some might consider the subtlety of this idiolectally highly variable data sufficient grounds for placing such cases outside the domain of core grammar. Those inclined to such a conclusion can skip the rest of this section.

65   Chomsky (1980) notes that changing *be allowed to* to *get permission for* disrupts the possibility of this control shift. Compare (72) with (i).

   (i)a.   John$_1$ asked Mary$_2$ PRO$_{?*1/2}$ to get permission to leave
      b.   John$_1$ promised Mary$_2$ PRO$_{1/?*2}$ to get permission to leave

   The cases in (i) are very infelicitous with the shifted readings, if acceptable at all.

66   I owe the following to discussion with Juan Uriagereka.

67   What of the second kind of partial control reading, the one involving *promise* in (72b). I sadly have little of interest to say about it. It appears, however, to be even more sensitive to minor perturbations than the *ask* cases are. See Landau (1999, pp. 212 ff.) for comments. He notes that Comrie (1984) rejects cases like (ib) and

Chomsky (1980) finds that substituting *get permission* for *be allowed to* in (ia) leads to only the non-shifted reading. It contrasts with the *ask* cases in several interesting ways, however.

First, it does not invert control so much as expand it. Thus, the examples in (i) allow both subject and object control.

(i)a.　?John promised Mary PRO to be allowed to go to the movies
　　b.　?John promised Mary PRO to be healthy at game time

This contrasts with the *ask* cases where the object control disappeared under control shift.

In other respects, however, it patterns like *ask/beg/petition*. The PRO does not require an antecedent.

(ii)　It was promised to be allowed to wash before dinner

It allows split antecedents.

(iii)　John promised Mary PRO to be allowed to wash themselves before dinner

It seems to permit a strict reading under ellipsis.

(iv)　John promised Frank to be allowed to rest before the talk and Mary too (Frank promised Mary that Frank would be allowed to rest)

These data support the idea that *promise* also involves NOC under control shift. However, why it contrasts with *ask* remains unclear.

68　His diagnostic properties are largely similar to those outlined above but there are some differences regarding the status of split antecedents. For current purposes I assume that PC and EC differ only on this single dimension made evident in the capacity of the PRO to license collective predicates like *meet*.

69　Actually, if this is an AGREE operation, then it is likely that the Probe is T-Agr and it AGREEs with the goal PRO prior to movement of PRO to Spec TP. This would be the standard AGREE configuration.

70　Landau (1999, p. 18) observes that he must revise the PIC to allow PRO to be visible but the embedded T-Agr to be outside the purview of the matrix probe. There are no apparent ill effects of doing this, he notes, but it is unclear why it should be that the Specifier of IP should be "visible" while the head of IP should not be, given that the label of the IP projection is identical to the head on bare phrase structure assumptions.

71　There is one more curious fact. The proposal must be assuming that AGREE is not a checking operation but an assignment operation. Consider why. Say that all AGREE did was see if features matched up to non-distinctness. Then in (76a) the DP could match F on all phi-features while PRO could match F only on person and gender features being unspecified for number. This would then allow PRO to be unspecified for number in (76a) and so, it would seem, permit a PC reading. So the assumption must be that this is not possible, that in such a case AGREE implies identity not non-distinctness. Now consider (76b). If AGREE were identity then the T-Agr must have the same phi-features as F and PRO must as well. But then F, PRO and DP must all have the same number specification. But then PC should not hold. So, AGREE cannot be feature checking.

That means that the current technology requires that AGREE involve assigning features, not merely checking them. This, you will recall, appears at odds with inclusiveness if we interpret this to mean that the semantic properties of an expression cannot be changed derivationally. In sum, AGREE cannot be feature checking and must involve feature assignment.

72   Recall that control is a much tighter relation than co-reference. The relation between a controller and a PRO in OC structures is quite different from the relation that holds between an antecedent to a bound or co-referential pronoun. Noting this is sufficient to establish that two expressions sharing identical features is not sufficient to establish the relation that underlies control in a way to distinguish it from pronominal binding.

73   See Castillo, Grohmann, and Drury (1999), Epstein and Seely (2000), Groat (1999), and Hornstein (2000) for discussion.

74   Such an approach to PC assumes that verbs like *meet* do not require *grammatically* plural subjects. This implies that sentences like (i) are grammatical though semantically deviant.

    (i)   John met

The restriction on *meet* is that there be understood to be a plurality of meeters, not that there be a plural subject. This seems correct; anyhow given the acceptability of sentences like (ii).

    (ii)a.   The committee met at 6
        b.   John met with the men at 6

75   Note that the gerundive structure of the adjunct is not the relevant factor given the possibility of PC with gerunds.

    (i)   John prefers meeting/gathering at 6

76   Landau (1999, p. 134) accounts for the absence of PC in these configurations by noting that the adjunct is an island and so not subject to AGREE. This would then block an AGREE relation between the T-Agr element in the adjunct and the higher T. The problem with this analysis, however, is that it does not explain two features of the indicated structures. First, they display all the other diagnostic properties of OC, as indicated. Second, it requires assuming that logophors (these occupy the subject position of infinitives within islands) cannot have PC-like readings. But this is incorrect.

    (i)   John said that PRO meeting/gathering together at 6 would be fine with him

The PRO in (i) can sustain a PC-like reading. If so, why cannot it do so in the adjunct case in the text? The movement theory answer is that the PRO in the purpose clause is an OC PRO and so patterns as such, while the PRO in (i) is not an OC PRO. See below for further discussion of PC readings and NOC interpretations.

77   The idea that PC structures are the result of a null *tachi*-like element that appears in Japanese PC structures has been suggested by Boeckx (p.c.). He suggests that *tachi* is an adjunct. He also assumes that adjuncts can be merged non-cyclically. In fact, given that *tachi* is phonetically null, it is possible that it gets merged *only* at LF. Let us also assume, following Boskovic (2001) that adjunction to elements in theta positions in prohibited. This implies that *tachi* can only be found on copies in non-theta positions. This would then yield a structure like (i) for (97).

    (i)   John wants [[[John]+tachi] to [John talk about himself] all together . . .

Note that the antecedent for *himself* is plausibly the lowest copy of *John* and it is singular. The matrix *John+tachi* is not the relevant binder.

This implementation is even consistent with the idea that adjunction is not acyclic. If we assume that Boskovic is correct in that adjunction to elements in thematic positions is blocked, we can adjoin *tachi* to *John* after copying it and before merging it to Spec TP. We could also distinguish EC constructions from PC constructions by supposing that the former have no TP projections while the latter do. Given that Spec TP is non-thematic, adjunction of *tachi* will be possible in the first case but not the latter.

This story might still have some problems. For example, it does not say why purpose clauses cannot have PC readings despite being tensed. However, the ideas behind this implementation are consistent with a movement analysis of control and would serve as well.

78   The facts as reported in Landau (1999) require some further elaboration, I believe. It is not correct that all semantically plural predicates permit a PC reading under verbs like *want* or *decide*. For example, the following seem to resist PC readings.

(i)   *John wants/decided to PRO be similar/be touching/to look alike/to sing alike/be a group/to be mutually supporting

These are all predicates that are fine with overt plural subjects. The cases in (i) contrast with Landau's examples in that the embedded verbs all resist additional commitative *with* adjuncts.

(ii)   *John is similar/is a group/sings alike with Bill

This suggests that the relevant generalization behind PC is that certain verbs can select embedded commitatives. How this is to be executed, however, is unclear at present. For further interesting discussion of PC and the subtleties that surround it see Pires (2001).

79   For a very good review, from which I have freely, (though selectively) borrowed here, see Culicover and Jackendoff (2000). I will not be able to deal with all the examples that this paper presents. Nor am I at all confident that the movement theory can be extended to cover all the complexities of the control facts in nominals. What I am more confident of is that there is too little theoretical structure to the proposal offered by Jackendoff and Culicover. What they suggest is that control is basically to be coded in terms of theta theory. But that is about *all* that they propose. Basically, the theory of control consists of a list of controllers coded by thematic role. For example, *try/attempt* is agent control, *tell* is addressee control, *persuade* is patient control, *promise* is source control, etc. (see Culicover and Jackendoff 2000, pp. 38 ff.). Thus, the theory of control is essentially a list. Perhaps they are correct. However, I believe it is worth resisting their conclusion for the time being for two reasons. First, if they are right, then it will be relatively easy to work out the details of the theory. Putting lists together is not all that difficult. Second, the grammatical relation between nominals and their verbal counterparts is not always well understood theoretically. Until the relation between the two is better understood it seems premature to conclude that the nominal tail should wag the verbal dog. Of course, it may well be that the nominal side is the dog and the verbal one the tail and, if so, perhaps the present movement approach to control is misconceived.

80   Randy Hendrick (private communication) notes that were OC a function of movement (as proposed here) then the absence of OC inside DPs leads us to expect the absence of raising as well. As is well-known, there is no raising within DP.

> (i)a. *John's$_1$ appearance [t$_1$ to leave]
>   b. John appeared to leave

Hornstein (2000) suggests a way of getting control (but not raising) within DPs via sidewards movement. The data reviewed here suggests that this view is incorrect. What then blocks sidewards movement? One possibility is to assume that the external arguments of DPs are not like those in verbs. The latter are licensed by *v*. It is plausible that Nouns do not have *v* projections and so do not have external thematic arguments. A similar claim is made by Williams (1994, p. 52). If so, the sidewards movement postulated in Hornstein (2000) would be barred by Greed and the absence of OC inside DPs would follow.

81 Juan Uriagereka and Ilhan Cagri (private communication) note that the distinction between raising and control within nominatives might not be as clean cut as generally assumed. Thus there are odd holes in the paradigm of OC structures.

> (i)a. *John's trial (from *try*) PRO to leave
>   b. *John's start PRO to leave
>   c. *John's finish PRO leaving

And there are some cases of apparent raising that seem remarkably acceptable.

> (ii) (?) John's likelihood PRO to break a leg rose considerably with the advent of the icy conditions on the slopes

These data suggest that the sharp contrast assumed to hold between raising and control in nominals might be somewhat more blurred than usually thought.

82 See, for example, Keenan (1987).

83 This sort of reasoning might also extend to "object" control cases.

> (i)a. John's order to Frank to wash himself/each other/ourselves
>   b. John's pressure on Frank to have himself/themselves/ourselves admitted

The cases involving *himself* strongly favor the object reading. This is not required, however, as the licensing of plural anaphors and *ourselves* indicates. Reasoning analogous to the one on the text could hold for the cases in (i). For example in (ii).

> (ii) I hated John's order to Frank to leave

This has as one reasonable paraphrase (iii).

> (iii) John ordered Frank to leave and I hated it.

Here, *Frank* is necessarily understood as the leaver. If (ii) is so understood, then we will have the appearance of object control.

84 NOC is the counterpart of what used to be called Super-Equi.

85 They are islands, at least, if the movement is upwards, as would be the case here, rather than sidewards, as would be the case with adjunct control.

86 Landau (1999, p. 134) offers a similar account for NOC. He proposes that AGREE cannot penetrate islands and so OC cannot be found within them. However, contrary to what is proposed here, Landau (1999) treats adjuncts as islands for A-movement. As noted above, this leaves the fact that they display the full range of OC properties unaccounted for. Nonetheless, Landau (1999) is parallel to the suggestion in Hornstein (1999, 2000) in that it treats the absence of OC in certain constructions as due to their island properties.

87 Randy Hendrick (private communication) points out that there are cases that look like control with overt pronouns:

(i)   John confessed that he/*Mary was lazy

Here it appears that we need the indicated coreference. I would assume that the indicated coreference is a consequence of the lexical meaning of *confess* and not really a kind of control similar to what is found in cases of OC discussed above.

88   One possible problem with treating this PRO as *pro* is that it runs foul of the generalization that *pro* does not exist in English which is not a pro-drop language. However, it is possible to interpret the pro-drop parameter in a slightly different way: not as banning *pro* from English, but as prohibiting *pro* from finite subject or case positions. *Pros* which are finite clause subjects can have referential functions, while *pros* in NOC configurations cannot be used referentially. Hornstein (2000) proposes that referential pronouns are lexical elements, in contrast with bound or expletive pronouns. The latter are treated as grammatical formatives while the former are assumed to be in the lexicon. If we assume that all DPs coming from the lexicon require case, then only pro-drop languages will allow *pro* to be referential. In particular, NOC *pro* will not have a referential or deictic use. This seems more or less correct empirically. Thus, (i) cannot be used in a context where NOC PRO is contextually understood deictically, as say John, in the relevant context.

(i)   PRO$_1$ washing would amuse Mary$_2$

89   See Landau (1999, pp. 137 ff.) and works therein cited.
90   Landau cites other cases as well. However, these are not clearly all of a piece. For example, his example (139, (69)) improves dramatically when the tenses are "sequenced."

(i)   John's wife thought that PRO to indulge himself in drinking *is/was inappropriate

Note further that the whole sentence improves again when we drop *in drinking*. It is unclear why this should make any difference, but it does. I similarly find the putative unacceptability of examples like (ii) (see p. 140) rather doubtful.

(ii)   Mary discussed with friends of John the possibility of him/*PRO divorcing her

Analogous cases with reflexives are fine.

(iii)   Mary discussed with friends of John the possibility of him/PRO dressing himself in a tux for dinner

I should add that both cases improve for me if *John* bears genitive case. But this is true in general as I find phrases like *friend of John* awkward.

(iv)   Mary discussed with friends of John's the possibility of him/PRO dressing himself in a tux for dinner

91   See Motomura (2001) for discussion.
92   One must, of course, control for binding restrictions such as being in the scope of the quantificational antecedent.
93   One more point. It might be that logophors are more like referential pronouns than bound pronouns. Hornstein (2000) argues that deictic pronouns are very different from "grammatical" pronouns like epithets and bound pronouns. If logophors are deictic, then they are not last resort expressions of the kind discussed in Hornstein (1999, 2000). It is interesting to observe that the examples in (102) are not particularly felicitous with quantificational antecedents for the overt pronouns.

(102)a.   ?*John said about nobody₁ that it would be easy for him₁ to pass the exam

   b.   *John sued every woman₁ for divorce because it was no longer possible for her₁ to support him

This suggests that logophors are not bindable and so may well be deictic pronouns of sorts, at least in the English examples provided.

94   Of course issues will remain. For example, why NOC PROs are logophors and not simple pronouns. See Sells (1987) for a fuller discussion of logophors. His discussion indicates that logophors (or what have been taken to be such) show quite a bit of cross linguistic variation. Thus, different "roles," in Sell's sense, serve as logophoric antecedents in different languages. As such, it is not clear what empirical consequences follow from saying that some expression is a logophor. This leaves the question of whether NOC PRO is (ever) a logophor or a pronoun somewhat up in the air.

95   Landau (1999, p. 134) makes an analogous suggestion concerning AGREE.

96   See Hornstein (1999, 2000) for discussion of this in the context of both control theory and binding theory. See Aoun, Choueri, and Hornstein (2000) for a discussion of movement as last resort in the context of resumptive pronoun constructions. See also Hornstein (2000) for a general discussion of pronouns along these lines.

97   There are other issues concerning interpretation within control clauses that this chapter ignores. For example, we say nothing about arbitrary control except to say that it is a species of NOC. Note that it is compatible with the views presented here that arbitrary control is a species of OC with an implicit controller (see Epstein, 1984). However, I am skeptical that this is always so given examples like (i).

(i)a.   John thinks that shaving oneself is important to Bill
   b.   John thinks that shaving oneself would amuse Bill

It is not clear where the implicit controller would reside in these cases and yet an arbitrary reading is available.

98   Landau (1999) can be read as making a similar distinction. For him OC PRO is anaphoric and requires Agreement. This, in conjunction with the assumption that Agree does not see into islands forces non-anaphoric PRO within islands. What Landau (1999) does not address is why non-anaphoric PRO cannot occur where the reflexive can. One can answer this by assuming that anaphors must be used where they can be used. One complication within Landau's (1999) theory is that OC PRO is not an anaphor in the sense of being subject to binding principle A. The requirement that anaphors be used in preference to pronouns is typically cast against the background of the binding theory.

99   Polinksy and Potsdam (2000) note that this phenomenon has also been documented in other languages, including Brazilian Portuguese (Farrell, 1995) (see below for discussion), Japanese (Kuroda, 1965, 1978; Harada, 1973).

100   Polinsky and Potsdam note that these effects are similar to Perlmutter's (1970) account of *begin* in English.

101   This is similar to Boskovic (1994) argument concerning dative subjects in *want* constructions in Chilean Spanish discussed above.

102   This sentence is somewhat degraded due to the volitionality requirement placed on the subject of *-oqa*.

103   At the end of the paper, Polinsky and Potsdam suggest that the correct parameterization is not on the strength of theta features but on EPP features and

the pro-drop parameter. However, this suggestion leaves the main thrust of their proposal intact; movement offers an account of BC while standard approaches do not.

104   All the data are taken from Farrell (1995).

105   For further data see Farrell (1995).

106   This section is based on work by Ferreira (2000), Modesto (2000) and Rodrigues (2000).

107   This construction has one further interesting property. It appears to allow partial control readings.

> (i)a.   A Maria disse que ec se encontrou na   rua
>   Mary said that ec SE meet-3 SG in-the street
>
>   b.   A Maria disse que se encontrarem na   rua
>   Mary said that SE meet-3 PL   in the street

It appears that all speakers accept a PC reading for (ia). Some also accept it for (ib), some do not. What is interesting is that the availability of the PC reading seems unaffected by the number features on the verb. Note that in these cases these features are overt. Recall that Landau (1999) ties PC readings to inflections *unspecified* for number. This suggests that where number is overtly specified that partial control readings should be affected. However, as indicated in (i) this seems to be incorrect.

These constructions involve further quirky properties that go beyond the scope of this review. However, it seems clear that studying the properties of these sorts of "control" might well shed light on PC given the overt number morphology available.

108   This section is based on Kiguchi (2000) and Kiguchi and Hornstein (2001).

109   There remain several problems that have not been adequately addressed here. We very briefly noted (note 32) the facts concerning quirky case in raising and control structures in Icelandic. They still await complete analyses in a movement based account. Second, Randy Hendrick (private communication) reminds me of an argument in Lasnik and Saito (1992) that goes as follows. They observe the following contrasts:

> (i)a.   How likely to win is John
>   b.   *How likely to be men at home are there
>   c.   *How likely to be taken of John is advantage

They note that if *likely* could get a control as well as a raising analysis then we could analyze cases like (ia) as control. This would then make the relevant cut. As expletives and idioms are barred from control clauses, only (ia) could have a control structure. The raising would be barred by the requirement that traces be properly governed (the Proper Binding Condition).

Whatever the current status of the Proper Binding Condition, the asymmetry noted in (i) is unexpected on the present analysis unless we explain the differences in (ia) versus (ib,c) in some other way, without adverting to control. Consider the following.

Cases like (ia) have one further distinctive property. It appears that the subject is topic-like in being old information. Thus, (ia) is very odd discourse initially. It is felicitous only if we are talking about John's chances of finishing the race and someone then asks (ia). Note, further, that indefinites are not acceptable here, though definites are. This is what we would expect if the subject had to be a discourse topic.

(ii)a.   *How likely to finish the race is/a man someone/are many people
b.   How likely to finish the race is that man/the man/John/?everyone

Last of all, sentences like (ia) have distinctive intonations, unlike those found in conventional questions. There is a rising at *is* and falling at *John* in (ia). In fact, these questions are unacceptable in embedded contexts where normal questions are required (contrast (iiia) and (iiib)).

(iii)a.   ?*I wonder how likely to finish the race he is
b.   I wonder how likely he is to finish the race

What might this be telling us? Say that for some reason the subject in these constructions is actually a topic (maybe even in topic position and hence not easily embeddable under *wonder*). Then, we would need something that was topic-like here. On the (reasonable) assumption that expletives and idioms cannot be topics (old information) then the cases in (ib) and (ic) would be ruled unacceptable regardless of the control versus raising distinction.

There is some independent reason for thinking that this might be the case. Note that (iva) and (ivb) are about as voice transparent as the raising constructions in (v) (setting aside topicality issues).

(iv)a.   How likely to examine Mary is the Dr
b.   How likely to be examined by the Dr is Mary

(v)a.   The Dr is very likely to examine Mary
b.   Mary is very likely to be examined by the Dr

This is what we would expect if both (iv) and (v) were raising constructions.

There is surely more to say about these (and other) cases. However, this seems like a fine place to stop.

References

Aoshima, S. (2001). Mono-clausality in Japanese Obligatory Control Constructions. Unpublished manuscript. University of Maryland, College Park.

Aoun, J., Choueiri, L. and Hornstein, N. (2001). Resumption, movement and derivational economy. *Linguistic Inquiry*.

Belletti, A. and Rizzi, L. (1988). Psych-verbs and θ-theory. *Natural Language and Linguistic Theory, 6*, 291–352.

Bobaljik, J. and Brown, S. (1997). Interarboreal operations: head movement and the extension requirement. *Linguistic Inquiry, 31*, 357–66.

Boeckx, C. (2000). A note on contraction. *Linguistic Inquiry, 31*, 357–66.

Boskovic, Z. (1994). D-structure, theta-criterion, and movement into theta-positions. *Linguistic Analysis, 24*, 247–86.

Boskovic, Z. (1997). *The syntax of nonfinite complementation: An economic approach.* Cambridge, MA: MIT Press.

Boskovic, Z. (2001). Floating quantifiers and theta role assignment, *Proceedings of NELS, 31*.

Boskovic, Z. and Takahashi, D. (1998). Scrambling and last resort. *Linguistic Inquiry, 29*, 347–66.

Bouchard, D. (1984). *On the content of empty categories.* Dordrecht: Foris.

Bowers, J. (1973). *Grammatical relations*, PhD dissertation, MIT, Cambridge (reprinted as *The Theory of Grammatical Relations* (1981). New York: Garland).

Bresnan, J. (1982). Control and complementation. In J. Bresnan (ed.), *The mental representation of grammatical relations*. Cambridge, MA: MIT Press.

Brugger, G. (1997). Expletive auxiliaries. Unpublished manuscript. UCLA.

Burzio, L. (1986). *Italian syntax*. Dordrecht: Reidel.

Castillo, J. C., Drury, J. E., and Grohmann, K. K. (1999). Merge over move and the extended projection principle. *University of Maryland Working Papers in Linguistics*. Vol. 8, 63–103.

Chomsky, C. (1969). *The acquisition of syntax in children from 5 to 10*. Cambridge, MA: MIT Press.

Chomsky, N. (1957). *Syntactic structures*. The Hague: Mouton.

Chomsky, N. (1965). *Aspects of the theory of syntax*. Cambridge, MA: MIT Press.

Chomsky, N. (1980). On binding. *Linguistic Inquiry*, 11, 1–46.

Chomsky, N. (1981). *Lectures on government and binding*. Dordrecht: Foris.

Chomsky, N. (1993). A minimalist program for linguistic theory. In K. Hale and S. J. Keyser (eds.), *The View from Building 20. Essays in Honor of Sylvain Bromberger*. Cambridge, MA: MIT Press.

Chomsky, N. (1995). *The minimalist program*. Cambridge, MA: MIT Press.

Chomsky, N. (1998). Minimalist issues: the framework. *MIT Occasional Papers in Linguistics*. Vol. 15, Cambridge, MA. MITWPL. To appear in R. Martin, D. Michaels, and J. Uriagereka (eds.), *Step by step*, Cambridge, MA: MIT Press.

Chomsky, N. (1999). *Derivation by phase*. MS, Cambridge, MA: MIT.

Chomsky, N. and Lasnik, H. (1977). Filters and control. *Linguistic Inquiry*, 8(3).

Chomsky, N. and Lasnik, H. (1993). The theory of principles and parameters. In Joachim Jacobs, Arnim von Stechow, Wolfgang Sternefeld, and Theo Vennemann (eds.), *Syntax: An International Handbook of Contemporary Research*. Berlin and New York: Walter de Gruyter. Reprinted in Chomsky (1995), *The minimalist program*. Cambridge, MA: MIT Press. pp. 13–127.

Comrie, B. (1984). Subject and object control: syntax, semantics and pragmatics. *BLS*, 10, 450–64.

Culicover, P. and Jackendoff, R. (2000). *Control is mostly semantic*. MS. Ohio State and Brandeis University.

Culicover, P. and Jackendoff, R. (2001). Control is not movement. *Linguistic Inquiry*, 32, 493–511.

Enç, Murvet (1990). On the absence of the present tense morpheme in English. University of Wisconsin, Madison. Unpublished manuscript.

Epstein, S. D. (1984). Quantifier-pro and the LF representation of PRO-arb. *Linguistic Inquiry*, 15.

Epstein, S. D. and Seely, T. D. (2000). *SPEC-ifying the GF subject: eliminating A-Chains and the EPP within a derivational model*. MS, University of Michigan.

Epstein, S. D., Groat, E. M., Kawashima, R., and Kitahara, H. (1998). *A derivational approach to syntactic relations*. Oxford: Oxford University Press.

Farkas, D. F. (1988). On Obligatory Control. *Linguistics and Philosophy*, 11, 27–58.

Farrell, P. (1995). Backward control in Brazilian Portuguese. In J. M. Fuller, H. Han, and D. Parkinson (eds.), *Proceedings of ESCOL'94*. Ithaca, NY: Department of Linguistics and Modern Languages, Cornell University. (pp. 116–27).

Ferreira, M. (2000). *Hyperraising and null subjects in Brazilian Portuguese*. MS. Univesidade Estadual do Campinas, Campinas.

Fodor, J. (1975). *The language of thought*. New York: Thomas Y. Crowell.

González, N. (1988). *Object raising in Spanish*. New York: Garland.

González, N. (1990). Unusual inversion in Chilean Spanish. In P. Postal and B. Joseph (eds.), *Studies in Relational Grammar*. Chicago: University of Chicago Press.

Groat, E. (1999). Raising the case of expletives. In Samuel D. Epstein, and Norbert Hornstein (eds.), *Working minimalism.* (pp. 27–44). Cambridge, MA: MIT Press.

Harada, S.-I. (1973). Counter-equi NP deletion. *Research Institute of Logopedics and Phoniatrics Annual Bulletin, 7,* 113–47.

Higginbotham, J. (1980). Pronouns and bound variables. *Linguistic Inquiry, 11,* 679–708.

Higginbotham, J. (1992). Reference and control. In R. Larson, S. Iatridou, U. Lahiri, and J. Higginbotham (eds.), *Control and grammar* (pp. 79–108). Dordrecht: Kluwer.

Hornstein, N. (1990). Verb raising in Icelandic infinitives. *NELS, 20,* 215–229.

Hornstein, N. (1997). Control in GB and Minimalism. *Glot International, 2*(8) (reprinted in Cheng and R. Sybesma (eds.), *The first glot international state-of-the-article book* (2000). Berlin: Mouton de Gruyter.

Hornstein, N. (1999). Movement and control. *Linguistic Inquiry, 30,* 69–96.

Hornstein, N. (2000). *Move! a minimalist theory of construal.* Oxford: Blackwell.

Huang, C.-T. J. (1983). A note on the binding theory. *Linguistic Inquiry, 14,* 554–61.

Keenan, E. (1987). A semantic definition of "indefinite NP", in Eric Reuland and Alice ter Meulen (eds.), *The representation of (in)definiteness.* Cambridge, MA: MIT Press, (pp. 286–317).

Keenan, E. (1989). A semantic definition of indefinite NP. In E. Reuland and A. G. B. ter Meulen (eds.), *The representation of (in)definiteness.* Cambridge, MA: MIT Press.

Kiguchi, H. (2000). PRO-gate and movement, Generals Paper, University of Maryland, College Park.

Kiguchi, H. and Hornstein, N. (2001). *PRO-gate and (sidewards) movement.* MS, University of Maryland, College Park.

Kitihara, H. (1997). *Elementary operations.* Cambridge, MA: MIT Press.

Koster, J. (1984). On binding and control. *Linguistic Inquiry, 15,* 417–59.

Kuno, S. (1975). Three perspectives in the functional approach to syntax. *Papers from the Parasession on Functionalism: Chicago Linguistics Society,* April 17, 276–336.

Kuroda, S. Y. (1965). Generative studies in the Japanese language. Doctoral dissertation. Cambridge, MA: MIT.

Kuroda, S. Y. (1978). Case marking, canonical sentence patterns, and counter-equi in Japanese. In John Hinds and Irwin Howard (eds.), *Problems in Japanese syntax and semantics.* Tokyo: Kaitakusha. (pp. 30–51).

Lakoff, G. (1970). *Irregularity in syntax.* New York: Holt, Reinhart and Winston.

Landau, I. (1999). *Elements of control.* PhD Dissertation, MIT, Cambridge.

Larson, R. (1988). On the double object construction. *Linguistic Inquiry, 19,* 335–91.

Lasnik, H. (1995a). Last resort. In S. Haraguchi and M. Funaki (eds.), *Minimalism and linguistic theory* (pp. 1–32). Tokyo: Hituzi Syobo.

Lasnik, H. (1995b). Last resort and attract F. In *Proceedings of FLSM 6* (pp. 62–81). Bloomington, IN: Indiana University Linguistics Club.

Lasnik, H. and Saito, M. (1992). *Move a: Conditions on its application and output.* Cambridge, MA: MIT Press.

Lasnik, H. and Uriagereka, J. (1988). *A course in GB syntax.* Cambridge, MA: MIT Press.

Lebeaux, D. (1984–5). Locality and anaphoric binding. *The Linguistic Review,* 343–63.

Lidz, J. and Isardi, W. J. (1997). Chains and phonological form, in A. Dimitraidis, H. Lee, C. Moisset, and A. Williams (eds.), *Proceedings of the 22nd annual Penn Linguistics Colloquium. University of Pennsylvania Working Papers in Linguistics, 8,* 109–25.

Manzini, M. R. (1983). On control and control theory. *Linguistic Inquiry, 14,* 421–46.

Manzini, M. R. and Roussou, A. (2000). A minimalist theory of A-movement and control. *Lingua,* 409–47.

Martin, R. (1996). *A minimalist theory of PRO and control.* PhD dissertation, University of Connecticut, Storrs.

Modesto, M. (2000). Null subjects and rich agreement. In M. Kato and E. Negão (eds.), *Brazilian Portuguese and the null subject parameter*. Frankfurt am Main: Verbuert.

Motomura, M. (2001). Zibun *as a Residue of Overt A-Movement*. Generals Paper, University of Maryland, College Park.

Nunes, J. (1995). The copy theory of movement and linearization of chains in the minimalist program, PhD dissertation, University of Maryland, College Park.

O'Neill, J. (1995). Out of control. In J. N. Beckman (ed.), *Proceedings of NELS 25* (pp. 361–71). GLSA, University of Massachusetts, Amherst.

Perlmutter, D. (1970). On the article in English. In Manfred Bierwisch and K. E. Heidolph (eds.), *Progress in linguistics* (pp. 233–48). The Hague: Mouton.

Pires, A. (2001). Clausal and TP-defective gerunds: control without tense. In *NELS 31*.

Pires, A. (forthcoming). *The syntax of gerunds and infinitives: subjects, case and control*. PhD dissertation, University of Maryland, College Park.

Polinsky, M. and Potsdam, E. (2000). Long-distance agreement and topic in Tsez. *Natural Language and Linguistic Theory, 19*, 583–646.

Polinsky, M. and Potsdam, E. (2001). *Backwards control*. MS, University of California San Diego and University of Florida, Gainsville.

Rodrigues, C. (1990). *Deriving Brazilian referential null subjects from movement*. Generals Paper, University of Maryland, College Park.

Rodrigues, C. (2000). Deriving Brazilian Portuguese null subjects from movement. Unpublished manuscript. University of Maryland, College Park.

Rosenbaum, P. (1967). *The grammar of English predicate complement constructions*. Cambridge, MA: MIT Press.

Rosenbaum, P. (1970). A principle governing deletion in English sentential complementations. In R. Jacobs and P. Rosenbaum (eds.), *Readings in English Transformational Grammar* (pp. 20–9). Waltham, MA: Ginn.

Roussou, A. and Manzini, R. (1997). Null arguments in early child grammars. *GALA Proceedings UK*. Durham, UK: University of Durham. (pp. 142–7).

Saito, M. (1992). Long distance scrambling in Japanese. *Journal of East Asian Linguistics, 1*, 69–118.

Salmon, N. (1986). Reflexivity. *Notre Dame Journal of Formal Logic, 27*, 401–29.

Sells, P. (1987). Aspects of Logophoricity. *Linguistic Inquiry, 18*, 445–80.

Sigursson, H. A. (1989). *Verbal syntax and case in Icelandic*. PhD dissertation, University of Reykjavik, Reykjavik.

Sigursson, H. A. (1991). Icelandic case marked PRO and the licensing of lexical arguments. *Natural Language and Linguistic Theory, 9*, 327–63.

Stowell, T. (1982). The tense of infinitives. *Linguistic Inquiry, 13*, 561–70.

Thráinsson, H. (1986). On auxilliaries, AUX and VPs in Icelandic. In L. Hellan and K. K. Christensen (eds.), *Topics in Scandanavian Syntax*. Dordrecht: Reidel.

Uriagereka, J. (1998). *Rhyme and reason*. Cambridge, MA: MIT Press.

Williams, E. (1980). Predication. *Linguistic Inquiry, 11*, 203–38.

Williams, E. (1982). The NP cycle. *Linguistic Inquiry, 13*, 277–93.

Williams, E. (1994). *Thematic structure in syntax*. Cambridge, MA: MIT Press.

Wurmbrand, S. (1998). *Infinitives*. PhD dissertation, Cambridge, MA: MIT.

Chapter two

On Logical Form*

Danny Fox

2.1 Introduction

A Logical Form (LF) is a syntactic structure that is interpreted by the semantic component. For a particular structure to be a possible LF it has to be possible for syntax to generate it and for semantics to interpret it. The study of LF must therefore take into account both assumptions about syntax and about semantics, and, since there is much disagreement in both areas, disagreements on LF have been plentiful. This makes the task of writing a survey article in the field fairly difficult, a difficulty that is amplified by the amount of material that needs to be covered if the result is going to be in any way representative. My response to this difficulty is to limit my objectives. As a start, I will confine myself to issues relating to the syntactic positions of Quantificational Noun Phrases (QNPs) at LF and to various interpretive consequences. But even within these relatively narrow confines, I will not attempt anything close to a comprehensive survey. Instead my goal will be restricted to the presentation of one leading idea and to the discussion of some evidence that might bear on it.[1]

Much research on the nature of LF has consisted in attempts to account for the meaning of sentences containing QNPs:

(1)a. A girl is tall.
   b. Many girls are tall.
   c. Every girl is tall.
   d. No girl is tall.

Since it is generally assumed that the meaning of sentences is related to the meaning of their parts, it might be useful to come up with a hypothesis about the meaning of QNPs.

So let us think about the sentences in (1) and how their meanings might result from the meaning of the predicate *tall* combined with the meaning of the QNP (*a girl* in (1a), *many girls* in (1b), *every girl* in (1c), and *no girl* in (1d). Basic predicates express properties of individuals. The predicate *tall* expresses the property that an individual has if the individual is tall, and not otherwise.

This can be modeled if we think that semantically the predicate is a function that maps individuals to truth values. Under standard terminology, the predicate *denotes* a function that maps an individual to TRUE if the individual is tall and to FALSE otherwise (to TRUE if and only if the individual is tall). If the subject of the predicate denotes an individual, the predicate can take the subject as its argument. But there is no straightforward way to think of QNPs as *denoting* individuals. So what can QNPs denote in order to combine with the predicate *tall*?

One way to deal with this problem is to assume that QNPs denote second order predicates. They convey information about basic (first order) predicates like *tall*; they tell us something about the set of individuals that a given (first order) predicate is true of. So in the sentences in (1) the relevant predicate is *tall*. And, given the meaning of the specific QNPs, the sentences convey the information that the predicate is true of at least one girl, (1a), many girls, (1b), every girl, (1c), or no girl, (1d).[2]

Assuming that this is correct, we will say that QNPs denote functions that take predicates as arguments and map these predicates to truth value:

(2)a.   *a girl* denotes a function, f (from predicates to truth values), that maps a predicate, P, to TRUE if and only if (iff) there is at least one girl, g, such that $P(g) = \text{TRUE}$.

   b.   *many girls* denotes a function, f (from predicates to truth values), that maps a predicate, P, to TRUE iff there are many girls, g, such that $P(g) = \text{TRUE}$.

   c.   *every girl* denotes a function, f (from predicates to truth values), that maps a predicate, P, to TRUE iff every girl, g, is such that $P(g) = \text{TRUE}$.

   d.   *no girl* denotes a function, f (from predicates to truth values), that maps a predicate, P, to TRUE iff no girl, g, is such that $P(g) = \text{TRUE}$.

These statements raise an immediate question regarding the relationship between structure and interpretation:

(3)   How is the argument, P, of a QNP determined?

In the cases in (1) the argument of the QNP is its sister, the predicate *tall*:[3]

(4)

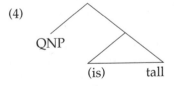

Therefore, if we limit our attention to cases of this sort, we have a fairly simple candidate for an answer to the question in (3):

(5)   The argument of a QNP is always the sister of the QNP.

This answer is not only a simple answer given the cases in (1). It is a simple answer given the fact that functions in general take their sisters as arguments. However, the answer (simple as it may be) is inadequate for the full range of constructions in which QNPs seem to occur. To see this, consider the following sentence:

(6)   I climbed every tree.

The meaning of the QNP is a function that maps its argument, P, to a truth value: TRUE iff P is true of every tree (see (2) above). This truth value would correspond to speakers' judgments about the sentence if P were the predicate that is true of exactly those things that I climbed (λx. I climbed x).[4] However, the sister of *every tree* doesn't seem to express a predicate of this sort:[5]

(6)′

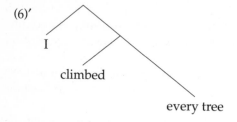

The answer given in (5) is sufficient only if the sister of a QNP is a one-place predicate (a function from individuals to truth values; the type of function that P in (2) has to be if the definitions are to make sense). Whenever this is not the case, it is not clear how the argument of the QNP is to be determined.

This problem becomes more acute when we attempt to account for the interpretations available for the sentence in (7). This sentence has two meanings; it can assert the existence of a single boy who climbed all of the trees or alternatively it can assert that for every tree there is a (perhaps different) boy such that the boy climbed the tree.

(7)   A boy climbed every tree.

This ambiguity, commonly referred to as a scope ambiguity, receives a very specific characterization given our assumption about the meaning of QNPs. The first interpretation results from the QNP *a boy* having as its argument or scope (terms that I will henceforth use interchangeably) the predicate which is true of exactly those individuals who climbed every tree (λx. x climbed every tree). The second interpretation results from the QNP *every tree* having as its argument (or scope) the predicate which is true of exactly those things that a boy climbed (λx. a boy climbed x). The problem is to find a procedure that will determine arguments/scopes for QNPs and will account for this ambiguity. More specifically we need a procedure that (in certain cases) allows for two possible interpretations: the subject QNP can be interpreted as part of the argument/scope of the object QNP (in which case we will say that the object QNP has wide scope), or alternatively the object QNP can be interpreted as part of the argument/scope of the subject QNP (in which case we will say that the subject QNP has wide scope).

So we started with a fairly simple mapping between syntax and semantics, (5), which allows QNPs to be interpreted whenever their sister is a one-place predicate. However, this procedure leaves us with two open questions:

(8)a. How does a QNP find its argument when its sister is not a one-place predicate (e.g. when the QNP is generated in object position)?

  b. How are arguments determined in constructions that involve multiple quantification so as to account for scopal ambiguities such as the one exemplified in (7)?

The questions in (8) take their particular form as a consequence of the assumptions that we made. It is definitely worthwhile to pursue alternative assumptions and to see whether the questions will subsequently be easier to address. In particular, one could attempt to relax our constrained assumptions about the syntax–semantics interface from which (5) follows or to revise our assumptions about the meaning of various constituents.

However, it is also interesting to search for answers that keep to our fairly minimal assumptions about the system. My goal in this chapter is to present one such answer and some of the evidence that has been gathered in its support. It is my impression that the evidence is fairly significant, and to the extent that I am correct, not only will the answer be corroborated but also the minimal assumptions that determined the form of the questions.

2.2   The relevance of movement

Consider the sentence in (9). This sentence has two interpretations. Under one interpretation, the speaker of the sentence asserts that he made a certain demand of his addressee, namely the demand that the addressee avoid reading any books. Under the other interpretation, the speaker of the sentence does not assert that he has made any demands of his addressee. All that he asserts is that there is no particular book such that he demanded that the addressee read it.[6]

(9) I demanded that you read not a single book.

Given our assumptions, this ambiguity can be attributed to two possible arguments/scopes that the QNP *not a single book* can take. Let us start with the second interpretation. This interpretation would result if the QNP could take as its argument the predicate which is true of exactly those things that I demanded that you read (λx. I demanded that you read x).[7] The result of the composition is the proposition that is true iff there is not a single book that satisfies the predicate, that is, not a single book that I demanded that you read. The first interpretation would result from *not a single book* taking as its argument the predicate which is true of exactly those things that you read (λx. you read x). The result of the composition is a proposition that is true iff you read not a single book. This proposition, in turn, serves as an argument of the matrix predicate *demanded* resulting in a predicate which is true of exactly those individuals that made a demand that you read not a single book. Finally, this predicate takes *I* as argument resulting in a proposition that is true iff I made the demand that you read not a single book.

This characterization is quite similar to the one that we provided for the ambiguity of the sentence in (7). In (7) there were two interpretations, one resulting from the subject QNP taking wide scope over the object QNP and the other resulting from the reversal of the scopal relation. Similarly, here, one interpretation results from the QNP, *not a single book*, taking scope over the verb *demand*, and the other resulting from the reversal of this scopal relation. Assuming that this characterization is more or less correct, the same questions arise. What is the procedure that allows the QNP to find its argument given that its sister is not a one-place predicate, (8a)? And, why is it that the relevant procedure can apply in two different ways, yielding two different arguments for the QNP, (8b)?

The sentence in (10), which is derived from the sentence in (9) by movement of the QNP, suggests a possible answer.

(10)   Not a single book did I demand that you read t.

This sentence is restricted to the interpretation resulting from wide scope for the QNP. It expresses the proposition that there is no particular book that I demanded that you read, and cannot be used to assert that I made the demand that you avoid reading any book.[8] What could this restriction follow from? To answer this question, let us look at the constituent that serves as sister of the QNP at its landing site (the derived sister of the QNP). This constituent is the IP *I demanded that you read t* (ignoring the effects of *do*-support and I to C movement). How is this IP interpreted? The restriction on the interpretation of the whole sentence would follow, if the IP were interpreted as the predicate λx. *I demanded that you read x*. Let us therefore assume that this is how things work, and state it (somewhat) explicitly in the following way:

(11)   In a structure formed by DP movement, $DP_n[_\varphi \dots t_n \dots]$, the derived sister of DP, φ, is interpreted as a function that maps an individual, x, to the meaning of $\varphi[x/n]$.

$\varphi[x/n]$ is the result of substituting every constituent with the index n in φ with some NP referring to the individual x.[9]

What we have learned is that a QNP can start out in a position other than the position in which it is interpreted. Movement takes the QNP to a position where its sister is a one-place predicate (given the rule in (11)) and it is in this new position that the QNP is interpreted. Can this help us address the questions in (8)? Well, it might, as long as we are willing to entertain the possibility that movement can sometimes occur without visible effects on word order.

Such movement, which is commonly referred to as "covert movement" or Quantifier Raising (QR), will allow a QNP to find its arguments when its base generated sister is not a one-place predicate, thus providing an answer to (8a). Similarly, this movement could account for scopal ambiguities (8b), under the assumption that more than one possible landing site is available.[10]

Stated somewhat differently, the rule in (11) allows a moved QNP to take its derived sister as its argument/scope.[11] This allows a QNP that is base generated in a position where its sister cannot serve as its argument/scope to move to a position where its argument/scope can be determined. In other words, it is predicted that the scope of a QNP will be its derived sister (i.e. its c-command domain in the structure derived by movement). If movement can be covert, that is if QR exists, and if there is some flexibility in landing sites, the questions in (8) would be answered.

To see this in more detail, consider the sentence in (6) repeated below. The problem with this sentence is that in the base generated structure, the sister of the QNP *every tree* (the base generated sister) is not a one-place predicate.

(6) I climbed every tree.

However, if we postulate covert movement, this does not have to be true of the structure that is interpreted by the semantic system. The QNP can move covertly, yielding the LF structure in (6').

(6)' [every tree]$_1$ [I climbed t$_1$]

In this new structure the derived sister of the QNP is interpreted by (11) as the predicate that, for every individual, x, yields the semantic interpretation of the derived sister, when t$_1$ is substituted by some name of the individual, x. This derived predicate is λx. *I climbed x*, and, as mentioned in the previous section, this is exactly the predicate we need as an argument of *every tree* in order to derive the correct truth conditions for the sentence.

Let us now go back to the sentence in (9).

(9) I demanded that you read not a single book.

Also in this sentence, the QNP cannot be interpreted in its base position, since, again, the base generated sister is not a one-place predicate. However, there are two positions to which the QNP can move where its derived sister would be interpreted as a one-place predicate (by (11)):

(9)'a. I demanded [that [Not a single book]$_1$ **[you read t$_1$]**]
    b. [Not a single book]$_1$ **[I demanded that you read t$_1$]**

It is easy to convince oneself that given our assumption in (11), the structures in (9) provide us with the basis to derive the two interpretations. Specifically, the derived sisters in (9'a) and (9'b) (which are marked in boldface) are interpreted as the one-place predicates $\lambda x.$ *you read x* and $\lambda x.$ *I demanded that you read x*, respectively. And as we reasoned above, these are precisely the predicates that are needed to derive the two interpretations.

Finally, consider the scopal ambiguity in (7).

(7)   A boy climbed every tree.

Here, just as in (6), the object QNP cannot be interpreted in its base position. However, once again, this problem can be addressed with the aid of covert movement. The object can raise covertly over the subject yielding the structure in (7′):

(7)′   [every tree]$_1$ [a boy climbed t$_1$]

Here the derived sister is interpreted as the predicate $\lambda x.$ *a boy climbed x* and after this predicate is interpreted as the argument of the universal quantifier one of the two interpretations is derived, namely the interpretation that we have called the object-wide-scope interpretation (sometimes also called Inverse Scope). To derive the alternative subject-wide-scope (or Surface Scope) interpretation, we would need to move the subject over the derived position of the object, yielding the representation in (7″).

(7)″   [A boy]$_2$ [[every tree]$_1$ [t$_2$ climbed t$_1$]]

Here the subject QNP takes as its argument the predicate which is true of an individual, y, if the QNP, *every tree*, yields TRUE when it combines with the predicate $\lambda x.$ *N climbed x*, where N, is some name for y. In other words, the derived sister of the subject QNP is the predicate which is true of an individual if the individual climbed every tree. Consequently, the sentence ends up being true iff there is a boy who climbed every tree.

So let us see where we are. We ended the previous section with two problems. Given the assumption that a QNP is a second order predicate (i.e. a function from first order predicates to truth values) and given a restrictive theory of the syntax–semantics interface (which stated that the argument of a function must be its syntactic sister), there was (a) no way to interpret a QNP in object position, and (b) no way to account for scope ambiguities. We started this section with the observation that overt movement of a QNP has consequences for the argument/scope of the QNP. We provided an account of this fact, with the aid of the semantic rule in (11). This semantic rule predicts that the derived sister of a moved QNP will serve as its argument/scope. In other words, it is predicted that the scope of a QNP is its c-command domain at LF. We then noticed that the puzzles in (8) can be resolved under the hypothesis that syntax allows movement that has consequences for LF but no consequences for phonology (covert movement). Our goal in the next section is to introduce additional considerations that might bear on the truth of the hypothesis.

But before we move on, I would like to make a short digression and say a few words about the hypothesis that subjects always move to a position higher than their base position. We will see that this hypothesis, known as the VP internal subject hypothesis (VPI), is relevant for determining some of the consequences of covert movement. Consider, again, the sentence in (7), *a boy climbed every tree*. Given our assumptions, the object QNP can be interpreted only if it moves to a position c-commanding the subject position:

(7)′ [every tree]₁ [a boy climbed t₁]

This, as we have said, yields the Inverse Scope interpretation. In order to get the Surface Scope interpretation, the subject must move over the derived position of the object, yielding the representation in (7″).

(7)″ [A boy]₂ [[every tree]₁ [t₂ climbed t₁]]

But notice that if we assume VPI, the subject moves over the derived position of the object independently of scope considerations. This means that (7′), which does not include subject raising, is not a possible LF.[12] Given VPI, the two scopal relationships would result from the following LFs:

(7)‴a. Surface Scope
        [$_{IP}$ [A boy]₂ [$_{VP}$ [every tree]₁ [$_{VP}$ t₂ climbed t₁]]]
    b. Inverse Scope
        [$_{IP}$ [every tree]₁ [$_{IP}$ [A boy]₂ [$_{VP}$ t₂ climbed t₁]]]

The important piece of this discussion is that our semantic framework in conjunction with VPI allows objects to be interpreted in a VP internal position. This position, which is higher than the base position of the subject but lower than its surface position, will play an important role in some of the discussion that follows.

2.3 Arguments in favor of covert movement

A principle such as (11) needs to be incorporated into our semantic system in order to account for the interpretation of constructions involving overt movement. Once the principle is in place, it turns out that certain correlations between sound and meaning are explained by the system as it stands, only if QR is part of grammar. However, one could imagine other ways to enrich the system in order to account for the relevant correlations. Indeed, the literature is full of competing proposals.

I will not attempt to evaluate these competitors. Instead I will try to go through various arguments that have been presented in favor of the idea that QR is the correct enrichment. This decision is due to space limitations, and is a significant shortcoming since arguments in favor of a proposal cannot be fully appreciated without an understanding of the nature of potential competitors. Nevertheless, I hope to be able to present a good picture of what has been achieved by the postulation of QR and of the challenges that ought to be considered when evaluating alternatives.[13]

How can we tell whether a certain operation takes place in the syntax? Well, we have to see whether there are any predicted consequences. Predictions, however, will not follow from the operation alone but only in conjunction with various other theoretical assumptions. We, therefore, have to search for various components of the theory that will yield predictions when combined with the operation. There are at least three components that could be relevant: phonology, semantics, and syntax. The claim that QR is a covert operation is essentially the claim that there are no predicted consequences that follow from phonology. So we need to ask whether there are predicted consequences given properties of semantics or syntax. We have seen in the previous section that certain consequences are predicted from the rules of semantics. Specifically, given the rule in (11), QR predicts that object QNPs will be interpretable and that scopal ambiguities will sometimes be attested. But the question we are asking now is whether there are further predictions.

So what we need to do is to identify additional principles of syntax or semantics that could tell us whether or not movement has taken place when there are no consequences for phonology. Two types of principles come to mind. First there are various constraints on movement that can serve as "movement detectors": if it turns out that scope is restricted by the movement constraints, this will suggest that scope is determined by movement. Second, there are various constraints on structure that can be taken as "structure diagnostics." We can use these diagnostics to see whether the output of QR provides the correct structural description of various sentences.[14]

2.3.1   Properties of movement

The claim that the scope of a QNP is determined by a (covert) movement operation leads to the expectation that constraints on movement will reveal themselves as constraints on scope. If this expectation turns out to be correct, it can be taken as evidence in favor of a theory that incorporates QR.

One case where the predictions of the theory are corroborated is the case of movement out of one of two coordinated conjuncts. Such movement is impossible as demonstrated in (12).

(12)a.   Which professor does John like t?
    b.   *Which professor does [[John like t] and [hate the dean]]?

This constraint (the Coordinate Structure Constraint, CSC; see Ross, 1967) can be used to test the predictions of a theory that postulates covert movement. The predictions are corroborated by the following contrast noted in Lakoff (1970) and Rodman (1976):

(13)a.   A (different) student likes every professor.
           (∃>∀)   (∀>∃)

   b.   A (#different) student [[likes every professor]

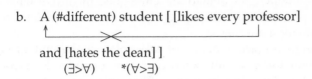

   and [hates the dean]]
           (∃>∀)   *(∀>∃)

(13) is a case of scope ambiguity that receives the analysis provided for (7) above. (13), by contrast, is restricted to the interpretation in which the object QNP is interpreted within the scope of the subject QNP: the sentence can express the proposition that there is a student who likes all of the professors and hates the dean, but not the proposition that for every professor there is a (perhaps different) student who likes the professor and hates the dean.[15] This restriction is a direct consequence of a theory that incorporates QR. Under such a theory, Inverse Scope requires the object to move by QR over the surface position of the subject, and this movement violates the CSC.

Of course, a theory that incorporates QR must also explain how Surface Scope is possible in (13)b. As noted in May (1985), this requires the assumption that QNPs can be interpreted within the VP. As mentioned, this assumption is a direct consequence of the rule in (11) once VPI is adopted. To see this in more detail, let us go over the derivation of the sentence, starting at a point at which two VPs are conjoined, (14). At this point, the object moves (covertly) by QR to a position internal to the first conjunct where it can be interpreted, (14). Since this movement does not cross a coordinated structure, the CSC is not violated. Finally, the subject moves (overtly) "Across the Board" to its surface position, [Spec, IP] yielding the LF representation in (14).[16]

(14)a.   [$_{VP}$ [$_{VP}$ a student likes every professor] and [$_{VP}$ a student hates the dean]]
    b.   [$_{VP}$ [$_{VP}$ **[every professor]**$_1$ [$_{VP}$ a student likes t$_1$]] and [$_{VP}$ a student hates the dean]]
    c.   [$_{IP}$ **[a student]**$_2$ [$_{VP}$ [$_{VP}$ [every professor]$_1$ [$_{VP}$ t$_2$ likes t$_1$]] and [$_{VP}$ t$_2$ hates the dean]]]

This is the representation of Surface Scope since the sister of the subject QNP (its argument/scope) contains the object QNP. To get the Inverse Scope interpretation the subject (in [spec, IP]) must be dominated by the derived sister of the object. The only way that this could be achieved is if the object were to move out of the coordinate structure violating the CSC.[17]

The observation that scope obeys the CSC serves as an important piece of evidence in favor of a theory that incorporates QR.[18] One would like to ask whether scope obeys other constraints on movement. Various people have argued that it does, but unfortunately I cannot go over the arguments in this context. Among the important references are Huang (1982), May (1977, 1985), Kayne (1981), Pesetsky (1987, 2000), Reinhart (1991, 1997), Aoun and Li (1993), and Richards (2001). If these arguments are successful, we might be able to conclude that all movement constraints indicate that QR should be dealt with by covert movement.

However, the situation is complicated by various factors, and there are many open questions for further research. For example, it has been argued that QR is more restricted than various forms of overt movement. But these arguments have received different interpretations, in part due to the fact that there are various restrictions that apply to some forms of overt movement but not to others. (Relevant references include Wilder (1997), Hornstein (1995), Kennedy (1997), Johnson and Tomioka (1997), Johnson (2000), Bruening (2001), Sauerland (2001), and Fox (2000, sect. 2.4).) Furthermore, some researchers have argued that the variability in overt movement is mirrored by a variability in covert movement (see, among others, Beghelli and Stowell, 1997; Szabolcsi, 1998; Aguero-Bautista, 2001). Finally, some have suggested that in certain environments QR is more flexible than overt movement and have attempted to provide an explanation for this fact (see Reinhart, 1991, and Fox, 2000, sect. 2.4).

These complications are inevitable given that the constraints on movement are not fully understood. Nevertheless, the fact that QR is demonstrably sensitive to certain specific constraints such as the CSC is encouraging. Still one would like to identify tests for QR that are based on better grounded auxiliary assumptions. As mentioned, one thing we can do is search for constraints on structure that can tell us whether or not the output of QR provides the correct structural description for various sentences. One such constraint, which we will use as a "structure diagnostic" in the next section, is a constraint on VP deletion, sometimes called Parallelism.

2.3.2   Parallelism as a "structure diagnostic"

The second sentence in (15) is missing a phonologically visible VP. Nevertheless, the sentence receives an interpretation. Specifically, it is interpreted as if it contained a VP identical to the VP of the preceding sentence (i.e. as if the interpretation were identical to that of *Then, Bill talked to Mary*).

(15)   First, John talked to Mary. Then, Bill did.

This interpretation is the only interpretation available: the second sentence cannot be interpreted as if it contained a VP which was different in interpretation from the preceding VP (at least as long as the discourse does not contain additional sentences).

A fairly simple way to characterize the situation would be to say that it is possible for a VP not to be pronounced but that this possibility is constrained by an identity condition:

(16)   *Parallelism*: VP_1 can be deleted only if the discourse contains a pronounced VP_2 (the antecedent VP) such that VP_2 is syntactically identical to VP_1.[19]

In light of Parallelism, consider the sentences in (17) (in which the deleted VPs are written inside angle brackets, <deleted VP>).

(17)a. I [$_{VP antecedent}$ read [a book [that you did <read t>]]].
   b. I [$_{VP antecedent}$ gave [every book [that you did <give t to Mary>]] to Mary].
   c. I [$_{VP antecedent}$ wanted to be in [the city [that you did <wanted to be in t>]]].

It appears that in these sentences the deleted VP is contained within its antecedent. This is reflected in the term commonly used to refer to the type of deletion involved: Antecedent Contained Deletion (ACD). But if Parallelism is to be satisfied, there can be no antecedent containment; the antecedent VP must be identical to the elided VP, but a syntactic constituent cannot be identical to one of its sub-constituents.[20] Therefore, if Parallelism holds, the deleted VP cannot contain the elided VP.

So the sentences in (17) cannot have the structures hinted at by the square brackets. What is their structure then? QR provides a possible answer. More specifically QR yields a structure in which the antecedent and the elided VP are identical:

(17)′a. [a book [that you did <read t>]]
          I [$_{VP antecedent}$ read t]
    d. [every book [that you did <gave t to Mary>]]
          I [$_{VP antecedent}$ gave t to Mary].
    e. [the city [that you did <wanted to be in t>]]
          I [$_{VP antecedent}$ wanted to be in t]

QR thus solves the problem that is posed by apparent cases of antecedent containment. Parallelism predicts that antecedent containment should be impossible.[21] If QR is not part of our theory, we have to posit structures that violate Parallelism, obviously not a good result. However, if we incorporate QR into the theory, the structures do not violate Parallelism, and the problem is eliminated.

Stated somewhat differently, assuming that Parallelism is established on independent grounds, we can use it as a "structure diagnostic." This diagnostic indicates that the output of QR yields a possible structural description for the sentences in (17). On the other hand, it is not obvious how the structural description might satisfy Parallelism if QR is not postulated.[22]

But the argument can be made even stronger. Right now QR has several independent effects in our system. If it turns out that these independent effects correlate with each other in non-trivial ways, it will suggest that we are on to something real. One significant correlation was pointed out in Sag (1976) (and discussed in Larson and May (1990) as well as much subsequent work). Given that QR yields a larger argument (or wider scope) for a QNP, and given that QR is necessary if ACD is to satisfy Parallelism, it is predicted that the two would correlate. More specifically it is predicted that the argument/scope of a

94   *Danny Fox*

QNP in an ACD construction would have to contain the antecedent VP. To see that this prediction is made consider the representation that an ACD construction has "before" QR:

(18)   ... [$_{VP}$Antecedent ... [$_{QNP}$ ... <deleted VP>] ...] ...

In order for the construction to satisfy Parallelism the QNP must move by QR and vacate the antecedent VP. This movement will place the QNP in some position where its derived sister contains the antecedent VP:

(18)'   [$_{QNP}$ ... <deleted VP> ...] [$_{DerivedSister}$ ... [$_{VP}$Antecedent ... t ...] ...]

This derived sister will be interpreted as the argument/scope of the QNP by the rule in (11), and since the antecedent VP is part of the Derived Sister, the resulting interpretation is the one we describe as involving wide scope for the QNP.

The prediction has been tested and corroborated in various ways. But they all share the following property: they involve a sentence with a QNP that can be interpreted either inside or outside of a certain VP; when this VP serves as the antecedent in an ACD construction (and when the deleted VP is dominated by the QNP), it is predicted that only the second option would be available.

Consider, from this perspective, the sentence in (19).

(19)   John refused PRO to read every book that I recommended.

Given our assumptions, there are at least two positions where the QNP can be interpreted. One position would result from QR to the matrix IP and the other from QR to the embedded IP:[23]

(19)'a.   [[every book that I recommended]$_1$ [John refused PRO to read t$_1$]].
    b.   John refused [[every book that I recommended]$_1$ [PRO to read t$_1$]].

Two different interpretations result from the two syntactic options (given the rule in (11)). If the QNP targets the matrix IP (wide scope for the QNP), as in (19'), the sentence asserts that every book that I recommended is a book that John refused to read (i.e. a book that the derived predicate λx. *John refused to read x* is true of). Under the alternative structure (19'), in which the derived sister of the QNP (the scope) is smaller (narrow scope for the QNP), the sentence asserts that John refused to the suggestion that he read all of the books that I recommended.

So we have an ambiguity here that can be used to test the prediction we characterized abstractly above. We have a QNP that can be interpreted either inside or outside of a certain VP ((19'a) or (19'b)), and, as mentioned, it is predicted that only the second option is available when the VP serves as the antecedent in an ACD construction.

Consider the following.

(20) I [refused to read [every book [that you did <read t>/<refuse to read t>]]].

In this sentence there are two interpretations for the elided VP. It could be interpreted with the embedded or matrix VP as antecedent (i.e. the elided VP could be *read* or *refuse to read*). Our prediction is that the matrix VP can be the antecedent, only if the QNP is interpreted outside of this VP. (This prediction follows since the QNP must move by QR outside of the antecedent VP for Parallelism to be satisfied.) That is to say, we predict that the QNP must outscope the verb *refuse*, (19′), if the elided VP is *refuse to read*. To test whether this is in fact the case, one has to access fairly complicated judgments. However, the results are pretty clear when an appropriate experiment is conducted.
So consider the following:

(21)a. John refused to read EVERY book that we thought he HAD <read>. He was willing to read only some of them.
   b. John refused to read EVERY book that we thought he would <refuse to read>. #He was willing to read only some of them.

Both (21a) and (21b) consist of two sentences uttered in succession. The second sentence ensures that the first sentence is understood with narrow scope for the QNP. (If there are books that John was willing to read than surely it's not the case that every book is such that he refused to read it.) It is a clear judgment that the two sentences contradict each other in (21b) but not in (21a). This indicates that the latter is restricted to the wide scope interpretation for the QNP, just as the theory predicts.
We started this subsection with a condition on the licensing of VP deletion, Parallelism. This condition was taken as a structure diagnostic, and as such it indicated that apparent cases of antecedent containment cannot be real cases of antecedent containment. If they really involved antecedent containment, there would be no way for Parallelism to be satisfied. This observation supported QR, which eliminates antecedent containment and provides structural descriptions that satisfy parallelism. Furthermore, QR predicted a non-trivial yet correct correlation between scope and the size of the elided VP. This suggested that the conflict between Parallelism and antecedent containment is a real one, and that it is resolved by the mechanism that accounts for scope.[24]

2.3.3 *Binding Theory as a "structure diagnostic"*

In the previous subsection we have seen that Parallelism (taken as a structure diagnostic) indicates that the structures derived by QR are real. In this subsection, we will see that Binding Theory appears to provide the opposite indication. This conflict will serve as the basis for the discussion in the following sections.

Consider the sentences in (22).

(22)a.   ??John and Bill said that [Mary bought every picture of each other/themselves].

b.   *He$_1$ likes every picture that John$_1$ saw.

The fact that (22) is unacceptable should follow from the locality conditions that restrict the distribution of anaphoric expressions such as *himself* and *each other*. Similarly, the unacceptability of (22b), on the intended interpretation, should follow from restrictions on co-reference between names and pronouns. This result is achieved by the following two conditions of Binding Theory:

(23)a.   *Condition A*: An anaphoric expression (*himself*, *each other*) must co-refer with (or be bound by) a locally c-commanding antecedent.[25]

b.   *Condition C*: A name and a pronoun cannot co-refer if the pronoun c-commands the name.

The unacceptability of (22a) follows if the matrix subject is outside the local domain for the binding of the anaphor, and the unacceptability of (22b) follows under the assumption that the subject c-commands the object.

The problem, however, is that the two assumptions are far from obvious the moment QR is postulated. To see this, consider the cases of overt movement in (24).

(24)a.   John and Bill know [[which picture of each other/themselves] Mary bought t].

b.   (Guess) [which picture that John$_1$ saw] he$_1$ likes t.

Once the wh-phrase moves over the embedded subject in (24a), the anaphor is close enough to its antecedent for Condition A to be satisfied. Similarly, in (24b), Condition C is satisfied since wh-movement removes the name out of the c-command domain of the pronoun.

A theory that postulates QR yields the structures in (22′) as possible LF representations of the sentences in (22). Consequently, it predicts incorrectly that these sentences, just like the sentences in (24), will escape violations of Conditions A and C.[26]

(22)′a.   J & B said that [[every picture of each other/themselves] Mary bought t].

b.   [Every picture that John$_1$ saw] He$_1$ likes t.

2.4   Binding Theory and QR – some recent research

In section 2.1 we have seen that QR together with the rule in (11) provides an explanation for various semantic properties of sentences that contain QNPs. Furthermore, we have seen that the explanation is supported by Parallelism and various locality conditions on movement (2.2.1, 2.2.2). However, we have seen in 2.2.3 that Binding Theory poses a challenge for the explanation.

In order to deal with this challenge, Chomsky (1981) suggested that Binding Theory applies at a level of representation at which the effects of QR are not visible (Surface Structure). However, in later work (Chomsky, 1993) he has criticized this suggestion on various grounds. I will not attempt to summarize the criticism. Rather, I would like to point out that given our limited perspective (namely the study of the syntactic position of QNPs), the appeal to Surface Structure is a cop-out (see note 26). There is conflicting evidence with respect to the syntactic position of QNPs, and the postulation of two syntactic representations each corresponding to a subset of the data is not much more than a restatement of the problem.[27] We would like to have one syntactic representation that captures all of the data. Following Chomsky's lead, various researchers have attempted to articulate a theory that would derive such a syntactic representation. In what follows, I will focus on a few suggestions I have made in recent work (Fox, 2000, 2002).[28] If there is something to these suggestions, it will turn out that (contrary to initial appearances) Binding Theory is a pretty reliable diagnostic of LF structures and as such it provides further evidence for a theory that incorporates QR.

2.4.1   Condition A and the position of QNPs

Let us go back to (22a), repeated below.

(22)a.   ??John and Bill said that [Mary bought every picture of each other/ themselves].

The unacceptability of this sentence is problematic for a theory that incorporates QR since, under such a theory, the embedded object QNP should be allowed to move covertly yielding a representation identical (in all relevant respects) to the representation of (24). Since in the latter representation Condition A is not violated, a theory that incorporates QR is not able to account for the unacceptability of (22). This conclusion follows under the assumption that the distribution of QR is identical to the distribution of wh-movement. This assumption in turn has been taken to be the null hypothesis, and has served as the basis for some of the arguments in favor of QR. However, it is not a necessary assumption (see p. 92 and note 29). It is possible that there are some constraints that apply to QR and do not apply to wh-movement. If that can be demonstrated on independent grounds, there might be a principled account for the unacceptability of (22a).

In Fox (2000) I have argued that such a constraint exists. More interestingly (for this context), I have tried to show that in environments where the constraint allows QR to apply, the covert operation has the expected consequences for Condition A (Fox, 2000, pp. 198–9). If these arguments are successful, it will turn out that (contrary to initial impressions) Condition A can serve to further motivate a theory that incorporates QR.[29]

The evidence in favor of a constraint that applies specifically to QR is based on a variety of considerations. Here I will present just one piece of data concerning the scope of QNPs in constructions that involve VP ellipsis. Consider the pair of sentences in (25).

(25)   A boy admires every teacher. A girl does, too <admire every teacher>.[30]

These sentences show a scopal ambiguity that we are by now very much familiar with. What I would like to focus on, though, is that the relative scope of the object and the subject is identical in the two sentences: if the object outscopes the subject in one of the sentences the subject cannot outscope the object in the other sentence. The way Parallelism was defined in section 2.3.2 is not sufficient to account for this demand for parallel interpretation, but it is pretty clear that parallel scope must be a consequence of the theory of ellipsis (see Fox, 2000, ch. 3 for a discussion of the necessary properties of the theory of ellipsis).

Now consider the pair of sentences in (26).

(26)   A boy admires every teacher. Mary does, too <admire every teacher>

The first of these sentences is restricted to subject-wide-scope. (It can only express the proposition that there is a boy who admires all of the teachers; i.e. it is false if each of the teachers is admired by a different boy.) This restriction would follow from Parallelism if there were an independent condition that blocked an application of QR in the second sentence in a way that would reverse the c-command relation between the subject and the object.

I will, therefore, assume that the independent condition exists. For current purposes it is not important to provide the correct characterization of the condition, and I will therefore keep to a statement of what must its consequences be if the facts in (26) are to follow from Parallelism:[31]

(27)   An object QNP can move over the subject when the subject is an indefinite but not when the subject is a name.

If (27) holds, (22) is no longer a problem. The object QNP must move by QR to a position where it can be interpreted, but given (27) this position must be below the embedded subject. The two requirements can be satisfied given VPI, and, assuming an appropriate definition of locality, Condition A of the binding theory would still be violated. The embedded subject still intervenes between the anaphor and its antecedent, thereby violating the specified subject condition or other characterizations of the relevant constraint.

(22)'a.   ??John and Bill said that [$_{IP}$ Mary$_1$ [$_{VP}$ [every picture of each other/ themselves]$_2$ [t$_1$ bought t$_2$]]].

But, more interestingly, we predict that the violation of Condition A that we have seen in (22a) could be circumvented if the embedded subject, the name

Mary, were replaced with an indefinite. This seems to be the case as the following contrast indicates:

- (28)a.   ??The two rivals hoped that Bill would hurt (every one of) each-other's operations.
  - b.   The two rivals hoped that someone would hurt (every one of) each-other's operations.   *∃>∀ ∃>∀

(28a), just like (22a), is a violation of Condition A resulting from an LF representation in which the name *Bill* intervenes between the anaphor and its antecedent. This intervention cannot be circumvented by QR given the constraint in (27). However, in (28b) the situation is different since the intervening subject is an indefinite, which QR is allowed to cross.

An additional interesting prediction is that (28b) would be acceptable only under the interpretation resulting from Inverse Scope in the embedded sentence. To understand the nature of the prediction, we start with the observation that (28b) is a proposition about the hopes that the two the rivals have. Under the Inverse Scope interpretation of the embedded clause these hopes would be satisfied if every one of the rivals' operations are hurt. Under the Surface Scope interpretation more needs to happen for the hopes to be satisfied, namely, the same person must hurt every one of the relevant operations.

Speakers I have consulted seem to feel that only the former interpretation is available. But this is a very delicate judgment (for reasons discussed in Abush (1994), among others). David Pesetsky (personal communication) proposed the following as a way to verify the prediction.

- (29)a.   The two friends hoped that someone would buy each-other's pictures of Mary.
  - b.   *The two friends hoped that someone$_i$ would buy each-other's pictures of himself$_i$.
  - c.   *The two friends hoped that someone$_i$ would buy each-other's pictures of his$_i$ mother.

(29a), like (28b), is a case where QR can circumvent a violation of Condition A. In (29b) and (29c), however, the embedded subject binds a variable dominated by the embedded object. Since (for obvious reasons) a QNP can only bind a variable within its scope, the intended variable binding would be impossible if the object were to QR over the embedded subject. It follows that in (29b) and (29c) QR cannot circumvent a violation of Condition A.

From all of this it seems reasonable to conclude that Condition A supports a theory that incorporates QR. More specifically, it turns out that Condition A indicates that QR applies in exactly those circumstances that we expect it to (exactly those in which an independently motivated structure diagnostics such as Parallelism indicates that it does).[32] Furthermore, there is a predicted correlation between scope and Condition A, which seems to hold (if the paradigm in (29) is indicative).[33]

2.4.2   *The problem with Condition C*

We have seen that Condition A, which at first appears to threaten the hypothesis that QR plays a role in deriving LF representations, turns out, under
careful scrutiny, to support the hypothesis. What about Condition C? We
mentioned above that the hypothesis might be threatened by the unacceptability
of (22b) (repeated below), which is unexpected if QR could derive the LF
representation in (22′b).

(22)b.   *He$_1$ likes every picture that John$_1$ saw.

(22)′b.   [Every picture that John$_1$ saw] He$_1$ likes t

But given our constraint in (27), (22′b) is not a possible LF and the problem is
eliminated. More specifically, the only LF structure that is available for (22b)
is one in which the object QNP adjoins to VP as in (22″b). This LF structure
still violates Condition C, and the unacceptability of the sentence is thereby
explained:

(22)″b.   He$_1$ [Every picture that John$_1$ saw]$_2$ t$_1$ likes t$_2$

However, things are not that simple. To see this, consider the sentence in
(30). The constraint in (27) allows the dative object to move by QR over the
subject, and it is thus incorrectly predicted that the sentence would not violate
Condition C. One might consider fiddling with the constraint in (27) so that
QR would not be allowed, but that does not seem very plausible given the
availability of Inverse scope in (30).[34]

(30)a.   *Someone introduced him$_1$ to every friend of John's$_1$.
      b.   Someone introduced John$_1$ to every friend of his$_1$.

So this is a genuine puzzle. It is clear that QR can move the dative object over
the pronoun in (30a), yielding the structure in (30′a). Yet this movement has
no consequences for Condition C.

(30)′a.   *[every friend of John's$_1$]$_2$ Someone introduced him$_1$ to t$_2$

How might we resolve this puzzle? We might want to appeal to Chomsky's
(1993) suggestion that movement is a copying operation (the copy theory of
movement), and is thereby never capable of circumventing Condition C.[35]
More specifically, the output of QR, under the copy theory of movement,
would be the structure in (30″a), in which Condition C is violated due to the
copy of the name *John*, which is not eliminated from the base position.[36]

(30)″a.   * [every friend of John's$_1$]$_2$ Someone introduced him$_1$ to [every friend
          of John's$_1$]$_2$

But this suggestion seems incompatible with some of the conclusions we have reached up to this point. First, consider our conclusion that movement (both overt and covert) is capable of obviating a violation of Condition A (see (22), (24), and (29)). We would be unable to understand this conclusion if a copy of an anaphor were to yield a violation of Condition A in the same way that a copy of a name yields a violation of Condition C. This is a problem that can be dealt with by an adaptation (with minor adjustments) of a proposal made in Belletti and Rizzi (1988).

Belletti and Rizzi argue that Binding Theory is sensitive to the structure of a sentence at every level of representation, and that our problem can be eliminated by a particular statement of the relevant type of sensitivity: Condition A requires an anaphor to be "bound" appropriately at *some* level of representation, whereas Condition C demands that a name be "free" at *every* level of representation.[37] Assuming the copy theory of movement, we can adopt this idea while eliminating reference to levels of representation other than LF (see Brody, 1995). Specifically, we will say that *one* copy of an anaphor must meet the locality condition in (23a) while *every* copy of a *name* must meet the anti-co-reference condition in (23b). Movement has affects on Condition A because it puts *one* copy of an anaphor in a local relation with what would otherwise be a non-local antecedent. By contrast, movement has no affect on condition C since (given the copy theory of movement) it does not put *every* copy of a name outside the c-command domain of a pronoun (which dominates the base position).

A more direct challenge comes from the observation made in (24b) that overt movement is capable of circumventing a violation of Condition C:

(24)b.   (Guess) [which picture that John$_1$ saw] He$_1$ likes t.

Under the copy theory of movement, the representation of (24b) should be that in (24'b), and the sentence is therefore expected, incorrectly, to violate Condition C.

(24)'b.   (Guess) [which picture that John$_1$ saw] He$_1$ likes [which picture that John$_1$ saw].

In order to deal with this challenge, Chomsky (1993) adopts Lebeaux's (1988) suggestion that relative clauses (and more generally adjuncts) can be merged ("counter-cyclically") with an NP after a DP that dominates the NP has undergone movement (late merger). (See also van Riemsdijk and Williams, 1981 and Freidin, 1986.) (24b) can thus have the following derivation, which results in a representation that does not violate Condition C.

(31)a.   He$_1$ likes [which picture] – wh-movement→
    b.   [which picture] He$_1$ likes [which picture] – adjunct merger→
    c.   [which picture that John$_1$ saw] He$_1$ likes [which picture]

So this type of derivation can account for the acceptability of (24b). But might it disrupt the account that the copy theory of movement provides for the unacceptability of (30)?

(30)a.   *Someone introduced him$_1$ to every friend of John's$_1$.

There are two potential reasons that we might appeal to in order to maintain the account. One reason would rely on certain assumptions about the architecture of the system that blocks late merger to an NP after the NP has been moved covertly. Under these assumptions, covert movement applies after "spell-out" and consequently after the merger of all constituents that need to be pronounced. It follows that covert movement cannot feed late merger of a constituent that dominates a name, and subsequently that a derivation similar to the one in (31a) would be impossible if it involved QR (instead of wh-movement). The second reason would rely on Lebeaux's (1988) hypothesis that late merger is restricted to adjuncts.[38] In (30a) there is no adjunct within the dative QNP that might be a candidate for late merger. Hence, even if covert movement could feed late merger, there would be no conceivable derivation for the sentence that would circumvent the violation of Condition C.

These two lines of reasoning can explain why late merger, which accounts for the acceptability of (24), cannot extend to covert movement in a way that would threaten the account provided for the unacceptability of (30a).

There are various questions that one should address in order to see which, if any, of these two lines of reasoning might be correct. We will get to some of this in section 2.5.1, where I will argue that only the latter line is correct. But first I would like to mention a third problem that arises once we adopt the account provided by the copy theory of movement for the unacceptability of (30a). The problem is that under the copy theory of movement, it is far from clear how QR could provide a representation for ACD sentences that would be compatible with the theory of VP deletion.

To the best of my knowledge, the problem was first noted in Lasnik (1993), and Hornstein (1994, 1995) (cf. Schmitt, 1995). To appreciate it, consider again a typical ACD sentence such as (32) (= (17a)). In this sentence, the antecedent and the elided VP do not appear to be identical, yet somehow the condition on VP deletion (Parallelism) is met.

(32)   I [$_{VPantecedent}$ read [a book [that you did <read t>]]].

QR solves this problem by providing an LF representation in which the two VPs are identical:

(32)′   [a book [that you did <read t>]
        I [$_{VPantecedent}$ read t].

However, if the copy theory of movement is adopted, it is not obvious that this solution can be maintained. The LF representation of (32) would be that in (32″) and here again the antecedent and the elided VP are not identical.

(32)″   [a book [that you did <read t>]]
        I [$_{VPantecedent}$ read [a book [that you did <read t>]]].

So we are left with a real problem. We have fairly good evidence for QR. This operation is needed if we want to keep to a simple theory of the interpretation of QNPs and at the same time to account for the locality of scope (section 2.2.1) for the properties of ACD (section 2.2.2), and for various Condition A effects (section 2.3.1). However, QR appears to get the wrong results for Condition C. This problem can be eliminated if we adopt the copy theory of movement, but then we lose our account for ACD. In the next section, I would like to present a solution to this conflict for which I have argued in recent work (Fox, 2002).[39]

2.5   Late merger and Antecedent Contained Deletion

We ended the previous section with a conflict between Condition C and the conditions on ellipsis (Parallelism). QR seems to have effects on Parallelism but not on Condition C. The facts pertaining to Condition C can be captured by the copy theory of movement. But then it is no longer obvious that QR should circumvent a violation of Parallelism in ACD constructions. The solution I would like to present for this puzzle is based on the idea that, contrary to initial appearances, QR on its own cannot circumvent a violation of Parallelism. An ACD construction is possible due to a combination of QR and the Late Merger of a relative clause.

In order to understand what I am trying to do, it is useful to return to (24b).

(24)b.   (Guess) [which picture that John$_1$ saw] He$_1$ likes t.

The initial response to this sentence is of course to suggest that Condition C can be obviated by wh-movement. But we have seen an alternative proposal consistent with the hypothesis that wh-movement cannot circumvent a violation of condition C, namely that (24b) is acceptable due to a combination of wh-movement and late merger. The proposal presented below for ACD is essentially identical: QR alone cannot circumvent a violation of Parallelism, and ACD is possible due to a combination of QR and late merger. But the proposal relies on a few auxiliary assumptions that need to be introduced. One assumption (defended in Fox and Nissenbaum, 1999) is that late merger can follow covert operations, contrary to common assumptions about architecture (p. 102). The second assumption concerns the interpretation of structures derived by movement, and the third concerns the representation of relative clauses.

2.5.1   QR and late merger

Why is QR covert? A commonly assumed answer is that it applies after a point of the derivation at which the phonological properties of a sentence are determined (spell-out). If this assumption is correct, nothing (at least nothing overt) can be merged after QR. It follows that there can be no derivation parallel to (31) that involved QR instead of overt wh-movement.

But let us consider the possibility that this consequence is false. Of course, if this turns out to be the case, something else needs to be postulated in order to derive the fact that QR is covert. Let us put aside the question of what this "something" might be,[40] and ask what a derivation parallel to (31) would look like if it involved QR instead of overt wh-movement. So let us start with (31) (slightly modified in (33) so as not to distract our attention with Condition C and the way it is satisfied):

(33)a.   Mary likes [which picture] – wh-movement→
    b.   [which picture] Mary likes [which picture] – adjunct merger→
    c.   [which picture that John saw] Mary likes [which picture]

(33) is the structure before the application of QR. QR yields the structure in (33), in which the wh-phrase, *which picture*, is in two positions. (The higher position – the position that according to notational convention is placed to the left – is the head of the chain; the lower position is the tail.) If the derivation ends at this point, the rules of phonology target the head of the chain, and the pronunciation is that of *which picture Mary likes*. If the derivations precedes, with late merger creating the structure in (33), the relative clause is pronounced where it was merged and we get *which picture that John saw Mary likes*.

Now let us consider the same derivation with QR.

(34)a.   Mary likes [every picture] – *QR*→
    b.   [every picture] Mary likes [every picture] – adjunct merger→
    c.   [every picture that John saw] Mary likes [every picture]

(34a) is the structure before movement. After QR, the QNP, *every picture*, is in two positions, (34b). But if the derivation ends at this point, the pronunciation is quite different from what we get from (33). QR is covert, which means that the sentence is pronounced as if it did not apply; that is, the tail of the chain is pronounced, not the head: *Mary likes every picture*.[41] If the derivation precedes, with late merger creating the structure in (33), the relative clause should be pronounced where it was merged and we might expect to get the following: *that John saw(,) Mary likes every picture*. Of course, we never get this pronunciation, which might suggest that late merger cannot follow QR.

But in Fox and Nissenbaum (1999), we argue for a different conclusion. Specifically, we argue that QR applies to the right and that this is the explanation for the missing pronunciation. Furthermore, we argue that the derivation in (34) is attested, yielding constructions traditionally analyzed as involving extraposition from NP (with the minor correction that QR normally targets VP, see p. 98).

To understand the nature of the claim, consider the sentence in (35). We argue that this sentence is derived by covert QR (to the right) followed by late merger; the DP *a painting* (the DP from which, under traditional accounts, the adjunct has extraposed, henceforth, the source DP) undergoes QR to VP yielding (35a), and then the NP, *painting,* is merged with the adjunct *by John,* resulting in (35c). (For related proposals, see Guéron and May, 1984, and Reinhart, 1991.) The pronunciation is expected under the assumption that QR is a rightward covert operation (see note 42). The fact that the movement is covert is indicated by the ~~strikethrough~~ format.

(35) We saw a painting yesterday by John.

(a)

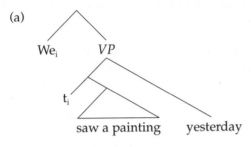

(b) *QR ("overt")*

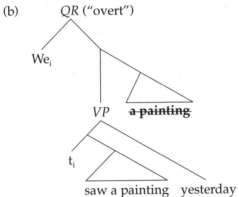

(c) *adjunct merger ("overt")*

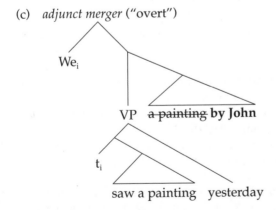

We present various arguments in favor of this proposal.[42] Here, I will limit myself to evidence pertaining to scope and Condition C. As for scope, there is a very obvious, though non-trivial, prediction. Because extraposition involves covert movement of the source DP to the position where the adjunct is merged, it is predicted that the scope of the source DP would be at least as high as the extraposition site.[43] That this prediction is correct was argued in Williams (1974, ch. 4) based on slightly different constructions, and it is stated below as Williams' generalization.[44] If the generalization is correct, it provides important evidence in favor of the account.

(36) Williams' generalization: When an adjunct β is extraposed from a "source DP" α, the scope of α is at least as high as the attachment site of β (the extraposition site).[45]

As a first step towards constructing an example that would test whether the generalization is correct, consider the ambiguity of (37).[46]

(37) John must teach no book about evolution in order to please the school committee.

One reading of this sentence asserts that if John is to please the school committee, it must be the case that he teaches no book about evolution. Under this reading the sentence might be used to convey something about the school committee's intolerance. The other reading of the sentence (which might be facilitated by replacing "no book" with "no *particular* book") asserts that there is no book such that pleasing the school committee requires that John teach *that particular* book. Under this reading, the sentence does not impute intolerance to the school committee, but rather indifference. The former reading results from the DP *no book about evolution* taking narrow scope with respect to the modal operator *must*, which the rationale clause restricts. The latter interpretation results from the reverse scope relation.

If Williams' generalization is correct then extraposition of an adjunct to a position dominating above the rational clause should disambiguate sentences similar to (37) towards the interpretation in which the source DP outscopes the modal. This disambiguation is expected since the rationale clause restricts the modal (see Williams, 1974). That the expectation is borne out is suggested by the contrast in (38).

(38)a. John must miss no assignment that is required by his math teacher in order to stay in school.
   b. #John must miss no assignment in order to stay in school that is required by his math teacher.
   c. John must hand in no assignment in order to stay in school that is required by his math teacher.

(38a) is – in principle – ambiguous in the same way that (37) is. However, in this case the interpretation in which the DP outscopes the modal is pragmatically odd. In particular, given our assumptions about the function of schools, we do not expect students to be required to miss assignments. Therefore it is not particularly informative to assert that there are no assignments (of a particular sort) that John must miss in order to stay in school. The fact that (38) has only this odd (non-informative) interpretation suggests that extraposition to the right of the rationale clause forces wide scope for the source DP, evidently an instance of Williams' generalization. This is reinforced by the relative naturalness of (38). This example, in contrast to (38), makes sense (only) under wide scope for the source DP, again given our assumptions about the function of schools, and thus is expected to be natural if Williams' generalization is the correct description.

Let us now move to the predictions that the analysis of extraposition has for Condition C. Because extraposition involves post-QR merger of adjuncts, it is predicted to have effects on Condition C of the binding theory (identical to the effects that were observed in the case of wh-movement, (24)). Evidence that this prediction is correct is provided by the following example from Taraldsen (1981) (compare with (30)):

(39)   I gave him$_i$ a book yesterday that John$_i$ liked.

The acceptability of this sentence is expected under Fox and Nissenbaum's (1999) approach to extraposition. In fact the account is identical to the account provided by Lebeaux and Chomsky for (24) above: Condition C is obviated because the adjunct *that John liked* is merged with the source DP at the landing site of QR, yielding a structure in which the name *John* is not c-commanded by the coindexed pronoun:

(40)   I [[VP t gave him$_i$ [a book] yesterday] [a̶ ̶b̶o̶o̶k̶ that John$_i$ liked]

The explanation that Taraldsen offers for the status of (39) is different; it is based on the assumption that extraposition is a movement operation and as such is capable of bleeding Condition C. Evidence against this explanation and in favor of an explanation based on late merger is provided by the contrast in (41).

(41)a.   ?I told him$_i$ about your new argument the other day that supports John's$_i$ theory.
   b.   *I told you about his$_i$ new argument the other day that supports John's$_i$ theory.

In (41a), extraposition obviates a violation of Condition C.[47] This follows from the standard explanation as well as from the one based on late merger. However, the fact that in (41b) extraposition does not obviate a violation of Condition C is extremely puzzling under Taraldsen's explanation; the pronoun *him$_i$* in (41a) is in a higher (surface) position than the pronoun *his$_i$* in (41b); therefore, if extraposition is a movement operation capable of bleeding Condition C in (41a), it should also be able to do so in (41b).

On the late merger account, the contrast in (41) is expected. If the effects on Condition C are due to late merger, there are very specific predictions: a violation of the condition should be obviated only if the problematic pronoun (*him$_i$* in (41a) and *his$_i$* in (41b)) is not contained within the source DP. This is seen by the representations of the sentences in (41) that are derived by post-QR merger:[48]

(42)a.   I [[$_{VP}$ t told him$_i$ about [your new argument] the other day] [~~your new argument~~ that supports John's$_i$ theory]].

   b.   I [[$_{VP}$ t told you about [his$_i$ new argument] the other day] [~~his new argument~~ that supports John's$_i$ theory]].

Additional evidence in favor of Fox and Nissenbaum's account comes from a consideration of Lebeaux's hypothesis that late merger is possible for adjuncts but not for complements (see p. 102). This hypothesis leads to the prediction that complement extraposition will differ from adjunct extraposition in failing to bleed Condition C. The contrast in (43) suggests that the prediction is correct.

(43)a.   I gave him$_i$ an argument yesterday **that supports John's$_i$ theory**.

   b.   ??/*I gave him$_i$ an argument yesterday **that John's$_i$ theory is correct**.

(43a) is derived by post-QR merger of the relative clause (in bold face), an operation which is expected to obviate Condition C. (43b), by contrast, cannot be derived by late merger of the bold faced phrase since this constituent is a complement. Instead, it is derived by rightward movement of a complement, which (given the copy theory of movement) does not obviate Condition C.[49]

Finally, the account in terms of late merger predicts a correlation between the ability of extraposition to circumvent Condition C and the scope of the source DP. To understand this prediction, consider the contrast in (44).

(44)a.   ?I wanted him$_i$ not to talk to a (certain) girl yesterday that John$_i$ has known for years.[50]

   b.   *I wanted him$_i$ not to talk to any girl yesterday that John$_i$ has known for years.

   c.   I wanted John$_i$ not to talk to any girl yesterday that he$_i$ has known for years.

In (44a), extraposition to the matrix clause is expected to yield the following structure in which Condition C is not violated:

(44)'a.   I [[$_{VP}$ t wanted him not to talk to [a (certain)] girl yesterday] [~~a (certain) girl~~ that John has known for years]]

However, an obviation of Condition C by extraposition has predicted consequences for the scope of the source DP; it must be at least as high as the extraposition site. In the case of (44), the indefinite *a (certain) girl that John has known for years* must outscope both negation and the intensional verb *want*. This predicted consequence seems to be correct (as far as speakers can access the judgments). More importantly, the unacceptability of (44b) verifies the prediction: the source DP is an NPI, which is not allowed to outscope negation, and thus brings about a conflict with the requirement imposed by Condition C. (44c) is acceptable since Condition C imposes no requirements and extraposition to the embedded VP is available.

What have we learned from this discussion? We saw that if we adopt a model of grammar in which overt and covert operations can be interspersed, we might expect covert movement to be followed by late merger of an adjunct. Furthermore, if we assume that covert movement applies to the right, extraposition from NP cries out for an analysis in these terms. Finally, we saw that there are various non-trivial predictions for scope and for condition C, as well as for their interaction, and that there is some evidence that these predictions are borne out.

Can this help us in resolving the conflict between ACD and the copy theory of movement? Given the copy theory, QR cannot circumvent the violation of Parallelism that ought to arise in ACD constructions. This, as we noted, is similar to the fact that movement cannot circumvent a violation of Condition C. But could the acceptability of ACD constructions rely on QR + late merger (extraposition) along the logic of our account for (24)?

So consider a simple ACD construction such as (32), repeated below.

(45)   I [$_{VPantecedent}$ read [a book [that you did <read t>]]].

Suppose that this sentence has the following derivation:

(45)'a.   I [$_{VPantecedent}$ t read a book] – QR→
     b.   I [[$_{VPantecedent}$ t read a book] ~~a book~~] – late merger→
     c.   I [[$_{VPantecedent}$ t read a book] ~~a book~~ [that you did <read t>]].

The elided VP and the antecedent look a little closer to each other in (45'c) than they do in an LF that involves QR without late merger (see (32)″). But it is still not obvious that Parallelism is satisfied. Parallelism requires that the trace/copy formed by QR be identical to the trace/copy inside the relative clause. But we have not said anything yet about the form that the latter has under the copy theory of movement. And, also, we have not talked about the way that structures derived by movement might be interpreted once the copy theory is adopted. Both issues will be relevant for the question of Parallelism, as we will see. I will begin with the latter.

2.5.2   Movement and interpretation

Chomsky (1995) points out that the copy theory of movement simplifies syntax in two ways. First, the theory eliminates the need to postulate new objects (traces) beyond run-of-the-mill lexical items. In this sense, it brings us closer to a view of syntax as a recursive procedure that does not access anything but the lexicon. Second, the copy theory turns movement into a simpler operation; it is practically identical to the elementary structure-building operation (*merge*), differing only in that it takes as input an object that has served as input for an earlier merger (*move* is *re-merge*).

How do the copy theory of movement and the traditional alternative (with traces) compare with respect to semantic interpretation? We spelled-out a semantic mechanism that interprets structures with traces in (11), repeated below with a minor, though insignificant, modification.

(46)   In a structure formed by DP movement, $DP_n[_\varphi \ldots t_n \ldots]$, the derived sister of DP, φ, is interpreted as a function that maps an individual, x, to the meaning of $\varphi[x/n]$.

$\varphi[x/n]$ is the result of substituting every constituent with the index n in φ with him_x, a pronoun that denotes the individual x.

It is fairly obvious that this rule does not depend on a theory that postulates traces instead of copies. The rule refers to the interpretation of structures derived by substituting indexed elements with pronouns of a certain sort. It, therefore, does not matter what properties the indexed elements have. In particular, it does not matter whether these indexed elements are traces or copies. So the rule might as well be stated as in (47), and it, therefore, cannot serve to distinguish between trace- and copy-theory.

(47)   In a structure formed by DP movement, $DP_n[_\varphi \ldots DP_n \ldots]$, the derived sister of DP, φ, is interpreted as a function that maps an individual, x, to the meaning of $\varphi[x/n]$.

$\varphi[x/n]$ is the result of substituting every constituent with the index n in φ with him_x, a pronoun that denotes the individual x.

We conclude that syntax is simplified by copy theory and that semantics is not affected. So we have a decent conceptual argument in favor of the theory. But notice that the rule in (47) ignores every property of the copy besides its index. In this sense, it might be viewed as mysterious that the content of the copy has relevance for Condition C of the binding theory. That is to say, we do not understand why Condition C is different from the rule in (47) in that only the former is sensitive to the fact that a name is dominated by a copy. Both the rule in (47) and in (46) treat traces the way that we treat variables in logic, and it is therefore somewhat surprising that Condition C "sees" something which is richer than a variable.

As a response to this, I have postulated a syntactic rule that converts lower-copies/traces into structures that contain variables. The rule was designed to convert a trace to a definite description, eventually yielding interpretations similar to those of the following paraphrases:[51]

(48)   Which boy Mary visited which boy?
Paraphrase: Which is the boy, x, such that Mary visited **the boy x**?

(49)   every boy A girl talked to every boy.
Paraphrase: For every boy, x, there is a girl who talked to **the boy x**.

The boy x in the paraphrase is modeled on definite descriptions in natural language such as *the man John*. These definite descriptions, I assume, are interpreted by predicate modification of $[[\text{man}]]$ and $\lambda x(x=[[\text{John}]])$ with the resulting predicate serving as argument of the determiner. The postulated rule, thus, involves two operations:

(50)   *Trace Conversion:*
     a.   Variable Insertion: (Det) Pred $\rightarrow$ (Det) [Pred $\lambda y(y=\text{him}_n)$][52]
     b.   Determiner Replacement:(Det) [Pred $\lambda y(y=\text{him}_n)$] $\rightarrow$ the [Pred $\lambda y(y=\text{him}_n)$][53]

Furthermore, I assumed that the output of this syntactic rule is interpreted by the semantic rule in (46). To see how this would work, consider the derived sister of *every boy* in (49), *A girl talked to every boy*. This constituent is converted by Trace Conversion to *A girl talked to the boy (identical to) him*$_n$, which is interpreted by the relevant semantic rule as λx. *A girl talked to the boy, x*.[54]

Once Trace Conversion is part of grammar (and the rule in (46) is maintained) it is pretty clear why QR cannot affect condition C. A sentence such as (30a), repeated below as (51), is unacceptable since the LF structure is one in which the name *John* is *semantically interpreted* in a position that is not licensed by Condition C. To make this clear (i.e. to make the interpretation clear together with the ramifications for Condition C), I will use the lambda notation to indicate a position in the structure where the rule in (46) applies. So the structure of (51b) is derived from (51a) by a combination of QR and trace conversion and it is clear that Condition C is ruled out in this structure.[55]

(51)a.   A boy introduced him$_1$ to every friend of John's$_1$.
     b.   [every friend of John's$_1$] λx. A boy introduced him$_1$ to [the friend of John's$_1$ identical to x].

Trace Conversion, I will argue, can also help us in accounting for Antecedent Contained Deletion. But before we get to this, I would like to make a short conceptual diversion. If Trace Conversion is viewed as part of syntax, there still needs to be a semantic rule that tells us how the structure is interpreted, for example the rule in (46). But if this is how things work, it seems to me that Chomsky's conceptual argument in favor of the copy theory of movement is undermined. It is true that a copying operation (*re-merge*) is simpler than an operation that moves an object and replaces it with a trace/variable. But if the copy has to be converted to an object that contains a variable, questions of simplicity are much harder to address. For this reason, I would like to mention the possibility that Trace Conversion is an artifact of the semantic rule that interprets the derived sister of a moved constituent, and that this rule should therefore be modified (see Elbourne, 2002):

(52)   In a structure formed by DP movement, $DP_n[_\varphi \ldots DP_n \ldots]$, the derived sister of DP, φ, is interpreted as a function that maps an individual, x, to the meaning of $\varphi[x/n]$.

$\varphi[x/n]$ is the result of replacing the head of every constituent with the index n in φ with the head the_x, whose interpretation, $[[the_x]]$, is, $\lambda P. [[the]](P \cap \lambda y.y =x)$.

This semantic rule interprets the derived sister of a moved constituent directly (without Trace Conversion). Nevertheless, the interpretation is identical to the one resulting from the standard rule, (46), when it applies to the output of Trace Coversion. This raises the possibility that ultimately Trace Conversion can be eliminated with no significant modification to the ideas outlined below. But at the moment, I will continue to employ Trace Conversion as a syntactic rule.

2.5.3 *Relative clauses*

I will assume (following Kayne, 1974; Cinque, 1982; Sauerland, 1998) that relative clauses are both head external and head internal (what Sauerland calls the "matching analysis;" see also Cresti, 1999; Kennedy, 2000). More specifically, I will assume that the derivation of relative clauses involves "movement to Comp" of a CP internal NP, which is deleted under identity with a CP external NP:

(53)   Every boy [CP ~~boy~~ Mary likes ~~boy~~].

Furthermore, I will assume (along with many) that the NP in [spec, CP] is not interpreted but that movement turns the relative clause into a predicate that combines with the CP external NP by predicate modification. More specifically, given Trace Conversion, we get the following structure:

(54)   Every [boy λx. Mary likes the boy x][56]

2.5.4 *Explaining Antecedent Contained Deletion*

If (54) is the interpreted structure of a DP containing a relative clause, and if the relative clause can be merged with NP after the QNP has undergone QR, then a sentence involving ACD can have the following derivation.

(55)   [$_{VP}$ John likes every boy] – *QR→*
       [[$_{VP}$ John likes] every boy] **every boy** – *adjunct merger→*
       [[$_{VP}$ John likes every boy] every boy **that Mary does <likes boy>**]

Trace Conversion transforms the structure to (56), which satisfies Parallelism.

(56)   [every boy λx Mary does <likes the boy x>]
                   λy John   likes the boy y]

So, here is what we have learned. Given the copy theory, ACD constructions do not escape a violation of Parallelism by virtue of QR alone. However, we have seen (in section 2.5.1), evidence in favor of the proposal that QR can be followed by later merger of an adjunct (extraposition).[57] Next, we asked whether Parallelism would be satisfied by a combination of QR and late merger. We could not address this question before we spelled out some specific assumptions about the structure of relative clauses and the methods that might allow chains to be interpreted. We saw that Trace Conversion together with a (version of a) head internal analysis for relative clauses (the matching analysis) provided a positive answer. But it is clear that quite a few assumptions are involved. We would therefore like some additional evidence.

In Fox (2002), I have attempted to provide various sources of evidence. Some of the evidence consisted in arguments (partially taken from previous literature) that extraposition is indeed needed for ACD resolution. There was also important evidence from work by Chris Kennedy and (in particular) Uli Sauerland that the effects of the copy theory of movement are visible in ACD constructions. In particular, there were specific environments in which the copy theory of movement predicted that late merger would be insufficient to obviate a violation of Parallelism, and there was evidence that the predictions come out the right way. Unfortunately, I will have to stop here.

2.6   Conclusions

We ended section 5 of this paper in a somewhat peculiar situation. We had a good deal of evidence in favor of LF structures in which QNPs are in their scope position (i.e. they are sisters of their argument/scope). The LF structures were needed for a simple semantic procedure to be possible (section 2.2). Furthermore, there was evidence from locality considerations (section 2.3.1), from Parallelism (section 2.3.2), and from Condition A of the Binding Theory (section 2.4.1). The nagging problem was Condition C. This condition contrasted with all the other evidence in showing no indication that the postulated LF structures were real. The Copy Theory of Movement provided a way out, which was consistent with our discussion of Parallelism, as long as we adopted a model of grammar in which an overt operation of late merger could follow the covert operation of Quantifier Raising (section 2.5).

Notes

*   Thanks to Jonathan Bobaljik, Noam Chomsky, Irene Heim, and Jon Nissenbaum.
1   The editor of this volume (Randall Hendrick) asked me to dedicate half of this paper to a discussion of some of the traditional arguments in favor of QR and to use the other half to present some of my own work. There is no clear point where the first half ends and the second begins, but the transition is somewhere in the middle of section 2.3.

2   The treatment of quantification as second order predication is due to Frege (see Dummett, 1977). The application to natural language semantics together with the observation that QNPs are restricted quantifiers comes from Montague. The presentation in this introduction follows the logic of Heim and Kratzer (1998). For a slightly different way of thinking about the semantics of QNPs, see Larson and Segal (1995, ch. 7), as well as Heim (1997).

3   I am ignoring the copula *is* assuming that it is semantically vacuous. To simplify the discussion, I am also ignoring "functional categories" that are not vacuous, such as tense.

4   $\lambda x.\phi$, where ϕ is a sentence, should be read as a function from individuals to truth values that assigns TRUE to x, iff ϕ is true.

5   The problem generalizes to all cases in which the QNP is in the non-external position of a predicate that has two or more arguments.

6   See Klima (1964), Kayne (1981). The latter interpretation is forced when *not a single book* is replaced with *no particular book*.

7   Notice that I am using the terms *I* and *you* to describe the meaning of the sentences (in the "meta language"). This practice would not be a good idea if it were adopted more generally. Sophisticated things need to be said in order to explain the way that first- and second-person pronouns depend on context to determine their meaning. Also, much more needs to be said about the meaning of verbs such as *demand*. To account for their scopal behavior, it is standard practice to treat them as quantifiers that range over possible worlds.

8   Notice, though, that what makes the semantic effects of movement visible is not very well understood. Once a broad array of movement constructions is taken into account, it is clear that a moved constituent can sometimes be interpreted as if it hasn't moved (scope reconstruction). Furthermore, it is not obvious (to me, at least) what blocks scope reconstruction in (10). But there are also arguments (for the rule in (11)) that do not depend on the unavailability of scope reconstruction. These arguments rely on environments in which (again for ill-understood reasons) QR – the operation that we will introduce shortly – is more restricted than overt movement (see Fox, 2000, p. 144 and references therein). Also, strong evidence comes from the effects of scrambling in scope rigid languages (see Kuroda, 1971; Hoji, 1985) or from other languages in which QR might be overt (see note 14).

9   According to Sauerland and van Stechow (2000), this rule is due to Cooper (1979), though the idea that the semantic objects formed by this rule should be made to serve as arguments of quantifiers goes back to Frege. The statement that I provide in (11) yields undesirable results when certain constructions that involve more than one operation of movement are taken into account. These problems could be circumvented by a constraint against "meaningless coindexation" of the type argued for in Heim (1997). See Heim and Kratzer (1998) for extensive discussion of a different implementation. On other concerns associated with reference to substitution, see Larson and Segal (1995, section 7.2) and references therein.

10   The hypothesis that QNPs move to "their scope position" (Quantifier Raising) is due to Chomsky (1976) and May (1977). It is, of course, related to the hypothesis of McCawley (1970) that QNPs start out in their scope position and move from there to their surface position (Quantifier Lowering). In fact, the argument in favor of QR based on the Coordinate Structure Constraint (see section 2.2.1, below) was originally framed in terms of Quantifier Lowering. See also Postal (1974). Quantifier Raising also bears some resemblance to the rule of Quantifying In proposed by Montague. For a recent comparison of the various approaches, see Jacobson (in press).

11 As long as the result is interpretable. This will be the case as long as the derived sister denotes a one-place predicate, that is as long as $\phi[x/n]$ denotes a truth value.

12 Notice that this is not the case once scope reconstruction is acknowledged (see note 8). See Hornstein (1995) and Johnson and Tomioka (1997) for an interesting exploitation of this observation. See also notes 17 and 29.

13 See Hendriks (1993), Jacobson (1999), Brody (1995), Williams (1986), and Barker (2001).

14 I will not discuss the argument in favor of QR presented in Chomsky (1976), which was based on Weak Crossover. I will also not present various arguments based on languages in which Quantifier Raising might be overt. Among the relevant references are Kiss (1991), Szabolcsi (1998), Pesetsky (1987, 2000) Hoji (1985), Huang (1982), and Johnson (2000).

15 The use of the adjective, *different*, makes the difference between surface and inverse scope fairly transparent.

16 This derivation is cyclic and as such is incompatible with models of grammar in which covert operations must "follow" all overt operations. This incompatibility is, of course, not significant; the relevant structures could be derived in two different cycles; one overt and one covert. However, see section 2.5.

17 One might wonder whether scope reconstruction (cf. notes 8 and 12) could circumvent the effects of the CSC. See Fox (2000, pp. 58–62).

18 Ruys (1992) observes that the CSC applies somewhat differently in the case of overt and covert movement. See Lin (2001) for arguments that overt A-movement patterns with covert movement.

19 I haven't said what it means for two VPs to be identical. There are very difficult questions relating to the way the condition should apply to traces and pronouns that I cannot go over in this context. What I have in mind is something along the lines of the theory of Parallelism in Rooth (1992) as it is outlined in Heim (1997).

20 Since syntactic constituents are finite.

21 Notice that the predictions of Parallelism go beyond the exclusion of antecedent containment. So it is not enough to postulate a structure for the sentences where antecedent containment does not exist; one has to make sure that the postulated structure satisfies Parallelism.

22 There are, however, alternative proposals. One type of proposal involves a relaxation of Parallelism (Vanden Wyngaerd and Zwart, 1991; Brody, 1995). Another involves the assumption that the constituant that is elided is not a traditional VP but something else (Jacobson, 1999). Space limitations do not allow me to discuss these alternatives (but see note 24).

23 Given the VPI and the consequence that a QNP can be interpreted in VP, there are other positions that would yield the same interpretation, namely the matrix and embedded VP. The argument would not be affected if these other positions are taken to be the landing sites for QR. This had better be the case since in section 4 we will argue that VP is the common landing for a QNP.

24 This conclusion is shared by some researchers who do not agree that QR is the relevant mechanism. Thus Jacobson's (1999) mechanism for ACD resolution is not movement but a mechanism that has consequences for scope (function composition). Furthermore, it is a mechanism she uses (following many others) to account for cases of overt displacement. (Jacobson's position, if translated to a theory that postulates movement – a translation that she would strongly object to – would be the position that ACD involves overt movement to the right. In this sense her position is rather close to that of Kayne (1998).) Similarly, for Brody ACD resolution,

although not dependent on movement, is dependent on a pattern of "scope mark-ing" that derives the correlation with scope.

25 I wish to ignore the question of whether Condition A is satisfied by co-reference or requires variable binding as argued for in Reinhart (1983). If Reinhart is correct, we will need to be a little more careful in the way we re-state Belletti and Rizzi's idea.

26 Williams (1986) and more recently Brody (1995) pointed out, correctly in my view, that the contrast between (24) and (22) argues against the postulation of QR. How-ever, the facts discussed in the remainder of the paper might reverse the argument.

27 This is one of the points that Chomsky (1993) makes. But he argues that the appeal to Surface Structure is a cop-out from a broader perspective as well. He also provides some empirical evidence that Binding Theory must apply at LF. This evidence has been supported by the discovery of a correlation between scope reconstruction and condition C (Heycock, 1995; Lebeaux, 1991). For discussion, extensions, and various additional references see Fox (2000, ch. 5), Romero (1997), and Sportiche (2001).

It is also important to note that the claim that Binding Theory applies at Surface Structure is an incoherent position if the approach to Condition C advocated in Reinhart (1983) is adopted.

28 The latter draws heavily on Fox and Nissenbaum (1999). For alternative proposals, see Lasnik (1993) and Brody (1995).

29 It is important to point out that other researchers have provided evidence that QR is more restricted than wh-movement. In particular, Johnson and Tomioka (1997) and Hornstein (1995) have suggested that a QNP can never move over the surface position of the subject. These theories can account for the paradigm I present below (under certain assumptions about the Local Domain for Condition A) if the constraint in (27) is viewed as a constraint on the reconstruction of the subject. Hornstein, in fact suggested such a constraint on independent grounds (related to the theory of Diesing, 1992). For a few challenges to the claim that inverse scope depends on reconstruction, see Fox (2000, pp. 44–6, 51–62).

30 In Sag (1976) and Williams (1977) it was assumed that a QNP cannot take scope outside of an elided VP. However, this assumption was based on examples such as (26), and has been challenged by ellipsis sentences in Hirschbühler (1982) similar to (25):

(i)   An American flag is hanging from every window, and a Canadian flag is, too.

For discussion and further references, see Fox (2000).

31 In Fox (2000) I argued that the condition is more general favoring the shortest instance of QR needed for a given semantic interpretation. I also tried to make sense of the fact that the condition applies to QR and not to overt movement. But see Tomioka (2001).

32 As mentioned there are other pieces of evidence converging on the same results discussed in Fox (2000), for example the CSC. Note, however, that there is a poten-tial problem here. The following ACD construction doesn't seem as bad as ex-pected given the unacceptability of (22)a:

(i)   John said that you were on every committee that Bill did <say that you were on>.   (Wilder 1997)

It is interesting to see what happens in constructions that combine ACD and Con-dition A. The judgments are at the moment too subtle to support any conclusion:

(ii) (??)John and Bill said that I was in every picture of each other that you did.

If it turns out that (ii) is unacceptable, one might consider the possibility that the universal quantifier can QR to the matrix clause but that the relevant constraint forces the embedded subject to move to a higher position yielding a violation of Condition A.

33 The contrast in (i) is similar to the contrast between (22) and (24), and it raises (more or less) the same theoretical dilemma. It has led some (e.g. Chomsky, 1981) to assume that Condition A applies at Surface Structure and others to assume that there is no covert wh-movement (e.g. Chomsky, 1993; Brody, 1995). But Nissenbaum (2001) provides an intriguing third possibility. He provides various arguments that the contrast follows from a locality condition on a second instance of wh-movement (argued for in Richards (2001) on independent grounds). Under Nissenbaum's analysis, the paradigm turns out to provide additional support for covert movement, very similar in its nature to the support that is provided by the paradigm in (29).

(i)a. John and Bill know which picture of each other Mary bought.
b. *John and Bill know who bought which picture of each other.

34 A possible way out of this puzzle, which I will not discuss, invokes the hypothesis that the LF position of the pronoun is higher than the position of the two QNPs. This hypothesis is challenged by the arguments presented in section 2.5 (see the discussion of (39) below).

35 Section 2.5.2 discusses various ways in which the semantic component could treat the syntactic objects derived under the copy theory of movement. This discussion, I believe, is relevant for Condition C.

36 Of course, only one copy is realized phonologically. In the case of overt movement it is the copy at the higher position; in the case of covert movement it is the lower copy. The principles that determine which copy is pronounced (i.e. whether the movement is overt or covert) are not relevant at the moment, but they will be. Very shortly.

37 It is sometimes suggested that that distinction would be more natural if we distinguish between "positive" and "negative" conditions. Under such a distinction, we might say that Condition A is a *positive* condition which is *satisfied* by the existence of a level of representation that meets the *required* structural configuration. By contrast, Condition C is a *negative* condition which is *violated* by the existence of a level of representation that meets the *prohibited* structural configuration. See also Lebeaux (1995). See Chomsky (1993) for an alternative approach.

38 See Lebeaux (1988), Chomsky (1993), and Fox (2002) where some theoretical justification is provided for the hypothesis.

Lebeaux's empirical argument relies on the following contrast:

(i)a. Guess which argument that supports John's$_1$ theory he$_1$ adopted.
b. ??Guess which argument that John's$_1$ theory is correct he$_1$ adopted.

For some skepticism regarding the significance of this contrast, see Kuno (1997) and Lasnik (1998). For some discussion and counter-arguments see Safir (1998). See also (43) below. Additional data that are not covered by the proposal made here are discussed in Munn (1994).

39 For alternatives, see Lasnik (1993), Hornstein (1994), and Schmitt (1995).

40 Two types of proposal have been made in the literature. One is the proposal that principles of phonology sometimes target the tail of the chain for pronunciation

118 Danny Fox

(cf. Brody (1997), Bobaljik (1995, in press), Groat and O'Neil (1996), and Pesetsky (1998)). Another proposal involves multiple points of spell-out, which are followed by some covert operations. (Such a proposal was made in Chomsky (2000) and was developed with particular attention to late merger in Nissenbaum (2001). See also Chomsky (2001).) By now, various arguments have been presented against the traditional architecture, which is committed to a "covert component". (Some of the arguments focus on the commitment to "multiple cycles" advocating a single cycle grammar.) To the best of my knowledge, the initial arguments are presented in Brody (1995), who argues for a theory that dispenses with derivations.

41 The claim that the tail is pronounced is none other than the claim that QR is covert; it, therefore, does not presuppose a particular account of covert movement. See note 40.

42 But various questions remain unanswered. One question is what accounts for the (apparently necessary) assumption that QR applies to the right. (See Chomsky (2001) for some criticism and for an alternative proposal.) Another question relates to cases of extraposition for which the analysis does not extend straightforwardly (such as extraposition from subjects and overtly moved wh-phrases).

43 One might question this prediction under the assumption that QR can reconstruct. But if an adjunct is present only at the head of a chain, and if reconstruction results from interpreting only the tail of a chain (i.e. the head of the chain is deleted at LF), then late merger will block reconstruction; the adjunct would not be interpretable as a modifier of the source NP. Exactly these considerations are needed independently (as pointed out by Fox, 2000, ch. 5) to account for correlations between scope reconstruction and Condition C. Notice that in both cases there is an argument against "semantic reconstruction." If semantic reconstruction (via type shifting operations or higher type traces) were possible (see Jacobson, 1999; Sternefeld, 2001 and references therein), it would not conflict with late merger of an adjunct.

44 Williams, in contrast to Fox and Nissenbaum, focused on comparative- and result-extraposition, and not on extraposition from NP. For an account of the former in terms of late merger see Bhatt and Pancheva (2001).

45 Of course, if Fox and Nissenbaum's proposal is correct, it is (strictly speaking) wrong to refer to the attachment site of EC (since under the proposal, EC is adjoined to *NP* in the raised position rather than raised to VP). The intention is to refer to what is taken to be the attachment site of EC under traditional analyses. A statement of Williams' generalization consistent with Fox and Nissenbaum proposal would be the following: When an adjunct β is "extraposed" from a "source DP" α, every node that c-commands the base position of α and does not c-command β will be interpreted in the scope of α.

46 The discussion of this ambiguity was inspired by Williams (1974).

47 The sentence is slightly marginal, but this is unrelated to Condition C: replacing the R-expression with a pronoun does not improve the status of the sentence. In any event, the contrast between (a) and (b) is pretty sharp.

48 The relations that are relevant for Condition C might be more transparent when we consider the way the structures are interpreted, section 2.5.2. Thus we can characterize the interpretation of (42), with the structure in (i), in which the violation of Condition C is fairly transparent.

(i) [his₁ new argument that supports John's₁ theory] λx. [I told you about his₁ new argument, x]

49 A derivation of adjunct extraposition via rightward movement needs to be blocked; otherwise the explanation of Williams' generalization would be lost. This blocking

is achieved in Fox and Nissenbaum (1999) with appeal to the observation that in general movement out of NPs is restricted to complements. See Fox and Nissenbaum (1999) for a variety of arguments that complement extraposition and adjunct extraposition have a very different analysis.

50 (44) is marginal for some speakers. However, it is definitely better than (44). See Fox (2002).

51 The suggestion was based on a proposal made in a different context by Rullmann and Beck (1997).

52 Where n is the index of the moved QNP.

53 For the sake of accessibility the rule is stated somewhat informally using objects of the semantic theory (the "meta language") as if they were syntactic objects (in the "object language"). This informal practice will continue throughout this paper. Furthermore, sometimes the output of trace conversion will be stated as *the Pred x* (as in (48)), and sometimes to aid the reader I will add the words "identical to" between *Pred* and *x* (as in (51)).

54 The lamda-expression is a partial function defined only for boys. (It maps a boy to TRUE iff Mary likes that boy). There are no semantic problems with this rule since natural language determiners denote conservative two-place predicates (D(A, B) = D(A, A∩B)). My hope is that this rule could play an interesting role in accounting for the conservativity.

55 So, if Reinhart's (1983) perspective on Condition C is right, the sentence could be ruled out on the grounds that the derived predicate (the derived sister of the raised QNP) would be the same if *John* were replaced by a variable bound by the pronoun *him*. The same story could not be told if the name *John* does not contribute to semantic interpretation, as in the rule in (47).

56 The meaning of this QNP is the following: $\lambda P \forall x ((boy(x) \ \& \ \text{Mary likes the boy } x) \rightarrow (P(x) = 1))$.

57 The idea that extraposition is necessary for ACD has been proposed in Baltin (1987) and has resurfaced in various forms (see Lasnik, 1995; Wilder, 1995; Abe and Hoshi, 1999). For some comments on the differences and similarities between the proposals, see Fox (2002).

References

Abe, J. and Hoshi, H. (1999). A generalized rightward movement analysis of Antecedent Contained Deletion. *Journal of Linguistics, 35,* 451–87.

Abush, D. (1994). The scope of indefinites. *Natural Language Semantics, 2,* 83–135.

Aguero-Bautista, C. (2001). On pair list readings. *North East Linguistics Society, 30,* 95–110.

Aoun, J. and Li, A. (1993). *The syntax of scope.* Cambridge, MA: MIT Press.

Baltin, M. (1987). Do antecedent contained deletions exist? *Linguistic Inquiry, 18,* 579–95.

Barker, C. (2002). The dynamics of vagueness. *Linguistics and Philosophy, 25,* 1–36.

Beghelli, F. and Stowell, T. (1997). Distributivity and negation. In A. Szabolcsi (ed.), *Ways of scope taking* (pp. 71–107). Dordrecht, The Netherlands: Kluwer.

Belletti, A. and Rizzi, L. (1988). Psych-verbs and theta theory. *Natural Language and Linguistic Theory, 6,* 291–353.

Bhatt, R. and Pancheva, R. (2001). *Variable height of adjunction and the LF licensing of degree complements.* Unpublished manuscript. University of Texas at Austin.

Bobaljik, J. (1995). *Morphosyntax: the syntax of verbal inflection*. Doctoral dissertation, MIT, MITWPL.

Bobaljik, J. (2002). A-chains at the interface: copies, agreement and "covert movement". *Natural Language and Linguistic Theory, 20*, 197–267.

Brody, M. (1995). *Lexico-logical form*. Cambridge, MA: MIT Press.

Brody, M. (1997). Perfect chains. In L. Haegeman (ed.), *Elements of grammar: Handbook in generative syntax. Kluwer International Handbooks of Linguistics, vol. 1*. Dordrecht: Kluwer.

Bruening, B. (2001). QR obeys superiority: ACD and frozen scope. *Linguistic Inquiry, 32*, 233–73.

Chomsky, N. (1976). Conditions on rules of grammar. *Linguistic Analysis, 2*, 303–51.

Chomsky, N. (1981). *Lectures on Government and Binding*. Dordrecht, The Netherlands: Foris.

Chomsky, N. (1993). A minimalist program for linguistic theory. In K. Hale and S. J. Keyser (eds.), *The view from Building 20*. Cambridge, MA: MIT Press; re-printed as chapter 3 of Chomsky (1995).

Chomsky, N. (1995). *The minimalist program*. Cambridge, MA: MIT Press.

Chomsky, N. (2000). Minimalist inquiries: the framework. In R. Martin, D. Michaels, and J. Uriagereka (eds.), *Step by step: Essays on minimalist syntax in honor of Howard Lasnik* (pp. 89–155). Cambridge, MA: MIT Press.

Chomsky, N. (2001). *Beyond explanatory adequacy*. Manuscript. MIT.

Cinque, G. (1981–2). On the theory of relative clauses and markedness. *The Linguistic Review, 1*, 247–94.

Cooper, R. (1979). Variable binding and relative clauses. In F. Guenthner and S. J. Schmidt (eds.), *Formal semantics and pragmatics for natural languages*. Dordrecht, The Netherlands: Reidel.

Cresti, D. (1999). Ellipsis and reconstruction in Relative Clauses. In *Proceedings of NELS 30*, Amherst: GLSA Publications.

Diesing, M. (1992). *Indefinites*. Cambridge, MA: MIT Press.

Dummett, M. (1977). *Elements of intuitionism*. Oxford: Clarendon Press.

Elbourne, P. (2002). *Situations and individuals*. Doctoral dissertation, MIT.

Fox, D. (2000). *Economy and semantic interpretation*. Cambridge, MA: MIT Press.

Fox, D. (2002). Antecedent contained deletion and the copy theory of movement. *Linguistic Inquiry, 33*, 63–96.

Fox, D. and Nissenbaum, J. (1999). Extraposition and scope: a case for overt QR. Unpublished MS.

Friedin, R. (1986). Fundamental issues in the theory of binding. In B. Lust (ed.), *Studies in the acquistion of anaphora*. Dordrecht: Reidel.

Groat, E. and O'Neil, J. (1996). Spellout at the LF interface. In W. Abraham, S. D. Epstein, H. Thráinsson, and C. J.-W. Zwart (eds.), *Minimal ideas: Syntactic studies in the minimalist framework* (pp. 113–39). Amsterdam and Philadelphia: John Benjamins.

Guéron, J. and May, R. (1984). Extraposition and logical form. *Linguistics Inquiry, 15*, 1–31.

Heim, I. (1997). Predicates or formulas? evidence from ellipsis. In A. Lawon and E. Cho (eds.), *Proceedings of SALT 7*. (pp. 197–221). Ithaca, NY: CLC Publications.

Heim, I. and Kratzer, A. (1998). *Semantics in generative grammar*. Oxford: Blackwell.

Hendriks, H. (1993). *Studied flexibility*. Amsterdam: ILLC Dissertation Series.

Heycock, C. (1995). Asymmetries in reconstruction. *Linguistic Inquiry, 26*, 547–70.

Hirschbühler, P. (1982). VP deletion and across the board quantifier scope. In *Proceedings of the North East Linguistics Society, 25*, 425–40.

Hoji, H. (1985). *Logical form constraints and configuration structures in Japanese*. Doctoral dissertation, University of Washington.

Hornstein, N. (1994). An argument for minimalism. The case of antecedent contained deletion. *Linguistic Inquiry, 25*, 662–88.

Hornstein, N. (1995). *Logical form: From GB to Minimalism.* Oxford: Blackwell.

Huang, J. (1982). *Logical relations in Chinese and the theory of grammar.* Doctoral dissertation, MIT.

Jacobson, P. (1992). Comment flexible categorial grammar, questions and prospects. In R. Levine (ed.), *Formal grammar, theory and interpretation.* Oxford: Oxford University Press.

Jacobson, P. (1997). Where (if anywhere) is transderivationality located? In P. Cullicover and L. McNally (eds.), *The limits of syntax: Syntax and semantics* (pp. 303–66). San Diego, CA: Academic Press.

Jacobson, P. (1999). Toward a variable free semantics. *Linguistics and Philososphy, 22*, 117–84.

Johnson, K. (2000). How far will quantifiers go? In R. Martin, D. Michaels, and J. Uriageka (eds.), *Step by step.* (pp. 187–210). Cambridge, MA: MIT Press.

Johnson, K. and Tomioka, S. (1997). Lowering and mid-sized clauses. In *Proceedings of the Tübingen Workshop on Reconstruction*, ed. G. Katz, S. S. Kim, and W. Haike. University of Tübingen, pp. 185–206.

Kayne, R. S. (1974). French relative que. In M. Lujan and F. Hensey (eds.), *Current studies in romance linguistics.* Washington, DC: Georgetown University Press.

Kayne, R. S. (1981). Two notes on the NIC. In A. Belletti, L. Brandi, and L. Rizzi (eds.), *Theory of markedness in generative grammar: Proceedings of the 1979 Glow Conference.* (pp. 475–516). Pisa: Scuola Normale Superiore.

Kayne, R. S. (1998). Overt vs. covert movements. *Syntax, 1*, 128–91.

Kennedy, C. (1994). *Argument contained ellipsis*, Linguistics Research Center Report LKC-94-03, Santa Cruz: University of California.

Kennedy, C. (1997). Antecedent contained deletion and the syntax of quantifiers. *Linguistic Inquiry, 28*, 662–88.

Kennedy, C. (2000). *Comparative deletion and optimality in syntax.* Unpublished MS. Northwestern University.

Kiss, E. K. (1991). Logical structure and syntactic structure: the case of Hungarian. In C. T. J. Huang and R. May (eds.), *Logical structure and syntactic structure: Cross-linguistic perspectives.* (pp. 111–48). Dordrecht, The Netherlands: Reidel.

Klima, E. (1964). Negation in English. In J. Fodor and J. Katz (eds.), *The Structure of Language.* (pp. 246–323). New York: Prentice-Hall.

Kuno, S. (1997). *Binding theory and the minimalist program.* MS. Harvard University.

Kuroda, S.-Y. (1971). Remarks on the notion of subject with reference to words like also, even, or only, Part II. *Annual Bulletin, 4*, 127–52.

Lakoff, G. (1971). On generative Semantics, in Danny D. Steinberg, and Leon A. Jacobovits (eds.), *Semantics: An interdisciplinary reader: Linguistics and psychology.* Cambridge: Cambridge University Press. pp. 232–96.

Larson, R. and May, R. (1990). Antecedent containment or vacuous movement: reply to Baltin. *Linguistic Inquiry, 21*, 103–22.

Larson, R. and Segal, G. (1995). *Knowledge of Meaning: An introduction to semantic theory.* Cambridge, MA: MIT Press.

Lasnik, H. (1993). *Lectures on minimalist syntax.* Working Papers in Linguistics: Occasional Papers Issue 1 (reprinted in H. Lasnik (1999), *Minimalist Analysis*, Blackwell).

Lasnik, H. (1995). A note on pseudogapping, In R. Pensalfini and H. Ura (eds.), *Papers on Minimalist Syntax.* (pp. 143–64). MIT Working Papers in Linguistics 27. MITWPL, Department of Linguistics and Philosophy, MIT, Cambridge, MA.

Lasnik, H. (1998). Reconstruction Riddles. *UPenn Working Papers in Linguisitics, 5*(1).

Lebeaux, D. (1988). *Language acquisition and the form of the grammar*. Doctoral dissertation, University of Massachusetts, Amherst.

Lebeaux, D. (1991). Relative clauses, licensing, and the nature of the derivation. In S. Rothstein (ed.), *Syntax and semantics 25: Perspectives on phrase structure: Heads and licensing.* (pp. 209–39). Orlando, FL: Academic Press.

Lebeaux, D. (1995). Where does the binding theory apply? *University of Maryland Working Papers in Linguistics, 3,* 63–88. University of Maryland, College Park.

Lin, V. (2001). A way to undo A movement, in K. Megerdoomian and A. Bar-el (eds.), *Proceedings of the West Coast Conference in Formal Linguistics.* Sommerville, MA: Cascadilla Press. pp. 358–71.

May, R. (1977). *The grammar of quantificiation*. Doctoral dissertation. MIT.

May, R. (1985). *Logical form*. Cambridge, MA: MIT Press.

May, R. (1988). Ambiguities of quantification. *Linguistic Inquiry, 19,* 118–35.

McCawley, J. (1970). English as a VSO language. *Language, 46,* 286–99.

McCawley, J. (1988). *The syntactic phenomena of English*. Chicago: Chicago University Press.

Munn, A. (1994). A minimalist account of reconstruction asymmetries. In M. Gonzalez (ed.), *Proceedings of NELS 24.* (pp. 397–410). GLSA, University of Massachusetts, Amherst.

Nissenbaum, J. (2001). *Investigations of covert phrase movement*. Doctoral dissertation. MIT, Cambridge, MA.

Pesetsky, D. (1987). WH-in situ: movement and unselective binding. In E. Reuland and A. ter Meulen (eds.), *The representation of (in)definiteness* (pp. 98–167). Cambridge, MA: MIT Press.

Pesetsky, D. (1998). Some optimality principles of sentence pronunciation. In P. Barbosa, Danny Fox, Paul Hagstrom, Martha McGinnis, and David Pesetsky (eds.), *Is the best good enough? Optimality and competition in syntax?.* Cambridge, MA: MIT Press.

Pesetsky, D. (2000). *Phrasal movement and its kin*. Cambridge, MA: MIT Press.

Postal, P. (1974). *On raising: One rule of English grammar*. Cambridge, MA: MIT Press.

Reinhart, T. (1983). *Anaphora and semantic interpretation*. London: Croom Helm.

Reinhart, T. (1991). Non-quantificational LF. In A. Kasher (ed.), *The Chomskian turn* (pp. 360–84). Cambridge, MA: Blackwell.

Reinhart, T. (1997). Quantifier-scope: how labor is divided between QR and choice functions. *Linguistics and Philosophy, 20,* 335–97.

Richards, N. (2001). *Movement in language: Interactions and architecture*. Oxford: Oxford University Press.

Riemsdijk, H. van, and E. Williams (1981). NP-structure. *The Linguistic Review, 1,* 171–217.

Rodman, R. (1976). Scope phenomena, movement transformations, and relative clauses. In B. Partee (ed.), *Montague Grammar.* (pp. 156–76). New York: Academic Press.

Romero, M. (1997). The correlation between scope reconstruction and connectivity effects. *Proceedings of the West Coast Conference in Formal Linguistics, 16,* 351–66. Stanford, CA: CSLI Publications.

Rooth, M. (1992). Ellipsis redundancy and reduction redundancy. In S. Berman and A. Hestvik (eds.), *Proceedings of Stutgart Ellipsis Workshop.* Arbeitspapiere des Sonderforschungsbereichs 340, Bericht 29, Heidelberg: IBM Germany.

Ross, J. R. (1967). Constraints on variables in syntax. Doctoral dissertation. Cambridge, MA: MIT.

Rullmann, H. and Beck, S. (1997). Presupposition projection and the interpretation of which-questions. In Devon Strolovitch and Aaron Lawson (eds.), *Proceedings from Semantics and Linguistic Theory VIII* (pp. 215–32). Department of Linguistics, Cornell University.

Ruys, E. (1992). *The scope of indefinites.* Doctoral dissertation. Utrecht University.

Safir, K. (1998). Symmetry and unity in the theory of anaphora, in H. Bennis, P. Pica, and J. Rooryck (eds.), *Atomism and Binding.* Dordrecht, the Netherlands: Foris.

Safir, K. (1999). Vehicle change and reconstruction of A-bar-chains. *Linguistic Inquiry,* 304, 587–620.

Sag, I. (1976). *Deletion and logical form.* Doctoral dissertation, MIT, Cambridge, MA: MITWPL.

Sauerland, U. (1998). *The making and meaning of chains.* Doctoral dissertation, MIT, Cambridge, MA: MITWPL.

Sauerland, U. (2001). Syntactic economy and quantifier raising. Unpublished MS, Tübingen.

Sauerland, U. and Steckow, A. von (2000). The syntax–semantics interface. In N. Smelser and P. Bates (eds.), *International encyclopedia of the social and behaviorial sciences.* Amsterdam: Elsevier.

Schmitt, C. (1995). Antecedent contained deletion meets the copy theory. *Proceedings of the North East Linguistics Society,* 25, 425–40.

Sportiche, D. (2001). *Reconstruction, binding and scope.* Unpublished manuscript. UCLA.

Sternefeld, W. (2001). Semantic vs. Syntactic Reconstruction. In H. Kamp, A. Rossdeutscher, and C. Rhorer (eds.), *Linguistic form and its computation* (pp. 145–82). Stanford: CSLI Publications.

Stroik, T. (1992). Adverbs and antecedent contained deletion. *Linguistics,* 30, 375–83.

Szabolcsi, A. (1998). *Ways of scope taking.* Dordrecht: Kluwer.

Taraldsen, T. (1981). The theoretical interpretation of a class of marked extractions. In A. Belletic, L. Brandi, and L. Rizzi (eds.), *Theory of markedness in generative grammar: Proceedings of the 1979 Glow Conference.* (pp. 475–516). Pisa: Scuola Normale Superiore.

Tiedeman, R. (1995). Some remarks on antecedent contained deletion. In S. Haraguchi and M. Funaki (eds.), *Minimalism and linguistic theory.* Hituzi Linguistics Workshop Series no. 4. Japan: Hituz Syobo.

Tomioka, S. (2001). Information structure and disambiguation in Japanese. In K. Megerdoomian and A. Bar-el (eds.), *Proceedings of the West Coast Conference in Formal Linguistics.* Sommerville, MA: Cascadilla Press. pp. 552–64.

Vergnaud, J.-R. (1974). *French relative clauses.* Doctoral dissertation. MIT, Cambridge, Mass.

Wilder, C. (1995). Antecedent containment and ellipsis. *FAS Papers in Linguistics,* 4, 132–65.

Wilder, C. (1997). Phrasal Movement in LF: *de re* readings, VP Ellipsis and Binding. *Proceeding of NELS 27,* 425–40.

Williams, E. (1974). *Rule Ordering in Syntax.* , Doctoral dissertation. MIT, Cambridge, MA: MITWPL.

Williams, E. (1977). Discourse and logical form. *Linguistic Inquiry,* 8, 101–39.

Williams, E. (1986). A reassignment of the functions of LF. *Linguistic Inquiry,* 17, 264–300.

Wyngaerd, Vanden G., and C. J. W. Zwart (1991). Reconstruction and Vehicle Change. In F. Drijkoningen and A. van Kemenade (eds.), *Linguistics in the Netherlands.* (pp. 151–60). Amsterdam: John Benjamins.

Chapter three

Steps toward a Minimal Theory of Anaphora

Howard Lasnik and Randall Hendrick

3.1 Introduction

The theory of anaphora has occupied a central place in Principles and Parameters theories of syntax. In Chomsky (1981), for example, the Binding Theory
carried the burden of accounting for a wide range of empirical phenomena. It
limited the free distribution of reflexive pronouns in (1), independent pronouns in (2), and proper names in (3).

  (1)a. Jill criticizes herself too much (Jill = herself)
    b. *Jill said that Jamie criticized herself too much (Jill = herself)

  (2)a. *Jill criticizes her too much (Jill = her)
    b. Jill said that Jamie criticizes her too much (Jill = her)

  (3)a. *She criticizes Jane too much (she = Jane)
    b. *She said that Jamie criticizes Jill too much (she = Jill)

The basic outlines of this influential theory of anaphora will be familiar to
most readers. It contains three distinct theoretical statements, Principles A, B,
and C, to regulate the distribution of reflexives, independent pronouns, and
proper names, respectively.

  (4)   *Binding Theory*
    a. Anaphors must be bound in their governing category
    b. Pronouns must be free in their governing category
    c. R-expressions must be free

An element is "bound" if it is c-commanded by a co-indexed element; otherwise it is "free." A "governing category" is understood as in (5). This particular theoretical construct defines a locality condition on anaphora. In (1) the
governing category of the reflexive anaphor is identified by this definition as
the main clause in (1a) and the embedded clause in (1b).

(5) *Governing Category*
    γ is a governing category for α if and only if γ is the minimal category containing β, a governor for α, and a SUBJECT accessible to α.

(6) SUBJECT = Agr where present, or a subject DP otherwise

(7) α is accessible to β if and only if α is in the c-command domain of β and the assignment to α of the index of β would not violate the i-within-i filter.

The reflexive in (1a) is licensed as an anaphor because it is bound by the c-commanding expression, *Jane*, which is in the same locality domain (i.e. governing category). Sentence (1b) is ungrammatical because the reflexive and its antecedent are in distinct locality domains. The independent pronoun has the complementary distribution. It can be understood as co-referential to a c-commanding antecedent only when the two expressions are in separate locality domains. Hence only (2b) is grammatical. Proper names can never have c-commanding antecedents regardless of the locality domain, and for this reason, neither (3a) nor (3b) are acceptable.

The Binding Theory in (4) simultaneously played an important role in constraining the general transformational operation (Move α). The trace of the raised DP, *there*, in (8) was identified as an anaphor, like the reflexive in (1).

(8) There$_i$ seems [[e]$_i$ to have been trouble here]

(9) *There$_i$ seems it appears [[e]$_i$ to have been trouble here]

(10) *Who$_i$ did she$_i$ say [[e]$_i$ left]

This was held responsible for the unacceptability of the "super-raising" structures like (9). Traces of raised wh-phrases were classed with proper names under Principle C as R-expressions. This explained the unacceptability of cross-over facts in (10). The use of the Binding Theory to capture limitations on movement entailed that the constraints of the theory were applied to a given structure at some level of representation after d-structure when Move α had the opportunity to apply. This claim jibed with the interaction of movements and the licensing of anaphors. Raising, for example, could transform a d-structure like (11), in which the anaphor *each other* does not yet satisfy Principle A of (4), into the s-structure (12) which does satisfy Principle A.

(11) [[DP e]$_i$ seem to [each other]$_i$ [[DP the contestants]$_i$ to be anxious]]

(12) [[DP the contestants]$_i$ seem to [each other]$_i$ [[DP e]$_i$ to be anxious]]

From examples like this, one could also infer that the Binding Theory in (4) applied at some level of representation after d-structure.

There have, of course, been a number of proposals to improve facets of this general theory. Nevertheless, the central ideas of binding (i.e. c-commanding antecedent), a locality restriction (such as a governing category) that limits the structural domain relevant to the constraints, and the application of those constraints at a particular level of syntactic representation after d-structure remained unchanged through Chomsky and Lasnik (1993).

The purpose of this chapter is to ask what, if anything, needs to be rethought in this influential account. In particular, we ask whether we are led to any empirical or conceptual advances in our understanding of the phenomena classed under (4), when we look beyond explanatory adequacy as assumptions about minimalist syntax urge us to do, and attempt to limit syntactic theorizing to elements plausibly interpreted at the interface with other cognitive systems. It has already been suggested in Chomsky (1995) that such considerations entail that the movement structures in (8)–(9) should be dissociated from the theory of anaphora and instead be attributed to derivational metrics of economy. The issue we take up here is whether a theory of anaphora can be assembled exclusively of primitives that have plausible functions at Logical Form, where a syntactic representation is made available for semantic interpretation.

One of the most fascinating topics in this search for a minimal theory of anaphora concerns the question of levels of representation relevant to the determination of anaphoric connections. In terms of the Binding Theory in (4), the question reduces to the level (or levels) of representation that must satisfy (4). Over the years, a variety of proposals have been put forward, none of them conceptually very satisfactory. Moreover, "minimalist" characterizations of the general form of syntactic theory render most of those proposals not just unsatisfactory but inexpressible, since those proposals crucially rely on a level of representation, s-structure, which is claimed not to exist. We will consider the quite strong evidence motivating those early proposals and ultimately suggest a way of capturing the apparent s-structure effects without direct appeal to s-structure. We take this conclusion to provide a powerful argument for a major tenet of minimalism. Before embarking on this, our central exploration, we will address two other conceptual cornerstones of the binding theory: the notion of being "bound," and the locality restriction encapsulated in the definition of "governing category." Both of these concepts are liable to minimalist revisions, though in both cases, the achievement of this goal remains, as yet, incomplete.

3.2   On being bound in a governing category

3.2.1   *Existential constructions and binding*

The theory of Chomsky (1981) represents binding via the formalism of co-indexing two elements in a c-command relation. Each of these conceptual building blocks can be scrutinized with minimalist concerns in mind. The notion of c-command can potentially be reduced to the method of phrasal composition, as suggested in Epstein et al. (1998). The practice of co-indexing two phrases is potentially more mysterious, especially if we ask what function it has at the LF interface. Although other suggestions have been made in the past (see, e.g., Higginbotham, 1983), the simplest way to understand co-indexing is as identity. The copy theory of movement adopts this view explicitly, avoiding the resort to the representational device of a co-indexed trace by instead employing an identical copy of the moved element. However, an active debate has been joined over whether identity of grammatical features (Φ features) alone is sufficient to establish a binding relation. This debate involves differing conceptions of the *there* construction in (13).

(13)   There is a book on the table.

At issue is the licensing relation between the expletive *there* and its "associate," the post-verbal indefinite DP.

Covert movement (at LF) was initially proposed by Chomsky (1976) to explain why certain items that appeared in situ in a surface representation behaved in some respects as if they had undergone movement. May (1977) and (1985) developed the idea in greater detail. Their analyses relied on a type of covert movement that closely paralleled overt movement, primarily the movement of an XP.

Covert movement of this sort was chiefly used to explain scope phenomena, principally the scope of quantifiers and that of in situ interrogative operators. These were all covert A-bar movements.[1] However, Chomsky (1986) introduced an instance of covert A-movement: covert movement of the "associate" indefinite DP to the position occupied in overt syntax by the expletive *there*, as illustrated in (14).

(14)a.   There is a woman here   **s-structure**
    b.   A woman$_i$ is [$_{DP}$ e$_i$] here   LF

For Chomsky, the expletive replacement operation had at least two positive consequences: it allowed for the Case of the associate to be properly determined (since Chomsky assumed that the surface position of *a woman* in (14a) is not a Case position[2]) and it appropriately established the agreement relation between the associate and Infl.

It is important to recognize that, for a variety of purposes, the associate in an existential sentence does not behave as if it is Spec of Infl. Chomsky (1991) pointed out that this was true for the scope of the associate, and den Dikken (1995) did the same for the binding properties of the associate. We can add to this list the pattern of negative polarity items (NPIs) and bound pronouns noted in Lasnik (1995b). The examples in (15) contrast with the corresponding examples in (16), demonstrating that the associate in (16) does not show the behavior of the same DPs when in Spec of INFL as in (15).

(15)a. *Many* **has wider scope than the negative**
Many linguistics students aren't [[e] here]

b. *Each other* **is bound by the raised DP**
Some linguists seem to each other [[e] to have been given good job offers]

c. **NPI is licensed by the raised DP**
No good linguistic theories seem to any philosophers [[e] to have been formulated]

d. **Bound pronoun interpretation is available**
Some defendant$_i$ seems to his$_i$ lawyer [[e] to have been at the scene]

(16)a. *Many* **has narrower scope than the negative**
There aren't many linguistics students here

b. **Binding of** *each other* **is not achieved**
*There seem to each other [[e] to have been some linguists given good job offers]

c. **Licensing of the NPI is not achieved**
*There seem to any philosophers [[e] to have been no good linguistic theories formulated]

d. **Bound pronoun interpretation not available**
*There seems to his$_i$ lawyer [[e] to have been some defendant$_i$ at the scene]

To accommodate the scope difference in (15a) vs. (16a), Chomsky (1995, p. 273) suggests a revised theory of the LF movement involved in expletive constructions, as part of a revised theory of LF movement more generally. Proceeding from the minimalist assumption that all movement is driven by the need for formal features to be checked, Chomsky argues that, all else being equal, movement should never be of an entire syntactic category, but only its formal features.[3] PF requirements will normally force overt movement of a category containing the formal features, via a sort of pied-piping, under the reasonable assumption that a bare feature (or set of features) is an ill-formed PF object. For covert LF movement, on the other hand, pied-piping will not be necessary. Hence, only the formal features of a phrase will move covertly, and they will move exactly to the heads that have matching features. In an existential sentence, then, the associate does not move to *there*. Rather, only the formal features move, and only to a corresponding functional head (or heads). Chomsky's feature movement analysis of existential constructions has the potential to solve the scope problem. If in LF, only the formal features of *many linguistics students*, rather than the entire expression, move to a functional head or heads above negation (presumably the Agr$_S$ head), it is reasonable to conclude that the quantificational properties remain below negation. Then, if it is this structure that determines scope, the desired results are obtained. On the other hand, Chomsky suggests that anaphoric relations are licensed by formal feature movement.

While this line of explanation is not unattractive, raising constructions pose a serious empirical obstacle to its success. The kinds of examples that den

Dikken used to argue against expletive replacement are equally telling here. Consider the reciprocal facts of (17)–(18).

(17) Some linguists seem to each other [[e] to have been given good job offers]

(18) *There seem to each other [[e] to have been some linguists given good job offers]

When the entire DP has raised, as in (17), whatever properties of the DP are relevant to licensing an anaphor are in the appropriate structural position to do so (both at s-structure and at LF). When, by hypothesis, only the formal features have raised, as in (18), the reciprocal is not licensed. If raised formal features were sufficient to bind an anaphor, (18) should have the same status as (17), contrary to fact. Parallel arguments can be constructed on the basis of NPI licensing, as in (19), and bound pronoun interpretation, as in (20), if these do not already fall under the scope generalization.

(19)a. No good linguistic theories seem to any philosophers [*t* to have been formulated]
    b. *There seem to any philosophers [*t* to have been no good linguistic theories formulated]

(20)a. Some defendant$_i$ seems to his$_i$ lawyer to have been at the scene
    b. *There seems to his$_i$ lawyer to have been some defendant$_i$ at the scene

These observations lead us to conclude that the referential properties relevant to licensing an anaphor remain below the raising predicate and cannot be the raised formal features exclusively.[4]

As mentioned above, Chomsky (1995), in contrast, takes the position that the elements of anaphora are precisely formal features. There are two bases for Chomsky's position. One is a theory internal argument that concerns ECM facts which we will return to in section 3.2.2. The other argument is an empirical one that warrants careful consideration at this juncture.

Chomsky's empirical argument is based on control. He presents an example suggesting that the associate of *there* behaves as if it is "high" (either in the specifier of INFL or AGR if INFL is decomposed), by virtue of its ability to control PRO in an adjunct:

(21) There arrived three men (last night) without [PRO] identifying themselves

In contrast, sentences like (22) suggest that a typical object cannot control PRO in this construction:

(22) *I met three men (last night) without identifying themselves

In (21) *three men* is, like the direct object in (22), arguably too low to control PRO, but the raising of the formal features to replace *there* provides a controller for PRO. From this consideration Chomsky reasons that feature raising generally can create new control configurations, and hence, new binding configurations. However, even if Chomsky turns out to be correct about the generality of the control phenomenon in (21), that would not warrant the broader conclusion about binding. There are significant differences between control and binding.[5] For example, languages which, unlike English, have only "subject oriented" anaphors still have structures of "object control" (cf. Lasnik, 1992a).[6] Examples (23)–(24) illustrate this fact on the basis of Polish.

(23) Jan$_i$ opowiada Marii$_j$ o   swoim$_{i/*j}$ zachowaniu
      John telling   Mary about self's   behavior
      "John was telling Mary about his/*her behavior."

(24) Jan$_i$ kaza Marii$_j$ [PRO$_{j/*i}$ napisa artyku_]
      John told Mary   write   article
      "John told Mary to write an article."

A second reason for drawing a distinction between anaphor binding and control is that control has well-known thematic aspects that are lacking in other instances of anaphora.[7]

Further exploration of the very control phenomenon in (21) suggests that it does not support the conclusion about binding by raised formal features. Chomsky implies that the associate of *there* in (21) is behaving just as an overtly raised subject, such as in (25), would.

(25) Three men arrived (last night) without PRO identifying themselves

But there is a perceptible difference between (21) and (25). While (25) is perfect, (21) is somewhat degraded for many speakers.[8] This contrast is heightened if the adverbial is fronted:

(26) Without identifying themselves, three men arrived

(27) ?*Without PRO identifying themselves, there arrived three men

Further, under raising, the contrast between structures like (21) and (25) intensifies greatly. In the following examples, the adverbial is intended as being in the higher clause, along with the raised subject or *there*:

(28) Someone seems to be available without PRO seeming to be eager to get the job

(29) *There seems to be someone available without PRO seeming to be eager to get the job

There is no reason this should be so if raised features of the associate of *there* can serve as a controller. Finally, while (22) is clearly unacceptable, it is not only complements of unaccusatives like (21) that are reasonably acceptable as controllers. The following example is considerably better than (22), even if not quite as good as (21):

(30)   The news upset John while reading the paper

Taken together these facts invite the speculation that thematic properties are involved in control into an adjunct just as they seem to be into a complement: from this perspective the object might be a possible controller because the subject is itself too low on the thematic hierarchy. In (21), the subject is not thematic at all. In (30), it is low relative to the object.

Taking stock of our discussion so far, the covert LF raising analysis of the relation between the expletive *there* and its associate provides three important inferences relevant to the theory of anaphora. First, the covert raising of formal features does not create new binding or scope relations. Second, the properties that license anaphoric relations include more than just the identity of formal features. And third, binding should be distinguished from control because they have distinct properties with control being more sensitive to thematic relations.

3.2.2   ECM constructions and governing categories

We explore in this section the proper characterization of the locality condition so central to the theory of anaphora. In the Binding Theory of Chomsky (1981) this restriction is modeled by the definition of "governing category." Because minimalist syntax attempts to replace appeals to government with appeals to concepts necessary at the interface levels of PF or LF, we will search for a more explanatory specification of the locality condition.

The bold face DP in examples like (31) has a dual nature that has figured prominently in the development of generative grammar. In some respects, that DP behaves like the subject of the lower predicate, *convinced*, while in other respects, it behaves like the object of the matrix verb, *believe*, as Rosenbaum (1967) observed.

(31)   I believe **John** to have convinced Bill

Rosenbaum argued persuasively that at least in underlying structure, *John* in (31) must be a subject. He observes that the synonymy between infinitival embedding and finite embedding, as in (32), will follow if *John* is the subject of the lower clause in both (31) and (32).

(32)   I believe that John convinced Bill

Rosenbaum also pointed to the contrast between *believe*-type constructions, on the one hand, and clear instances of DP + S complementation, on the other hand, with respect to semantic import of active vs. passive voice in the complement. (33) is synonymous with (31), but (35) is not synonymous with (34).

(33)   I believe Bill to have been convinced by John

(34)   I compelled the doctor to examine John

(35)   I compelled John to be examined by the doctor

The underlying subject status of the DP in question is confirmed by the fact that the existential *there* and idiom chunks associated with the embedded clause can appear in this position (cf. Rosenbaum, 1967; Bach, 1974). Thus, (36)–(37) contrast with (38)–(39), which are instances of DP + S complementation.

(36)   I believe there to be a man in the garden

(37)   I believe advantage to have been taken of John

(38)   *I forced there to be a man in the garden

(39)   *I forced advantage to have been taken of John

Alongside these arguments for the lower subject status, Postal (1974) marshalled other "traditional arguments" for higher object status, based on reflexivization, and reciprocal marking. Both of these processes typically establish a relation between an object position and a subject position in the same clause. But they can also form a relation between the underlying subject of the complement clause and the subject of the matrix under certain limited circumstances including, in particular, the infinitival constructions under discussion. The following examples are from Postal (1974, pp. 40–2).

(40)   *Jack$_i$ believed him$_i$ to be immoral

(41)   Jack$_i$ believed himself$_i$ to be immoral

(42)   They believed each other to be honest

This class of arguments centrally involves the nature of the boundary separating the two linked DP positions. For Postal, any clause boundary would suffice to block the relevant relations, hence the second DP position must have become a "clausemate" of the first (via "raising to object"). Chomsky (1973) took a different approach to these phenomena. For Chomsky, the relevant structural property is not *whether* there is a clause boundary separating the two DPs, but rather *what sort* of clause boundary there is. Metaphorically, an infinitival clause boundary is weaker than a finite clause boundary. While the latter is strong enough to block the relations in question, the former is not.

Chomsky formulated this relative inaccessibility of material in finite clauses (and of non-subjects of infinitives) in terms of his Tensed Sentence Condition and Specified Subject Condition. In the same spirit, the notion of governing category in (5) continues to pursue the definition of stronger and weaker clausal boundaries.

Lasnik and Saito (1991) propose that the exceptionally Case-marked subject of an infinitival clause moves into the higher clause. The arguments for this conclusion are to the effect that ECM subjects act as if they are actually higher than some elements in the higher clause. In addition to the much discussed phenomena alluded to above, where boundary strength at least potentially provides the needed distinctions, Postal (1974) sketched another class of argument for raising in which the actual surface structure height of the deep structure subject is implicated. One such argument is based on a scope difference between (43) and (44):

(43)   The FBI proved that few students were spies

(44)   The FBI proved few students to be spies

Postal indicates that *few students* can have wide or narrow scope in (43) while it can have only wide scope in (44), and that this distinction is best described in terms of the hierarchical notion "command." While the precise semantic difference between (43) and (44) is not well understood, there does seem to be some meaning difference. If it is correct to assume that this difference has something to do with scope, it is plausible to conclude, with Postal, that some sort of transformational reorganization is implicated since notions of hierarchical clause membership, such as command, are independently known to play a role in describing quantifier scope.

It is important to note that the distribution of reciprocals, NPIs, and binomial *each* displays a similar pattern that leads us to the same conclusion. Consider first the distribution of reciprocal expressions. One facet of this distribution formed the basis of Postal's "traditional argument," as in (42) above. This aspect of the argument was essentially neutral between a raising analysis and one in terms of boundary strength because the relative height of reciprocal and antecedent was not at issue in such constructions. But there is another facet of the distribution where relative height is significant. Note that (45) is not significantly worse than (46).

(45)   ?The DA proved [the defendants to be guilty] during each other's trials

(46)   ?The DA cross-examined the defendants during each other's trials

They both are considerably better than (47), the finite counterpart of (45).

(47)   ?*The DA proved [that the defendants were guilty] during each other's trials

Given the usual assumptions, the antecedent of a reciprocal must bear a command relation to the reciprocal (e.g. c-command). But an embedded subject does not c-command an adverbial in the matrix clause. This indicates that at the point in the derivation relevant to the licensing of reciprocals, or anaphors in general, the structure of (45) has changed in such a way that the position of *the defendants* is comparable to what it is in (46).

NPI licensing is known to display asymmetries that have also been attributed to c-command. Thus, a negative subject of a simple sentence can license *any* in the object, but not vice versa:

(48)   No one saw anything

(49)   *Anyone saw nothing

Further, a negative object can, to a reasonably acceptable extent, license *any* in an adverbial:

(50)   The DA cross-examined none of the defendants during any of the trials

It is highly significant that, to roughly the same extent, a negative subject of an infinitival can license *any* in an adverbial attached to the higher VP.

(51)   ?The DA proved [none of the defendants to be guilty] during any of the trials

This again is in rather sharp contrast to a corresponding finite complement:

(52)   ?*The DA proved [that none of the defendants were guilty] during any of the trials

Once again, we find reason to believe that, at the relevant level of representation, the subject of the infinitival complement is approximately as high in the structure as a DP complement would be.

"Binominal *each*," a construction presented in Postal (1974) and explored in detail by Safir and Stowell (1987), also involves c-command relations (at least for many speakers). The "antecedent" of *each* must c-command it:

(53)   The students solved three problems each

(54)   *Three students each solved the problems (on the reading "The problems were solved by three students each")

Postal shows that there is what we have been calling a boundary strength effect with this *each*, presenting the following contrast, among others.

(55)   *The students proved that three formulas each were theorems (on the reading "Each of the students proved that three formulas were theorems")

(56)   ?The students proved three formulas each to be theorems

But there is an additional finite/non-finite asymmetry displayed by binominal *each*. Safir and Stowell present the "small clause" in (57); the full infinitival in (58) seems equally good.

(57)   Jones proved the prisoners guilty with one accusation each

(58)   Jones proved the defendants to be guilty with one accusation each

(57) and (58) are comparable to (59).

(59)   Jones prosecuted the defendants with one accusation each

However, the finite counterpart of (57) and (58) is degraded:[9]

(60)   ??Jones proved that the defendants were guilty with one accusation each

In this paradigm, it is apparently not (just) boundary strength that is at issue, but, once again, structural height.

The examples discussed so far indicate that the subject of the embedded infinitival has roughly the height of the matrix object at some level of representation where the possibility of pronominal co-reference is explained and where anaphors, negative polarity items and binominal *each* are licensed.

In Chomsky (1981) structural Case assignment (or checking) appears to take place in two distinct basic configurations. Assuming that Agreement (or some related functional category) is responsible for nominative Case assignment/checking, such Case assignment can be regarded as an instantiation of SPEC-Head agreement. Accusative Case assignment, on the other hand, had been viewed as arising from a government relation between a verb and the accusative DP. Chomsky (1991) speculates that the second type of Case assignment might be reducible to the first if, inside of the subject agreement (AGR-S) projection, there is an object agreement (AGR-O) projection. Then the structural relation necessary for accusative Case could once again be a SPEC-Head relation, this time holding between the SPEC and head of AGR-O (with the contribution of V to the Case assignment process presumably following from the amalgamation of V with AGR-O). Chomsky hypothesizes that, in a language like English, movement to SPEC of AGR-O does not take place between d-structure and s-structure. SPECs in English are phrase initial, but the accusative direct object of a verb follows the verb, and hence should follow the AGR head that takes the VP as its complement. But this leaves open the possibility that the movement takes place "covertly," between s-structure and LF. Chomsky thus suggests the following phrase structure for sentences:

(61)

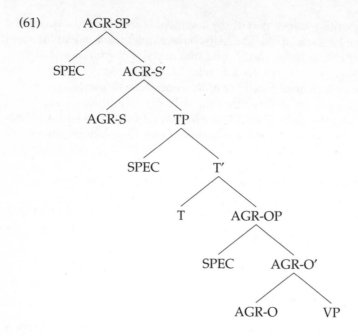

Assuming that in English, DPs with accusative Case must move to the SPEC position of AGR-OP in the LF Component for the purpose of Case assignment/ checking, this hypothesis, then, implies that the subject of the embedded infinitival and the matrix object are in the same position at the level of LF. That is to say, the possibility exists that the subject is raised covertly to the matrix not at s-structure but at LF.

We will now question whether the raising that we have already seen evidence for takes place after s-structure, along the lines of Chomsky's conjecture. There is some reason to believe that this raising operation is not covert LF movement to SPEC of AGR-O, but rather is an overt s-structure operation, much as Postal (1974) proposes.

The discussion of existential constructions above indirectly provided one reason for thinking the movement is overt. In that instance covert movement did not create new binding and licensing configurations. A second reason involves the complex verb *make out* in (62).

(62)   Jane made Bill out to be a fool.

On the assumption that the particle *out* is immobile, it would appear that (62) requires overt raising out of the infinitive as illustrated in (63). In this derivation, the verb *make* will also need to raise to a higher verbal shell to account for the linear ordering of *made* and *Bill*.

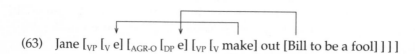

(63)   Jane [vp [v e] [AGR-O [DP e] [vp [v make] out [Bill to be a fool]]]]

From this raised position the subject of the infinitive will be able to c-command constituents of the higher clause. This will make available an explanation for the facts concerning reciprocals, NPIs, and binominal *each* catalogued above.

In this subsection we set out to ask whether we could improve on the theoretical construct "governing category" that encoded the locality restriction on binding. If it is correct to believe that the subject of infinitives under ECM verbs raises overtly into the higher clause, we would be in a position to conceptualize the locality condition as a requirement that two elements in a binding relation be, in Postal's terms, "clausemates" when the relevant principle of the Binding Theory is applied.[10] Such a conclusion begins to approximate minimalist standards of explanation since, unlike the concept of governing category, clauses have a natural reflex at LF as semantic propositions.

One significant consequence of adopting this view of the locality restriction is that it will not naturally make a distinction in the "picture DPs" like (64)–(65).

(64)   Jane doesn't like many pictures of herself/her

(65)   Jane doesn't like Bob's pictures of herself/her

The judgments often reported in the literature are that the reflexive pronoun is possible in (64), but relatively disfavored in (65). Such a distribution would not fall out from the locality condition formulated as a "clausemate" restriction. However, we do not believe that this paradigm constitutes a strong argument against the clausemate restriction we have advocated because there is some reason to doubt that reflexives have different distributions in (64) and (65). Recently Asudeh and Keller (2000) have provided some preliminary empirical evidence suggesting that reflexives are acceptable in both (64) and (65). Any remaining distinction between (64) and (65) might, from this perspective, be attributed to the effect of definiteness or other discourse properties.

3.3   Levels of representation

In this section we explore the question of which levels of representation are relevant to the determination of anaphoric relations. In terms of the theory of anaphora of Chomsky (1981) outlined in section 3.1, the question concerns the level (or levels) of representation that must satisfy the three principles of the binding theory. In keeping with recent minimalist characterizations of syntactic theory we will be unable to appeal to any non-interface level such as s-structure in this endeavor because such levels are claimed not to exist. We will begin this section by surveying the quite strong evidence that has suggested to many that the binding principles must apply at s-structure, thus challenging the empirical adequacy of any minimalist theory of anaphora. We will then weigh evidence that binding relations are determined after s-structure. Ultimately we suggest a way of capturing the apparent s-structure binding effects without direct appeal to s-structure.

The fact that anaphora has essential semantic aspects has always suggested that its syntax, the binding conditions, should be determined at LF, the syntax–semantics interface level. However, difficulties with such a theory were recognized early on. Discussing the following examples, Chomsky (1981, pp. 196–7) argues that Condition C must apply at s-structure:

(66)   Which book that **John**$_i$ read did **he**$_i$ like

(67)   **He*$_i$ liked every book that **John**$_i$ read

(68)   *I don't remember who thinks that **he**$_i$ read which book that **John**$_i$ likes

Chomsky's point is that following QR, the LF of (67) would be structurally parallel to the s-structure (and LF) of (66), where *John* is outside the c-command domain of *he*. Thus, as in (66), there should be no Condition C effect if LF is the level relevant to that condition. The same should be true for (68) following LF wh-movement. Contrary to the prediction of this LF theory, in both instances the hypothesized LF movement, unlike the overt movement creating (66), has no effect on binding possibilities. This strongly suggests Chomsky's conclusion: that Condition C is specifically a requirement on s-structure.

Barss (1986) draws the same conclusion for Condition A, based on examples like the following:

(69)   **John**$_i$ wonders which picture of **himself**$_i$ Mary showed to Susan

(70)   **John*$_i$ wonders who showed which picture of **himself**$_i$ to Susan

(69) shows that an anaphor within the embedded CP Spec can be licensed by an antecedent in the matrix subject position. Given this fact, the ungrammaticality of (70) is surprising if anaphors can be licensed by virtue of their LF positions. On the then standard theory, in LF, the wh-phrase in situ, *which picture of himself*, moves to the embedded CP Spec position, where it takes scope. Thus, at LF, the configurational relation between *himself* and its antecedent is virtually identical in (69) and (70). Hence, the ungrammaticality of (70) shows that anaphors must be licensed at a level prior to LF, for example s-structure (and possibly at LF as well). (70) is ruled out because the reflexive fails to be licensed at that level.

The three arguments sketched above suggest that the Binding Theory applies at s-structure. If there is no s-structure, they provide some reason to believe that LF raising does not create new binding configurations, possibly because such movement is movement of mere formal features. Such a conclusion is consistent with the results of our examination in section 3.2 of covert raising of the associate in the existential *there* construction and of the overt raising of an ECM subject. However, some apparent empirical difficulties have been identified with this conclusion. There are configurations in which constituents have been thought to lower at LF and which apparently alter s-structure binding relations.

Several classes of phenomena have been used to argue that at least some of the binding conditions are not tied to s-structure position and instead are determined after reorganization at LF. The sentences in (71) have been taken to require that the wh-phrase be "reconstructed" at LF into the position in which it receives a theta-role (its d-structure position in the terms of Chomsky (1981)). Only in this way will the reflexive be c-commanded by its antecedent *Bill*.

(71)   Jane wonders [which picture of **himself**$_{j]_i}$ [**Bill**$_j$ likes [e]$_i$]

Similarly the unacceptability of co-reference between *John* and *he* in questions like (72) suggests that the wh-phrase should also be reconstructed at LF.[11]

(72)   *[Which picture of **John**$_i$]]$_j$ does **he**$_i$ like [e]$_j$

After reconstruction the wh-phrase would be in its d-structure position where *John* would be c-commanded by *he* in violation of Principle C. At its heart, this kind of analysis proposes a lowering operation at LF that changes binding relations at s-structure.

We thus face two major questions: (a) can the binding principles apply successfully at LF without reference to s-structure?, and (b) can covert movement at LF change the licensing of binding relations?

Two avenues are available to reconcile the phenomena surveyed above both with each other and with the assumption central to the minimalist program that non-interface levels such as s-structure should not exist. The two analyses differ in whether they allow covert movements that derive LF to change binding relations. The first line of analysis would claim that only the quantificational head moves at LF, rather than the entire expression.[12] This proposal was first advocated by Hornstein and Weinberg (1990).[13] On this analysis the bold faced DPs relevant to the application of the binding theory in (66)–(72) would not alter their position at LF. Hence there would be no reason to expect either that access to s-structure was required for the correct application of the binding theory or that movement at LF would change binding relations. If, on the other hand, there were strong evidence to believe that the relevant DPs in fact change their binding relations at LF we could still deny that s-structure was relevant to the application of the binding theory. We could achieve this goal by pursuing a second line of analysis that would treat the binding principles as licensing constraints that need to be satisfied in the course of a derivation rather than at a specific level of representation. On this view, Principle A would be a positive constraint that needed to be satisfied "on line" which is to say, at any step in a derivation. Such an approach has already been advocated by Beletti and Rizzi (1988) to explain why, in Italian, anaphors functioning as arguments of psychological predicates seem to be licensed in non-s-structure positions. Principles B and C would be negative constraints that need to be satisfied at each step in a derivation. Variants of these ideas are used to some advantage in Kayne (1991) and Lebeaux (1992). At first glance this suggestion seems to run afoul of examples like (66). One might think that (66) should be unacceptable because the pronoun in subject position should bind the name in the relative clause at a point in the derivation where the object and its relative clause have not been raised yet. This objection assumes that the relative clause must be merged with its head before it undergoes wh-movement. Minimalist syntax makes no principled distinction between structure building operations and movement operations, making it possible to interleave the two. It is thus possible to raise the wh-phrase and then merge the relative clause with the wh-phrase. On this "late merger" account there would be a derivation of (66) that never includes a step where the subject pronoun binds the name.

Our choice between these two alternative conceptions will be based on whether covert movement is able to alter binding relations. At first glance the reconstruction phenomena in (71)–(72) would seem to argue in favor of allowing covert movement to alter binding relations. However, as Fox points out in his contribution to this volume, this conclusion is not necessary once we adopt the copy theory of movement that figures prominently in Chomsky (1993). On that view, movement of a targeted element involves copying that element in the landing site, followed by subsequent deletion only at PF. Crucially, both the moved element and its copy are available at LF. In (71)–(72) it would be possible to claim that the Binding Theory applies to the rightmost copy at LF, avoiding a lowering operation at LF that changes binding relations.[14]

Chomsky (1993) has outlined an argument that binding relations are changed at LF. Chomsky assumes that the interpretation of idiomatic expressions is done at LF. This assumption seems to demand that the components of an idiom are assembled at LF so that they can be assigned their idiomatic interpretation. In a sentence like (73) this would require that the wh-phrase *which pictures* appears in the VP with *take*, to produce the idiomatic interpretation of "to photograph." This process would not be required in a structure lacking an idiomatic expression, such as (74).

(73)   John wonders which pictures Mary took

(74)   John wonders which pictures Mary wanted

Chomsky notes that sentence like (74) can have anaphors referring to either John or Mary, as illustrated by the acceptability of both (77) and (78) below. In contrast, the idiomatic interpretation of (73) appears only to license the anaphor referring to Mary as in (76). Chomsky judges sentences like (75), in which the anaphor must refer to John, as unacceptable.

(75)   *John wonders which pictures of himself Mary took

(76)   John wonders which pictures of herself Mary took

(77)   John wonders which pictures of himself Mary wanted

(78)   John wonders which pictures of herself Mary wanted

The force of these observations is that the presence of the idiomatic interpretation in (73), (75), and (76) seems to correlate with a limitation on anaphors. Chomsky concludes that the process of idiom interpretation at LF effectively alters binding relations. Our own view of these facts is somewhat different. We are unconvinced that there is a significant difference in the relative judgments of (75)–(76), or that they differ substantially from those in (77)–(78). Moreover, the generality of the phenomena, in our view, is not wide enough to warrant the conclusion that idiom interpretation at LF can change binding relations, for reasons we will explain shortly.

Recently, Lebeaux (1998) has investigated another proposed lowering operation at LF and argued that this operation also changes binding relations. The phenomenon in question is exemplified in (79).

(79) Two senators seem to be obstructing justice

It has often been noted that sentences like (79) are ambiguous. On one interpretation (79) is a statement about two specific senators. On the second interpretation it states that there is evidence that two non-specific senators are interfering with the administration of the law. May (1985) proposes to explain this difference in meaning as a scope phenomenon with two different structures being derived from (79) by QR. The specific interpretation results from raising and adjoining *two senators* to the matrix clause. The non-specific interpretation is the product of lowering and adjoining *two senators* to the embedded clause.

We doubt whether LF lowering in fact provides an adequate explanation for this ambiguity. The account predicts, contrary to fact, that the quantified DPs in sentences such as (80) and (81) should be susceptible to lowering.

(80) Every coin is 3 percent likely to be heads

(81) No one is certain to solve this problem

Yet the sentences in (80) and (81) lack the "lowered" interpretations corresponding to (82) and (83).[15]

(82) It is 3 percent likely that every coin is heads

(83) It is certain that no one will solve the problem

Only indefinites appear to provide the ambiguous interpretation that the lowering analysis attempts to model, suggesting that a semantic treatment of the specificity/non-specificity of indefinites might be a better way of explaning the ambiguity of (79) than LF lowering.

However, Lebeaux accepts the correctness of May's lowering analysis and probes its interaction with anaphora. He observes that sentences like (84) appear to be unambiguous.

(84) Two senators seem to each other to be obstructing justice

Sentences like (84) appear only to have the specific reading. Lebeaux labels this phenomena "trapping" (see also Fox, 2000). He suggests that it has a straightforward account if we assume May's scope analysis of the ambiguity in (79) and if we also assume that the requirements of the binding theory must be met at LF in these sentences. Together these assumptions will prevent *two senators* from lowering to adjoin to the embedded clause.

Lebeaux argues that trapping correlates with other phenomena as well. The licensing of bound pronouns patterns with scope, idiom interpretation, and the licensing of anaphors. This conclusion is suggested by the following examples in which the (a) sentence is ambiguous but the (b) sentences loses one of its readings.

(85)a.   Two women seem to be attracted to every man
  b.   Two women seem to their mothers to be attracted to every man

Lebeaux explains the bundling of these properties by requiring that the interpretative processes responsible for these phenomena all apply to a single structural position in a tree.[16] On this hypothesis, it is not possible to distribute these interpretative processes to distinct members of a movement chain.

While this approach is conceptually appealing, there are significant problems with the claim that LF lowering bundles scope interpretation, idiom interpretation, bound pronoun interpretation, and anaphor interpretation. The claim predicts that there should be no grammatical sentences requiring high scope, while simultaneously allowing interpretation of anaphors or idioms in the lower clause. With this prediction in mind, consider the following sentences.

(86)   No picture seems to have been taken in poor light

(87)   Two pictures seem to have been taken in poor light

The universal quantifier in (87) is not subject to lowering and only has the high scope reading. Yet contrary to this requirement, *picture* can still form part of an idiom with *take*. By the same token the sentence in (87) remains ambiguous between the specific and non-specific interpretations of *two pictures* even though the idiom in the infinitive would require *pictures* to be adjacent to it at LF.

A similar puzzle is posed by (88). The reciprocal anaphor in (88) must be in the lower clause to be bound by *the two friends*. Despite this, the scope of *no criticism of each other* must be higher than *seem*.

(88)   No criticism of each other seemed to the two friends to be valid

Acceptable structures also exist in which a constituent must be high to license a negative polarity item, while the embedded clause contains an idiom that should attract that high constituent at LF. This situation is illustrated in (89)–(90). In both examples the negative expression must be higher than the negative polarity item it licenses. Yet at the same time, because it is part of an idiom in the embedded clause, it must be with the rest of the idiom at LF.

(89)   None of the pictures seem to any of the judges to have been taken in the appropriate light

(90)   No unfair advantage seems to any of the referees to have been taken of Jack

Further difficulties for Lebeaux's argument are posed by control structures. On the assumption that control structures are syntactically distinct from raising structures, Lebeaux would predict the absence of any "trapping" effects in control structures. Nevertheless, a trapping-like effect obtains even in control structures. This can be observed in the parallel status of the raising and control structures in (91)–(92).

(91)   Someone seems (to himself) to have read every book

(92)   Someone promised (himself) to read every book

In (92), as in (91), it is possible to construe the sentence lacking the reflexive pronoun as involving reference either to a specific or a non-specific individual. That ambiguity disappears when the reflexive is present: in such structures the only interpretation available is the one in which someone refers to a specific individual. Once again, these facts suggest that a semantic treatment of the specific/non-specific ambiguity of indefinites is at work, rather than the LF lowering of quantified expressions.

We have outlined a series of difficulties for Lebeaux's claim that idiom interpretation, scope interpretation, bound pronoun interpretation, and anaphoric licensing are invariably bundled and tied to a single position in a tree. Taken together these difficulties indicate that the bundling hypothesis is too strong. Apparently we need to admit a theory of LF in which distinct members of a movement chain can contribute to the interpretation of an element at LF. We now ask whether there is an alternative account better suited to the facts as we have described them.

Any successful explanation will minimally need to dissociate scope interpretation from the process involved in idiom interpretation and the licensing of anaphora. More specifically, scope interpretation should be segregated from other interpretative processes at LF (such as licensing of anaphora or NPIs) by requiring that scope interpretation be a function of the head of a chain. In contrast the other LF intepretative processes are free to apply to either the head of that chain or to the initial position where a nominal received its semantic role.[17] The licensing of anaphors, bound pronouns and NPIs will always be lower than scope. This view essentially permits "reconstruction" of all material other than the head D of a DP. The spirit of this proposal appears to be broadly consistent with the facts that our review of Lebeaux's proposal has uncovered. The task at hand is how best to capture this general intuition.

Minimalist syntax makes no privileged distinction between operations that build structure and operations that move constituents: both are the product of the same general operation – "merge." Movement structures are the result of applying merge to a target element already present in a syntactic structure. The idea that extraction involves merging a constituent DP already in a phrase marker, XP, by adjoining DP to XP has as a consequence the "copy theory of movement" because the operation results in two occurrences of the targeted DP. Thus (93) becomes (94) where there are two occurrences of DP. In the mapping to PF, subsequent operations will delete the rightmost DP.

(93)   [$_{IP}$ the police arrested [$_{DP}$ which suspect]]

(94)   [$_{DP}$ which suspect] the police arrested [$_{DP}$ which suspect]

What becomes of the rightmost copy (i.e. the "tail") of this chain at LF? In chapter 2 of this volume, Fox proposes that the tail of a chain is not deleted at LF as it is at PF. Instead it undergoes two interpretative operations: variable insertion and determiner replacement. Given a tail, [$_{DP}$ D NP], the NP will be treated as a predicate and a variable will be inserted in place of the D that the NP will be predicated of. This is the operation of "variable insertion." In addition, the determiner will be replaced by **the**. Operating together, these two operations will exchange a phrase [D [NP] for [the [PRED $\lambda y(y=x)$]. While (94) might have a PF something like (95), (where PF deletion is represented by striking through the rightmost DP), it will have an LF resembling (96). Notice that the head determiner is treated differently at LF than its NP sister.

(95)   [$_{DP}$ which suspect] did the police arrest [$_{DP}$ ~~which suspect~~]

(96)   which suspect λx did the police arrest [$_{DP}$ the [$_{NP}$ suspect x]

Fox's motivation for this treatment of the tail of a chain is rooted in an attempt to better explain the apparent interaction of QR and antecedent contained deletion facts. For our purposes here we hypothesize that the same account extends to raising structures like (97). This sentence has a copy in the infinitival clause, as illustrated in (98). The operations of variable insertion and determiner replacement discussed above will apply to exchange (98) for (99).

(97)   which student seems to be bored

(98)   which student seems which student to be bored

(99)   which student λx [seems [the [student x] to be bored]

This treatment of the copy of movement predicts that the determiner of a moved constituent will only occupy the higher position at LF, while the NP sister of the determiner will be present at LF in both elements of the chain. In essence we capture the intuition that a quantificational determiner does not reconstruct at LF, though the NP sister of the determiner may do so.

This explanation does not assume the existence of a movement account of the specific/non-specific ambiguity in (79). It is possible to imagine that a syntactic structure such as (100) forms the basis of both a specific and non-specific interpretation when an indefinite DP is involved.

(100)   [$_{DP}$ two senators] seemed [[$_{DP}$ two senators] to be obstructing justice

In this way we would also have available a way to explain the specific/non-specific ambiguity in the control structure (92). If, however, one found some way to avoid the empirical problem posed by the control structures and wanted to preserve May's movement analysis, one could do so. This is because the explanation has two crucial features: (a) scope is dissociated from the interpretation of idioms, bound pronouns, NPIs, and anaphoric interpretation, and (b) only the interpretation of idioms, bound pronouns, NPIs, and anaphoric interpretation can have their interpretation determined by the position of any member of a chain.[18] We have argued that only the constituent serving to mark scope has the requirement of being interpreted in the head of the chain. Indeed, there is no requirement that the licensing of anaphors, bound pronouns or NPIs be tied to a single member of a chain. They can be distributed between distinct members of a chain. This fact is observable in sentences like (101) where the bound pronoun is licensed from the subject of *seem*, but the idiom is licensed in the tail of the chain in the embedded clause.

(101)   Some picture seemed to its photographer to have been taken in poor light.

A similar dissociation is found in (102) where licensing of anaphors is achieved from the subject of *seem*, but the idiom is licensed in the embedded clause.

(102)   These pictures seem to each other's photographers to have been taken in poor light.

The fact that the presence of the idiom in the lower clause does not preclude the licensing of the anaphoric reciprocal weighs heavily against Chomsky's (1993) argument that idiom reconstruction at LF changes binding relations. In (102) the binding relations remain unaffected by the idiom in the lower clause.

The technical analysis just sketched for the basis of the asymmetry between a determiner and its nominal complement at LF is principally of interest because of its empirical consequences. Not only is it capable of explaining the phenomena in (80)–(90), it also makes novel predictions. In particular, it claims that we would expect NPI elements to behave differently depending on if they were to appear in the determiner system or if they were to appear elsewhere in a nominal expression. NPI determiners should always act as it they were "trapped" in their s-structure position. NPIs contained in non-determiners, on the other hand, should potentially behave as if they were in the position of the tail of a chain. There are at least two sources of evidence to corroborate this prediction.

It is well-known that the NPI *any* is unacceptable when it functions as the determiner of a subject that is not c-commanded by a NPI licensor. Thus, we find a contrast between (103) where *any* is not c-commanded by a negative and (104) where it is.

(103)   *Any doctors aren't available

(104)   Aren't any doctors available

Linebarger (1980) noted that *any* in a relative clause modifying a subject behaved differently.

(105)   *Doctors that know anything about acupuncture are available

(106)   Doctors that know anything about acupuncture aren't available

In (106) the NPI *anything* is acceptable even though it appears to parallel (103) where the negative licensor is too low to c-command the subject position. We can make sense of the asymmetry between (103) and (106) from the perspective of our analysis of raising and trapping. Only determiners are trapped in their s-structure position due to determiner replacement at LF. The remainder of the nominal is present in a position lower than the negative from which it has raised because of the VP internal subject hypothesis and the copy theory of movement. In this way *anything* in (106) is licensed by its copy within the VP.

A similar conclusion can be reached by considering the behavior of the NPI *at all*. This expression needs to be c-commanded at LF by an NPI licensor, and in that respect it is similar to *any*.

(107)   *They published many articles at all

(108)   They didn't publish many articles at all

(109)   *They published any articles

(110)   They didn't publish any articles

In subject position the two expressions diverge. While (111) is commonly observed to be unacceptable, the parallel example involving *at all* is much improved in comparison.

(111)   *Any articles weren't published

(112)   Many articles at all weren't published

This apparent contrast can begin to be understood if we assume that the structure of the nominal in (111)–(112) is [$_{DP}$ (m) any [$_{NP}$ articles (at all)]]. While the determiner is trapped in its s-structure position, the remaining NP is free to have its material licensed at the tail of its chain, where *at all* can be commanded, and thus licensed, by the negative. Hoeksema (2000) catalogs a series of empirical problems for the requirement that an NPI be c-commanded by its triggering element. Like (106) they mostly involve adjuncts and should be susceptible to an analysis similar to the one we have just outlined.

We have suggested that the operations responsible for inserting variables at LF have the property of keeping the determiner in its s-structure position while allowing the remainder of the DP to be interpreted in the tail of a chain where the DP was first merged. This view departs from Lebeaux's hypothesis that only a single element of a chain is visible for interpretative processes at LF.

3.4   Conclusion

The Binding Theory of Chomsky (1981) has three major features: (1) a general definition of the notion binding based on c-command and co-indexing; (2) a locality domain, "governing category," defined in terms of relative boundary strength; and (3) a privileged linguistic level at which the principles of the Binding Theory apply. Under the narrow explanatory strictures of the minimalist program, each of these features requires substantial revision. We can avoid stipulating the notion of c-command as a primitive component of binding by adopting the general composition of phrase structure suggested in Epstein et al. (1998). We have found some reason for believing that binding must refer to more than identity of formal grammatical features, suggesting that referential features of a nominal relevant at LF are essential to this concept. The locality restriction that limits the domain of the Binding Theory similarly requires revision to avoid appeal to the concept government. A notion like the "clausemate" restriction of Postal (1974) is more promising in this regard, though binding into DPs still presents residual empirical and conceptual problems not yet resolved. Finally we have examined the level at which the Binding Theory applies. We reexamined the evidence of Chomsky (1981) that s-structure was the relevant level for this purpose. We showed that the licensing conditions of the Binding Theory could apply at LF, as required by the Minimalist Program. We saw further that interpretative processes at LF could be sensitive to disparate members of a chain, and in this respect we disagreed with the hypothesis advocated in Lebeaux (1998) that required all LF interpretative processes to apply to a unique member of a chain. Instead we advocated a view in which the scope of a quantificational D was determined only by its raised position. The NP complement that serves semantically as a predicate restricting the D can potentially be interpreted in the position where the DP is initially merged into a structure and receives a semantic role. The interpretation of idiom chunks as well as the licensing of bound pronouns – anaphors as well as non-determiner NPIs – can be sensitive to the position of any member of a chain. The asymmetry of the behavior of the D and its complement NP can be given a natural account if the tail of a chain produced by the copy theory of movement is interpreted as Fox has proposed by two operations at LF, one inserting a variable, and the other replacing the determiner.

Notes

1 A-bar movements target as their landing site structural positions that are never assigned θ-roles by any lexical choice.

2 See Belletti (1988) and Lasnik (1992b), Lasnik (1995a) for a contrary point of view.

3 See Martin (1996) and Groat (1995) for related proposals.

4 Formal agreement features may well be relevant to the licensing of anaphors. The claim here is merely that more is involved.

5 Subject orientation remains a mysterious phenomenon. An intriguing possibility is that it relates to how Case is licensed (as suggested by Lasnik, 1993), or to *when* Case is licensed, with covert movement of (formal features of) objects to their Case position resulting in inability of those objects to license anaphors. At this point, however, this is just wild speculation.

6 Norvin Richards suggests that there is another way to look at this property of control on which it is less obviously relevant to the point at issue: "Subject orientation" seems to be a property of particular anaphors, rather than of languages per se. Given that perspective, PRO could be regarded as a lexical item without that specific property.

7 See Lasnik (1992a) for discussion.

8 Further, as Bob Fiengo pointed out in personal communication (21) itself degrades substantially with a slight change in the adverbial:

   (i)   ?*There arrived three men without saying hello

9 We do not fully understand why these finite complements are as good as they are. As far as we know, under no analysis do subjects of finite clauses undergo raising, so one would expect all such examples to be completely impossible.

10 More specifically we could say that α and β are clausemates if and only if every IP that contains α contains β and conversely.

11 Reinhart and Reuland (1993) attempt to side step the theoretical puzzles presented by these phenomena by denying that the Binding Theory is applicable to picture DPs. They suggest that anaphors in such DPs are interpreted as "logophors" sensitive to aspects of discourse, rather than sentence, grammar. This suggestion leaves unexplained why anaphors within picture DPs require antecedents as shown in (i)–(ii).

   (i)   Jill wanted to show Jane an old scrapbook.
   (ii)   *It contained [many pictures of each other]

Logophoric expressions typically do not need c-commanding antecedents, but in that respect anaphors in picture DPs do not seem to pattern like typical logophors.

12 Of course, it is also possible to deny the existence of the LF operations (such as QR, LF wh-movement or Focus movement) that Chomsky (1981) assumed. We will not explore here the far reaching consequences of such an assumption.

13 It is not immediately obvious how to extend this to the case of focus movement. Also, while it is easy to imagine how scope facts can be handled on the Hornstein and Weinberg theory (or, for that matter, on a theory with no LF A′-movement at all), one of the major arguments for QR, May's (1985) account of antecedent contained deletion, demands that the entire expression move. See Lasnik (1993), Hornstein (1994), and Lasnik (1995a) for discussion.

14 The theoretical issues posed by such "reconstruction" phenomena are somewhat more complex when one examines the interaction of relative clauses with Principle C. It has sometimes been suggested that relatives do not show Principle C effects in examples such as (i) (cf. Lebeaux, 1988).

(i)   Guess which argument that supports John's$_i$ theory he$_i$ adopted

Fox (ch. 2, this volume) shows that such structures can be generated if the relative clause is merged into this structure after *which argument* has been raised. In this way *he* will never c-command *John's* in the course of the derivation.

15   BoecRx (2001) attempts to save the lowering analysis by treating likely in (80) as a control structure when it has an adverbial modifier. If this is true, the lack of the lowered interpretation might be understandable. The problem with this line of analysis is that Lasnik and Saito (1991) provide evidence that expressions like "3 percent likely" and "how likely" are raising predicates by standard diagnostics such as the co-occurrence of expletive subjects and idiom chunks.

16   Lebeaux calls this requirement the "single tree condition" to capture the intuition that all the interpretative processes he is concerned with are bundled or tied to a single structural position, even if that position is one member of an extended chain.

17   This generalization is suggested in Lee (1994).

18   A second potential explanation requires a modification of May's scope analysis of the ambiguity of (79). The parallel between raising and control structures in (91)–(92) suggests that lowering of a quantified expression by QR only in the context of raising predicates is not the best way of explaining (91) (or (79)) because a similar ambiguity arises in the control structure (92) where no such movement analysis is available. The alternative treatment might try to locate the specific/non-specific interpretation of a constituent with whether the DP is lowered from its position as Spec of INFL into the VP. Non-specific DPs would lower into the VP while specific DPs would remain in Spec of INFL. We might correlate this movement of the non-specific DP with its status as a predicate of a free variable that is contextually bound. The specific interpretation would correlate with an entity, and belong syntactically to a DP outside of VP. An explanation for why the non-specific interpretation adhered to the lowered DP would still be required. On this score, we could, perhaps, make use of the work of Diesing (1992). The principal difficulty with this line of analysis is that it does not offer an elegant explanation for why the non-specific reading appears to be excluded when an anaphor is present in (91)–(92). Even in its lowered position the non-specific DP should be in a position to license the anaphor. This fact suggests that even a modified lowering account faces significant problems.

References

Asudeh, A. and Keller, F. (2000). Experimental evidence for a predication-based Binding Theory. In M. Andronis, C. Ball, H. Elston, and S. Neuvel (eds.), *CLS 37: The Main Session. Papers from the 37th meeting of the Chicago Linguistic Society, vol. 1*. Chicago, IL: Chicago Linguistic Society, pp. 1–17.

Bach, E. (1974). *Syntactic Theory*. New York: Holt, Rinehart and Winston.

Barss, A. (1986). *Chains and anaphoric dependence: On reconstruction and its implications*. Doctoral dissertation, MIT, Cambridge, MA.

Belletti, A. (1988). The case of unaccusatives. *Linguistic Inquiry*, 19, 1–34.

Belletti, A. and Rizzi, L. (1988). Psych-verbs and theta theory. *Natural Language and Linguistic Theory*, 6, 291–352.

Boeckx, C. (2001). Scope reconstruction and A-movement. *Natural Language and Linguistic Theory*, 19, 503–48.

Chomsky, N. (1973). Conditions on transformations. In S. Anderson and P. Kparksy (eds.), *A Festscrift for Morris Halle*. New York: Holt, Rinehart & Winston. pp. 232–86.

Chomsky, N. (1976). Conditions on rules of grammar. *Linguistic Analysis*. (Reprinted in N. Chomsky (1977), *Essays on Form and Interpretation*. New York: North Holland.)

Chomsky, N. (1981). *Lectures on Government and Binding*. Dordrecht: Foris.

Chomsky, N. (1986). *Knowledge of Language*. New York: Praeger.

Chomsky, N. (1991). Some notes on economy of derivation and representation. In R. Freidin (ed.), *Principles and Parameters in Comparative Grammar*. (pp. 417–54). Cambridge, MA: MIT Press.

Chomsky, N. (1993). A minimalist program for linguistic theory. In K. Hale and S. J. Keyser (eds.), *The View from Building 20: Essays in honor of Sylvain Bromberger*. (pp. 1–52). Cambridge, MA: MIT Press. (Reprinted in Chomksy (1995) *The Minimalist Program*. Cabridge, MA: MIT Press.)

Chomsky, N. (1995). Categories and transformations. In N. Chomsky (ed.), *The Minimalist Program*. (pp. 219–394). Cambridge, MA: MIT Press.

Chomsky, N. (2000). Minimalist inquiries: the framework. In R. Martin, D. Michaels, and J. Uriagereka (eds.), *Step by Step: Essays on minimalist syntax in honor of Howard Lasnik*. Cambridge, MA: MIT Press.

Chomsky, N. and Lasnik, H. (1993). The theory of principles and parameters. In J. Jacobs, A. von Stechow, W. Sternefeld and T. Vennemann (eds.), *Syntax: An international handbook of contemporary research*, vol. 1 (pp. 506–69). Berlin: Walter de Gruyter. (Reprinted in N. Chomsky (1995), *The Minimalist Program*. Cambridge, MA: MIT Press.)

Deising, M. (1992). *Indefinites*. Cambridge, MA: MIT Press.

den Dikken, M. (1995). Binding, expletives, and levels. *Linguistic Inquiry, 26*, 347–54.

Epstein, S. D., Groat, E., Kawashima, R., and Kitahara, H. (1998). *A Derivational Approach to Syntactic Relations*. Oxford: Oxford University Press.

Groat, E. (1995). English expletives: a minimalist approach. *Linguistic Inquiry, 26*, 354–64

Higginbotham, J. (1983). Logical Form, Binding, and Nominals. *Linguistic Inquiry, 14*, 395–420.

Hoeksema, J. (2000). Negative polarity items: triggering, scope, and C-command. In L. Horn and Y. Kato (eds.), *Negation and Polarity*. (pp. 115–46). Oxford: Oxford University Press.

Hornstein, N. (1994). An argument for Minimalism: the case of antecedent controlled deletion. *Linguistic Inquiry, 25*, 455–80.

Hornstein, N. and Weinberg, A. (1990). The necessity of LF. *The Linguistic Review, 7*, 129–67.

Huang, J. (1983). A note on the binding theory. *Linguistic Inquiry, 14*, 554–61.

Kayne, R. (1991). Romance clitics, verb movement, and PRO. *Linguistic Inquiry, 22*, 647–86.

Kayne, R. (1994). *The Antisymmetry of Syntax*. Cambridge, MA: MIT Press.

Lasnik, H. (1992a). Two notes on control and binding. In J. Higginbotham, S. Iatridou, U. Lahiri, and R. Larson (eds.), *Control and Grammar* (pp. 235–51). Amsterdam: Kluwer Academic.

Lasnik, H. (1992b). Case and expletives: Notes toward a parametric account. *Linguistic Inquiry, 23*, 381–405.

Lasnik, H. (1993). Lectures on minimalist syntax. UConn Working Papers in Linguistics: Occasional Papers Issue 1. (Reprinted, with minor revisions, in Lasnik, H. (1999) *Minimalist Analysis, Howard Lasnik*, Oxford: Blackwell.)

Lasnik, H. (1995a). Case and expletives revisited: On Greed and other human failings. *Linguistic Inquiry*, 26, 615–33.

Lasnik, H. (1995b). Last resort. In S. Haraguchi and M. Funaki (eds.), *Minimalism and Linguistic Theory* (pp. 1–32). Tokyo: Hituzi Syobo.

Lasnik, H. (1995c). Last resort and attract F. In L. Gabriele, D. Hardison, and R. Westmoreland (eds.), *Proceedings of the Sixth Annual Meeting of the Formal Linguistics Society of Mid-America* (pp. 62–81). Indiana University, Bloomington, distributed by the Indiana University Linguistic Club.

Lasnik, H. (1995d). A note on pseudogapping. In *Papers on minimalist syntax: MIT working papers in linguistics*, 27, 143–63.

Lasnik, H. (1999). Chains of arguments. In S. D. Epstein and N. Hornstein (eds.), *Working minimalism* (pp. 189–215). Cambridge, MA: MIT Press.

Lasnik, H. and Saito, M. (1991). On the subject of infinitives. In L. Dobrin, L. Nichols, and R. Rodriguez (eds.), *Papers from the 27th Regional Meeting of the Chicago Linguistic Society* (pp. 324–43). Chicago, IL: Chicago Linguistics Society.

Lebeaux, D. (1988). *Language acquisition and the form of the grammar*. PhD thesis, University of Massachusetts, Amherst.

Lebeaux, D. (1989). *Language acquisition and the form of the grammar*. PhD dissertation, University of Massachusetts, Amherst.

Lebeaux, D. (1992). Relative clauses, licensing, and the nature of the derivation. In S. Rothstein and M. Speas (eds.), *Perspective on Phrase Structure: Heads and licensing, syntax and semantics*, vol. 25 (pp. 209–39). New York: Academic Press.

Lebeaux, D. (1998). *Where does the binding theory apply?* Technical Report 98-044. Princeton, NJ: NEC Research Institute.

Lee, R. (1994). *Economy of representation*. Doctoral dissertation, University of Connecticut, Storrs, CN.

Linebarger, M. (1980). *The grammar of negative polarity*. PhD dissertation, MIT.

Martin, R. (1996). *Minimalist theory of PRO and control*. PhD dissertation, University of Connecticut, Storrs.

May, R. (1977). *The grammar of quantification*. Doctoral dissertation, MIT, Cambridge, MA.

May, R. (1985). *Logical Form: Its structure and Derivation*. Cambridge, MA: MIT Press.

Postal, P. M. (1974). *On Raising: One rule of English grammar and its theoretical implications*. Cambridge, MA: MIT Press.

Reinhart, T. (1983). *Anaphora and Semantic Interpretation*. London: Croom Helm.

Reinhart, T. and Reuland, E. (1993). Reflexivity. *Linguistic Inquiry*, 24, 657–720.

Rosenbaum, P. (1967). *The Grammar of English Predicate Complement Constructions*. Cambridge, MA: MIT Press.

Safir, K. and Stowell, T. (1987). Binominal *Each*. In *The Proceedings of the North Eastern Linguistic Society 18* (pp. 426–50). GLSA, University of Massachusetts, Amherst.

Chapter four

Syntactic Variation, Historical Development, and Minimalism

Höskuldur Thráinsson

4.1 Introduction

The concept of economy played a major role in the development that led to the proposal of the Minimalist Program (see, e.g., Chomsky, 1991, 1993, 1995).[1] Economy principles are reflected in various ways in the Minimalist Program (MP) and in different guises depending on the particular variant of MP. Informally, the basic content of the various economy principles can be stated as follows, at least in derivational principles:

(1) Do as little as possible.

Among well-known reflexes of economy principles in the MP one can mention Shortest Move ("only move as far as you have to," cf. Chomsky, 1993, p. 15, passim.), Procrastinate ("don't move overtly if you can do so covertly," cf. Chomsky, 1993, p. 30, passim) and even Greed ("don't help others," cf. Chomsky, 1993, p. 33, passim).

While the specific economy principles proposed in Chomsky's work leading up to the MP and in the earliest versions of the MP have been developed further and modified by him and other syntacticians working in the MP, the basic concept of economy has continued to play a role within the MP. One of its theoretical advances is that it calls for explicit explanations when one is faced with linguistic variation of the following two types:

(2)a. In language A we seem to have evidence for (overt) movement of X to Z whereas in language B we do not.
   b. In language C we seem to have movement of X to Z in some instances but not in others.

To some readers it might seem that looking for explicit explanations is just what linguists always do, or at least should do, so a theoretical principle calling for such explanations cannot really make much of a difference. But this is in fact not the case. First, a statement like the following can surely be found in many linguistic descriptions:

(3) In embedded clauses in Icelandic the finite verb typically precedes the negation whereas in Danish it follows the negation.

This can be, and frequently is, translated into (4), which is obviously a variant of (2a):

(4) In Icelandic we seem to have evidence for (overt) movement of V-to-I in embedded clauses whereas in Danish we do not.

The facts that statements of this sort are meant to describe include examples like the following:

(5)a. Hún spurði [hvort Jón hefði **ekki lesið**   bókina]   (Ic.)
        she asked if   Jón had   not   read (part.) book-the
        "She asked if John hadn't read the book."

   b. Hún spurði [hvort Jón myndi **ekki lesa**   bókina]
        she asked if   Jón would not   read (inf.) book-the
        "She asked if John wouldn't read the book."

   c. Hún spurði [hvort Jón **læsi**   **ekki** __ bækur]
        she asked if   Jón read (sbj.) not   books
        "She asked if John didn't read books."

   d. Hún vissi [að   Jón **las**   **ekki** __ bækur]
        she knew that Jón read (ind.) not   books
        "She knew that John didn't read books."

(6)a. Hun spurgte [om Jens **ikke** havde **læst** bogen.   (Da.)
        she asked   if Jens not   had   read book-the
        "She asked if Jens hadn't read the book."

   b. Hun spurgte [om Jens **ikke læste** bøger]
        she asked   if Jens not   read books
        "She asked if Jens didn't read books."

Here we see that the main verb *read* precedes the negation *not* in Icelandic when the main verb is in a finite form (subjunctive in (5c), indicative in (5d)) but the main verb follows the negation *not* when it is in a non-finite form (past participle in (5a), infinitive in (5b)). In Danish, on the other hand, the main verb follows the negation in embedded clauses of this sort, regardless of its finiteness.[2] Moreover, the "Danish" word order is unacceptable in the Icelandic embedded clause and the Icelandic word order is unacceptable in the

Danish embedded clause.[3] Given economy principles of the kind mentioned above, there must be a linguistic reason for variation of this sort and the syntacticians working on these languages should look for it.

Second, statements like the following could be found in linguistic descriptions and they would be factually correct, as we shall see below:

(7)   In Faroese embedded clauses the finite verb sometimes precedes the negation and sometimes (possibly more often) follows it.

Or to put it differently (cf. (2b)):

(8)   In Faroese embedded clauses, V-to-I movement is apparently optional (and possibly on the way out).

Now it must be admitted that one does not have to believe in economy principles to be puzzled by variation between languages and want to look for an explanation of it, like the (well-known) word order differences between Icelandic and Danish illustrated above. Thus the many accounts surveyed by Vikner (1995a, 1995b) are not always couched in economy terms, nor are all the proposals considered by Rohrbacher (1999), although some of them are. But it is important to note that simple optionality of the sort alluded to in (8) should not exist, given economy principles of the kind under discussion. Furthermore, it is not enough to simply appeal to Danish influence on Faroese to explain the apparent word order difference between Faroese and Icelandic embedded clauses. The increased frequency of the "Danish" word order may very well have something to do with Danish influence but the question is what the syntactic nature of that construction is and how this variation is possible, as it would appear to violate economy principles. In simplified terms the question is: "Why move if you don't have to?"

While many linguists have proposed accounts of the difference between Icelandic and Danish illustrated above (Norwegian and Swedish are virtually identical to Danish in this respect), I want to argue in section 4.2 below that these accounts are typically circular or ad hoc and hence non-explanatory. I will then review the account first outlined by Bobaljik and Thráinsson (1998) and argue that this account succeeds in explaining the variation precisely because it is a *minimalist account* where an *economy principle* plays a crucial role (and actually because it is a very *restrictive* minimalist account, cf. section 4.5). This account predicts that a language with "rich verbal inflection" (in a sense to be defined below) will have V-to-I movement but it leaves open the possibility that a language without rich verbal inflection can have V-to-I movement. In section 4.3 I will then show that this account forces the claim that apparent instances of lack of V-to-I movement in certain clause types in Modern Icelandic are different in nature from the observed "optionality" of V-to-I movement in Faroese and I will argue that this is, in fact, the correct conclusion. Section 4.4 then reconsiders the historical evidence that is frequently cited by linguists who have argued for a reciprocal (or biconditional) relationship between rich verbal inflection in Scandinavian and V-to-I movement and I will maintain that this historical evidence does indeed support the Bobaljik and Thráinsson (= Bobaljik-Thráinsson) account, where this relationship is only one way (i.e. an "if–then" relationship and not "if-and-only-if"). Finally, section 4.5 contains some concluding remarks.

4.2   Variation between the Scandinavian languages

4.2.1   *The best known basic facts – and some proposed generalizations*

It is well known that the so-called Principles and Parameters approach to syntax, usually traced back to Chomsky's Pisa-lectures (cf. Chomsky, 1981), has lead to an explosion in synchronic comparative syntax. One of the areas that has been studied very extensively in these terms is the syntax of the Scandinavian languages. This includes the type of variation illustrated above, as can be seen, for instance, in the works of Vikner (1995a), Holmberg and Platzack (1995), Bobaljik and Thráinsson (1998), Rohrbacher (1999), Thráinsson (2001b, 2001c) and references cited there. Most of the proposed accounts of this variation describe the position of the finite verb in Icelandic in terms of V-to-I movement, that is movement of the finite verb from the VP to the head position of the IP (or TP or AgrSP, assuming a split IP along the lines first proposed by Pollock, 1989, and Chomsky, 1991). The tree diagram in (9) illustrates the mechanics of the standard account of this phenomenon, using a part of the embedded clause in (5c) above as an example, and similar diagrams can be found in most of the works just cited (mutatis mutandis if a split IP (i.e. an IP split into an AgrSP and a TP) is assumed, cf. below):

(9)

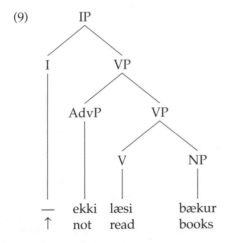

The difference between Icelandic, on the one hand, and Danish (and the other Mainland Scandinavian languages), on the other, is then supposed to be that

Icelandic has this type of V-to-I movement whereas Danish does not.[4] The proposed explanations of this difference then typically try to take into account the following set of facts:

(10)a.   Old Norse seems to have had V-to-I movement in embedded clauses and Old Norse had rich verbal inflection.
   b.   Modern Icelandic has preserved rich verbal inflection and V-to-I movement.
   c.   The system of verbal inflections has been simplified in Danish, Norwegian and Swedish and these languages appear to have lost V-to-I movement in embedded clauses (for the most part at least, but see sections 3 and 4 below).
   d.   One Swedish dialect, the dialect of the Älvdal valley (Älvdalsmålet), has preserved relatively rich verbal inflection and also V-to-I movement in embedded clauses.

The relevant facts are then partly illustrated by data such as the following (see e.g. Vikner, 1995b – the choice of verbs is partially determined by the existing linguistic evidence):

(11)

	Danish	Icelandic	Old Swedish (14th cent.)	Middle Swedish (16th cent.)	Älvdalsmålet
1sg.pres.	hører	heyr-i	kræf-er	kräv-er	hör-er
2sg.pres.	hører	heyr-ir	kræf-er	kräv-er	hör-er
3sg.pres.	hører	heyr-ir	kræf-er	kräv-er	hör-er
1pl.pres.	hører	heyr-um	kræf-um	kräv-a	hör-um
2pl.pres.	hører	heyr-ið	kræf-in	kräv-a	hör-ir
3pl.pres.	hører	heyr-a	kræfi-a	kräv-a	hör-a
1sg.past	hør-te	heyr-ð-i	kraf-þ-i	kräv-de	hör-d-e
2sg.past	hør-te	heyr-ð-ir	kraf-þ-i	kräv-de	hör-d-e
3sg.past	hør-te	heyr-ð-i	kraf-þ-i	kräv-de	hör-d-e
1pl.past	hør-te	heyr-ð-um	kraf-þ-um	kräv-de	hör-d-um
2pl.past	hør-te	heyr-ð-uð	kraf-þ-in	kräv-de	hör-d-ir
3pl.past	hør-te	heyr-ð-u	kraf-þ-u	kräv-de	hör-d-e
	"hear"	"hear"	"demand"	"demand"	"hear"

Here we see that in Icelandic, Old Swedish and Älvdalsmålet it is easy to distinguish the inflectional morphemes that mark tense on the one hand and subject–verb agreement on the other. In Danish there is just one form for the present tense and another for the past tense. In Middle Swedish, singular and plural are distinguished in the present tense but there is only one form for the past tense. Hence there was no obvious synchronic evidence in Middle Swedish for distinguishing between a past tense marker and an agreement marker, that is there was nothing that suggested to a Middle Swedish language acquirer that -*d*- was a past tense marker and -*e* a marker for person and number. It was just as plausible to interpret -*de* as a past tense marker.

If we now look at the word order in embedded clauses in these languages and dialects, we find an interesting correlation: in the languages where the agreement markers are easily distinguishable from the tense markers we find evidence for V-to-I movement but not in the others. Some relevant facts are given in (12)–(13) (see e.g. Platzack, 1988a; Platzack and Holmberg, 1989; Holmberg and Platzack, 1995; Vikner, 1995a, 1995b, 1997–98; Rohrbacher, 1999):

(12)a.   . . . af því   að   hann **vill**   **ekki** fylgja   honum.   (Ic.)
          because that he   wants not   follow him

b.   . . . at   Gudz ordh **kan ey** vara j   honom
          that God's word cannot be   in him
                              (Old Swedish, Holmberg and Platzack, 1995)

c.   . . . æn han **sivngærægh** thigianda messu
          if   he   sings not   silent   mass
                              (Old Swedish, Platzack, 1988a)

d.   Ba   fo dye   at   ig **uild**   **int** fy   om
      only because that I   wanted not follow him
                              (Älvdalsmålet, Platzack and Holmberg, 1989)

(13)a.   . . . hvorfor Jonas **ikke spiser** hval   (Da.)
          why   Jonas not   eats   whale

b.   wm annar   sywkdom **ey**   **krenker** nokon
      if   another sickness   not hinders anyone
                              (Middle Swedish, Platzack 1988a)

The conclusion reached by many linguists is that examples of the kind illustrated in (12)–(13), combined with the morphological facts shown in (11), indicate that there is a correlation between V-to-I in embedded clauses and "rich" verbal inflection. But if Middle Swedish reportedly did not have V-to-I in embedded clauses, despite the remnants of number distinction found there (distinction between singular and plural in the present tense, as shown in (11)), it is clear that just some remnants of subject–verb agreement are not enough to "trigger" V-to-I movement (more on this notion of "triggering" below). This is confirmed by the fact that the Norwegian dialect of the Hallingdal valley has similar remnants of number agreement as Middle Swedish has (number distinction in the present tense but a single form for the past tense) and it does not seem to have V-to-I movement in embedded clauses. This is typically illustrated by paradigms like those in (14) and sentences like the one in (15) (cf. Trosterud, 1989; see also Vikner, 1995b):

(14)   Verbal inflection in Hallingmål:

	present	past
1sg.	høyr-e	høyr-dæ
2sg.	høyr-e	høyr-dæ
3sg.	høyr-e	høyr-dæ
1pl.	høyr-æ	høyr-dæ
2pl.	høyr-æ	høyr-dæ
3pl.	høyr-æ	høyr-dæ

(15)   Kall me ko   ru   vill   bærre ru   **ikkji kalla** me æin dretukjæse
       call me what you want just if you not   call   me a   turd-rennet
                                        (Hallingmål, Trosterud, 1989)

Several linguists have tried to draw up appropriate generalizations about the correlation between rich verbal inflection and verb movement. Vikner has meticulously surveyed these attempts and his conclusion can be summarized as follows (cf. e.g. Vikner, 1997–98, p. 121 and references cited there):[5]

(16)   SVO languages have V-to-I movement in embedded clauses if and only if they show person distinction in both (or all) tenses.

A somewhat different descriptive generalization has been given by Rohrbacher (1999, p. 116):

(17)   The Paradigm-Verb Raising Correlate: A language has V to I raising if and only if in at least one number of one tense of the regular verb paradigm(s), the person features [1ST] and [2ND] are both distinctively marked [where "distinctively marked" means that forms bearing the feature in question are distinct from the forms lacking it].

Vikner's and Rohrbacher's generalizations are both meant to hold for the Scandinavian data we have seen so far. Thus the "reason" why Icelandic, Old Swedish, and Älvdalsmålet have V-to-I movement according to Vikner is that they have person distinctions both in the present tense and in the past tense (although some of them do not have person distinction in both numbers in both tenses). According to Rohrbacher, on the other hand, the crucial morphological fact about these languages in this connection is that they distinguish 1st and 2nd from the 3rd person in the plural (the fact that they do so both in the present tense and the past tense is presumably irrelevant for him).

As Vikner has shown (1995b, 1997–98), it is rather difficult to find clear empirical arguments that support one of these generalizations over the other. But there are two basic problems with both of them. The first one is that they are not explanations, just generalizations. Moreover, most explanations that linguists have tried to come up with to account for the observed generalizations have been ad hoc and circular. Most importantly, however, these generalizations are just plain wrong. As already mentioned, the correlation in question only goes in one direction, namely as follows:

(18)   If a language has rich verbal inflection (in a sense to be explained below) it has V-to-I movement in embedded clauses. The converse does not necessarily hold, however.

This will be shown in the next section.

4.2.2   Some (non-)explanations

Both Vikner (1995a, 1995b, 1997–98) and Rohrbacher (1999) survey and criticize previous accounts, such as those proposed by Roberts (1985, 1993), Kosmeijer (1986), Platzack (1988a), Platzack and Holmberg (1989), Holmberg and Platzack (1990), and Falk (1993) and argue that they make the wrong predictions, for example about Faroese. Thus they claim that previously proposed analyses typically predict that Faroese should have V-to-I movement since the relevant paradigms for Faroese look like this:

(19)   Verbal inflection in Faroese:

	present	past
1sg.	hoyr-i	hoyr-di
2sg.	hoyr-ir	hoyr-di
3sg.	hoyr-ir	hoyr-di
1pl.	hoyr-a	hoyr-du
2pl.	hoyr-a	hoyr-du
3pl.	hoyr-a	hoyr-du
	"hear"	

As indicated here, there are residues of subject–verb agreement left in modern Faroese. Under some of the theories surveyed by Vikner and Rohrbacher, this would predict that Faroese should have V-to-I movement like Icelandic, but Vikner and Rohrbacher claim that it does not. We will see in section 4.3 below that the Faroese facts are actually more complicated than this (as partially acknowledged by Vikner (e.g. 1997–98, p. 85, fn. 3) and Rohrbacher, 1999, pp. 141 ff.). It should be clear, however, that Vikner's account predicts that Faroese should *not* have V-to-I movement because there is no person distinction in the past tense and Rohrbacher's account predicts that Faroese should *not* have V-to-I movement because 1st and 2nd person are not both distinctively marked (distinguished from 3rd person for instance) in any number (cf. the generalizations stated in (16) and (17) above).

  Equally importantly, the proposed explanations surveyed by Vikner and Rohrbacher are typically circular and hence they would be non-explanatory even if they were correct. Many of the analyses attribute the V-to-I movement to the "strength" of I (or the Agr-part of it under a split IP analysis) in some sense. Thus references to "strength" of functional heads, or of the features associated with these heads, can be found, for example, in the above cited works by Roberts, Kosmeijer, Holmberg, and Platzack, for instance. Similarly, later work by Holmberg and Platzack (1995, p. 74) mentions a "strong [agree-ment] feature (or bundle of features)" in the languages that arguably have V-to-I movement, such as Icelandic and Old Swedish. The Mainland Scandinavian languages, on the other hand, have no agreement feature at all and hence no V-to-I movement. According to Holmberg and Platzack, it is also possible for languages to have a weak agreement feature and such a feature does not trigger verb movement.[6]

If one reads carefully the proposed accounts in terms of feature strength, the argumentation is typically circular. The structure of the argumentation tends to be as follows:

(20)a.   It is assumed that the inflectional head (I or its Agr-part) has to be "strong" in order to trigger verb movement.
   b.   It is assumed that there is a correlation between the strength of the inflectional head and the richness of the verbal inflection.
   c.   The verbal inflection of the languages that appear to have V-to-I is examined and attempts are made to come up with an empirically plausible generalization. This generalization is meant to describe the relevant morphological difference between the verb movement languages and the languages that do not exhibit V-to-I. Let us call the relevant type of verbal inflection Type X.
   d.   Then the argument goes like this: languages that have verbal inflec-tion of Type X have a strong inflectional head, and because they have a strong inflectional head the finite verb has to move to this inflectional head.

As Vikner has pointed out (e.g. 1995b, p. 6; 1997–8, p. 93), it is not particularly interesting to say that the inflectional head is strong and that this is somehow related to the morphological distinctions in the verbal paradigm unless one specifies which distinctions are needed. As we have seen, Vikner himself claims that person distinction in both (all) tenses is what is crucial. He does not, however, make any attempt to explain why it is exactly this distinction that is important. I want to argue below, however, that he is on the right track.

Rohrbacher, on the other hand, maintains that distinctive forms for 1st and 2nd person are crucial. While it is true, as Vikner has remarked (e.g. 1997–98, p. 98 ff.), that it is not entirely clear from which forms the 1st and 2nd person forms need to be distinctive or why, it must be admitted that Rohrbacher makes a serious attempt to relate (overt) verbal morphology to the relevant syntactic structure. His basic idea is that agreement affixes are only listed in the lexicon if agreement is "referential" in the language in question – and agreement is referential if 1st and 2nd person are distinctively marked in the relevant sense. If agreement affixes are listed in the lexicon, then they will project an Agr-phrase ("a second language-particular inflectional projection in addition to the universal TP" (Rohrbacher, 1999, p. 137)) and then the lan-guage in question will have V-to-I (that is V-to-T-to-Agr) raising. Languages without V-to-I movement ("V in situ languages," as Rohrbacher calls them) do not have an AgrP. As we will see below, this is somewhat similar to the idea proposed by Thráinsson (1996) and adopted by Bobaljik and Thráinsson (1998), namely that some languages have a split IP whereas others do not and that there is a correlation between the presence of a split IP and V-to-I. But there are two important differences between the accounts, one theoretical, the other empirical. They are worth outlining here.

First, the theoretical difference is that Rohrbacher has to assume that the verb movement in languages like Icelandic is movement of the verb stem to the relevant agreement affix and this movement is forced because morphologically realized affixes cannot be left unattended (in this connection he refers to a filter proposed by Lasnik, 1981; Rohrbacher, 1999, p. 132). For non-movement languages, like Faroese under Rohrbacher's account, the agreement affixes will not be represented syntactically, even though they exist in the language, and hence there will be no verb movement joining the stem to a dangling affix but just a spell-out rule ensuring the correct form. Thus Rohrbacher has to assume a lexicalist approach to morphology for languages like Icelandic and an interpretivist approach for languages like Faroese. Under the Bobaljik and Thráinsson account, on the other hand, the presence vs. absence of verb movement follows from structural differences because of independently proposed principles of checking, as we shall see in section 4.2.4.

Second, the empirical difference is that Rohrbacher maintains, as well as Vikner, that V-to-I occurs if and only if the verbal morphology is rich in the relevant sense (although they differ slightly in their accounts of what "the relevant sense" is). Thus it is the morphology that "drives" the syntax in this respect (cf. the title of Rohrbacher's 1999 book). Under the Bobaljik and Thráinsson approach, on the other hand, morphological evidence is only a part of the evidence accessible to the language acquirer trying to figure out the details of the syntactic structure. Thus Rohrbacher and Vikner predict that there should be no languages with "poor" verbal morphology and V-to-I movement, whereas the Bobaljik and Thráinsson approach does not rule this out, as we shall see. As partially acknowledged by Vikner and Rohrbacher (see, e.g., Vikner, 1995b, pp. 24–5; 1997–8, pp. 125–7; Rohrbacher, 1999, pp. 118–29 and note 17, p. 149), their predictions are empirically wrong. We now turn to the facts that are problematic for analyses of this sort.

4.2.3   Problematic facts?

First, it has been known for some time that the so-called Kronoby-dialect of Finland Swedish appears to have V-to-I movement but poor morphology. The following example is usually cited in the literature to show this and the reader is then told that the dialect in question has no subject–verb agreement at all (Platzack and Holmberg, 1989, p. 74; see also Vikner, 1995b, p. 24, 1997–98, p. 126):

   (21)   He va   bra   et   an **tsöfft**   int   bootsen.   (Kron.)
         It   was   good   that   he   bought   not   book-the
         "It was good that he didn't buy the book."

Similarly, the Tromsø-dialect in northern Norway reportedly has no subject–verb agreement but V-to-I movement appears to occur there too (cf. Vikner, 1995b, p. 25, 1997–8, p. 126, who also cites Iversen's grammar from 1918):

(22)a. Vi va' bare tre støkka før det at han
    We were only three pieces for it that he
    Nielsen **kom ikkje**. (Troms.)
    Nielsen came not
    "There were only three of us because Nielsen didn't come."

   b. Han kom så seint at dørvakta **vilde ikkje**
     he came so late that guard-the would not
     slæppe han inn. (Troms.)
     let him in
     "He came so late that the guard wouldn't let him in."

Although one could argue that the syntax of these dialects has not been investigated in detail, the examples just given indicate that the prediction of the strong hypotheses proposed by Vikner (1995b, 1997–8) and Rohrbacher (1994, 1999) is wrong but Bobaljik and Thráinsson's prediction is right: Languages *can* have V-to-I raising even if they have poor verbal morphology. Furthermore, Vikner (1995b, p. 25, 1997–8, p. 126) also shows that V-to-I movement was apparently not obligatory in the Tromsø dialect even when it was described by Iversen in the early 19th century. This is indicated by examples like the following (cited by Vikner from Iversen, 1918):

(23) . . . at dæm **ikkje måtte** klive op på det taket. (Troms.)
       that they not could climb up on that roof-the
   "that they couldn't climb on the roof"

We see, therefore, that V-to-I appears to be optional in some sense in the Tromsø dialect and Vikner states further that the "Icelandic" order of the finite verb and adverb (the Vf–Adv order) in embedded clauses is "not . . . the most common one" in that dialect.[7] In this respect the situation in the Tromsø dialect is very similar to the historical developments that will be discussed in sections 3 and 4 below. In that connection, one could also mention the fact that Vf–Adv order can apparently still be found in some Danish dialects, despite their poor verbal morphology (see, e.g., Pedersen, 1996 and also Gregersen and Pedersen, 1997), even in relative clauses like the one in (24) (cf. Pedersen, 1996):

(24) Der kan jo være nogen der **kan itte** tåle det.
     there can of-course be somebody that can not stand it
   "There can obviously be somebody who cannot stand it."

So, still another problem for the biconditional accounts: rich morphology ⊉ verb movement which is not a problem for the Bobaljik and Thráinsson account. Let us look at the Bobaljik and Thráinsson account in more detail to see why.

4.2.4   *The Bobaljik and Thráinsson account and Scandinavian verbal morphology*

Two of the most important theoretical assumptions underlying the Bobaljik and Thráinsson account can be summarized as follows (cf. Bobaljik and Thráinsson (1998) and references cited there):

(25)a.   Languages vary with respect to the functional projections instantiated. In particular, the IP can be split into an agreement projection (AgrP (possibly more than one)) and a tense projection (TP), along the lines first discussed in detail by Pollock (1989) and Chomsky (1991). Other languages may have an unsplit (or fused) IP, as mentioned above.

b.   Since functional projections are not universally instantiated, the child needs evidence for their "presence" in the language being acquired. This evidence can both be syntactic and morphological. In most languages the child will be presented with various kinds of syntactic evidence for a functional projection "above" the VP and "below" the CP, for instance, such as facts having to do with the position of subjects in finite clauses, possibly also the position of sentential adverbs, etc. But the child will not "assume" that this projection is split into two (or more) unless presented with syntactic or morphological evidence for it. Clear morphological distinction between tense and agreement markers on finite verbs will count as morphological evidence for this split. But evidence for "V-to-I movement" in embedded clauses would also count as evidence for a split IP, for reasons having to do with the nature of feature checking, as will be explained presently.

As already mentioned, a crucial property of this account is that it predicts that the correlation between rich verbal morphology and V-to-I movement is one way only. This is so because a "rich verbal morphology" of the appropriate kind provides evidence for split IP, as stated in (25b), and a split IP "causes" V-to-I (or, more precisely, V-to-T, as will be discussed presently) under a feature-checking (or matching) approach. But a language *could* also have a split IP even if it had poor verbal morphology. The evidence for the split would then be purely syntactic but it would be compatible with the morphological properties of the language, basically because (relatively) poor morphology can allow for competing analyses, partly because of the possibility of null morphemes. This obviously needs to be explained so let us look into the Bobaljik and Thráinsson account in some detail.

First, Bobaljik and Thráinsson make the following assumptions (1998, p. 39):

(26)a.   The features of a projection are those of its head.

b.   Movement occurs solely for the purposes of feature checking.

c.   Features are checked in all and only local relations to a head (viz., head–specifier, head–complement, head–head (adjoined heads)).

First, it should be fairly clear that (26a) is a standard assumption in X'-theory, as Bobaljik and Thráinsson point out (1998, p. 39). It is sometimes expressed in terms of feature percolation: the features of a head percolate to its maximal projection. The mechanics of this are unimportant here, however. The important thing is to note that (26a) underlies the whole X'-theory. Otherwise VPs could have N-heads, NPs could have P-heads, etc.

Second, (26b), in one form or another, is a basic assumption within the MP. It partly follows from economy principles of the sort mentioned above: if a given movement is not "necessary" in some sense, then it is disallowed, because one should "do as little as possible." But (26b) states furthermore that feature checking is the only legitimate purpose of movement. As Bobaljik and Thráinsson note (1998, p. 40), the movement operation could result in the checking of features of the moved element, features of the target or both, depending on your favorite version of checking theory. What is crucial, however, is that if a given movement does not result in feature checking of some sort, then it is disallowed by economy principles. This is obviously a very strong claim and it has generated lively discussion in recent years. One of the reasons is that it rules out truly optional movement. Hence it calls for an explanation or a different analysis whenever "optional movement" seems to occur. As is well known, many instances of XP-movement appear to be related to differences in interpretation having to do with topicality, specificity, or some such. This is true of Topicalization in English, Scrambling in Dutch, German, Japanese and Korean, Object Shift in Icelandic, etc. (see, e.g., the discussions in Kim, 1996; Diesing, 1997; Vikner, 1997; Thráinsson, 2001a and references cited there). While differences of this sort can be very subtle and one must try to avoid simplistic ad hoc accounts (i.e. accounts of the type: "Movement is triggered by feature checking, hence Topicalization must involve checking of a Topic feature, even though I don't have any independent evidence for its existence"), there are at least some indications that the movement operations in question have something to do with interpretation and thus they are not entirely vacuous or "truly optional," as it were. V-movement, on the other hand, does not seem to have anything to do with interpretation. Hence "optional V-movement" should not exist at all under the assumptions of MP in general or the assumptions listed in (26) above in particular, since it would be an instance of "truly optional" movement, unrelated to any interpretative differences. To put it differently: the theory proposed here predicts that there should not be any optional V-movement and I want to argue below that this is the correct prediction. But we have not yet shown how the Bobaljik and Thráinsson theory predicts this.

As mentioned above, Bobaljik and Thráinsson assume that languages may differ with respect to the "richness" of their functional projections in the syntax. More specifically, they assume the *Split IP Parameter* (SIP) first proposed by Thráinsson (1996, p. 262; see also Bobaljik and Thráinsson, 1998, p. 38):

(27)   Languages that have a positive value for the SIP have AgrSP and TP as separate functional projections whereas languages with a negative value of the SIP are characterized by an unsplit IP.

This difference is illustrated by the familiar but simplified[8] diagrams in (28a,b) (cf. Bobaljik and Thráinsson, 1998, p. 37):

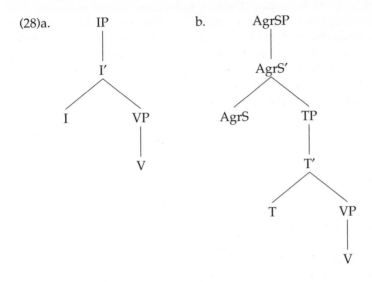

To see how the Bobaljik and Thráinsson account works, assume first that the V needs to check some features against I (or against some features in I, or match features in I and V or whatever – terminological (and other minor theoretical) details are unimportant here) in a language with an unsplit IP as in (28a). Given the (standard) assumption in (26a), the features of the head V will be present in VP and since VP is the complement of I it is in the checking domain of I under assumption (26c). Hence V does not have to move to I for checking purposes (nor do any of its features, assuming a feature-attracting implementation) and since it does not have to, it cannot under the economy principles implied by (26b). In other words, V-to-I movement cannot occur in a language that has an unsplit IP (negative value for the SIP).

Assume now that V needs to check some features against AgrS in a language with a split IP as in (28b), for example a language where AgrSP and TP are separate projections. Since VP is not in the checking domain of AgrS, the features of V cannot be checked in situ. Hence V-movement is triggered by the need to check features in a language with a split IP. Under the standard assumption that V-to-T involves adjunction of the V-head to the T-head, one may assume that the features of the TP will not only contain the features of T but also the features of the adjoined V "after" V-to-T movement. Under that assumption the V would only have to raise as far as to T and not all the way to AgrS to have its features checked by the AgrS head. We will return to this issue below.[9]

We have now seen how the Bobaljik and Thráinsson account relates split IP and V-raising: V-raising is forced if the language has a split IP (separate AgrS and T heads) but impossible if the language has an unsplit IP. But how does the language-acquirer know whether the language in question has a positive or a negative value for the SIP? According to the Bobaljik and Thráinsson account, the verbal morphology can provide crucial evidence. As mentioned above, the basic idea is that if a language has clearly separable tense and agreement morphemes in the verbal inflection, then that counts as morphological evidence for separate tense and agreement projections. Referring back to the verbal paradigms given in (11) and (14) above, we see then that Icelandic, Old Swedish, and Älvdalsmålet provide morphological evidence for a split IP. Hence these languages/dialects should have V-movement (V-to-T movement, more precisely) under the Bobaljik and Thráinsson approach, and they do.

The important thing to note here is that this well-known relationship between rich verbal morphology and verb movement follows under the Bobaljik and Thráinsson account from a principled theory of how checking and movement interact and what the relationship is between morphology and functional projections: first, movement occurs for the purposes of feature checking and it is only necessary (and hence only possible) if the relevant features cannot be checked in situ, that is if they are not already in the appropriate checking domain. Second, overt distinct tense and agreement morphemes require distinct tense and agreement projections in the syntax, where the inflectional features corresponding to these morphemes can be checked.[10] This is very different from most of the approaches outlined in section 4.2.2 above, where it was simply assumed that because verb movement appeared to occur, the relevant morphological features had to be strong, and because the relevant morphological features were strong, they triggered verb movement.

Now it could be argued that so far we have only considered the simple and straightforward cases that "everybody" claims to have an account for and the advantages of the Bobaljik and Thráinsson account so far are mainly theoretical or conceptual and not empirical. While that is by no means trivial, it is also clear that the less straightforward cases like Faroese would provide a very interesting testing ground here. As already mentioned in section 4.2.2, Vikner (1995a, 1995b, 1997–8) and Rohrbacher (1994, 1999) both present analyses that "require" that Faroese should not have V-to-I (or V-to-T) movement in embedded clauses, whereas many previous analyses assumed that Faroese did in fact have verb movement. Hence it would be interesting to see what the approach advocated here would predict about Faroese. The supposedly crucial facts about Faroese verbal morphology were presented in (19) above and they are repeated here for convenience:

(19)   Verbal inflection in Faroese:

	present	past
1sg.	hoyr-i	hoyr-di
2sg.	hoyr-ir	hoyr-di
3sg.	hoyr-ir	hoyr-di
1pl.	hoyr-a	hoyr-du
2pl.	hoyr-a	hoyr-du
3pl.	hoyr-a	hoyr-du
	"hear"	

Assuming for the time being that this is a fair representation of verbal morphology in Faroese (we will see presently that the facts are somewhat more complicated), we note that although it is not *necessary* to take the *-d-* in the past tense forms as a tense marker separate from a singular agreement marker *-i* and a plural agreement marker *-u*, it would seem *possible* that the language acquirer would interpret the forms in this way rather than "assuming" that *-di* is a fused marker for past tense singular and *-du* a fused marker for past tense plural. The "fusional" interpretation is not at all far fetched either, however, since many morphological markers in inflectional languages like Faroese express two or more grammatical categories at the same time. Thus the ending *-ur* is a fused marker for nominative singular and *-ar* a fused marker for nominative (or accusative) plural in strong Faroese nouns like *hund-ur* "dog," pl. *hund-ar* (cf. e.g. Thráinsson et al., 2002).

In the light of past discussion of Scandinavian morphosyntax (cf. the overview in section 4.2.2 above and references cited there), it is important to try to figure out how a child acquiring Faroese could set the value for the SIP given ambiguous morphological facts of the sort illustrated in (19). What would be the deciding factor in this case? Under the Bobaljik and Thráinsson approach advocated here, evidence from the syntax should come into play. Since verbal morphology of the type illustrated in (19) is clearly compatible with a split IP as it *can* be analyzed as involving separate tense and agreement morphemes, salient syntactic evidence for a split IP, like V-to-T movement in embedded clauses for instance,[11] would be expected to disambiguate the situation, as it were. Consequently one might expect speakers of Faroese to have a split IP grammar if (19) is a fair representation of regular verbal morphology in Faroese. That does not quite correspond to the observed facts, however, as pointed out above. Hence Vikner (1995a, 1995b, 1997–8) and Rohrbacher (1994, 1999) have argued that Faroese does not in fact have V-to-T movement (or at least only to a very limited extent). Similarly, Petersen (2000, p. 80) concludes that the younger generation of Faroese speakers "has generally lost V-to-I movement in the complements of non-bridge verbs" whereas Jonas (1996b) and especially Thráinsson (2001b, 2001c) show that there is considerable variation among Faroese speakers in this respect. How is this compatible with the Bobaljik and Thráinsson approach advocated here? Why does not the (apparently ambiguous) Faroese verbal morphology illustrated in (19) combined with syntactic evidence suffice to trigger a positive value of the SIP for all speakers of Faroese?

One very important reason is the fact that (19) is actually a rather misleading presentation of regular verbal morphology for the following reason: many speakers of Faroese do not distinguish unstressed /i,u/ at all and others only make a distinction between these sounds before /n/. More specifically, the situation is like this with respect to forms like the ones in (19) (cf. Hagström, 1967; Weyhe, 1996; Thráinsson, et al., 2002):

(29)		Sandoy, Vágar, Nothern Streymoy, Eysturoy, Kalsoy	Elsewhere
	Singular and plural distinguished in the past tense of regular verbs	Yes	No

The "elsewhere" area includes Southern Streymoy, which is Tórshavn and the area around it, and also the southernmost island, Suðuroy, and the outer (or easternmost) nothern islands. This means, then, that for a large part of the speakers of Faroese (presumably the majority), the morphological distinctions made in the verbal inflection are comparable to those made in Middle Swedish (cf. the paradigms in (11)) and Middle Swedish reportedly did not have V-to-I (but see the discussion in section 4.4). To the extent, then, that speakers of these morphologically "poor" dialects of Faroese have a V-to-I (or V-to-T) movement grammar, namely a split-IP grammar under the Bobaljik and Thráinsson account, it is clear that the positive setting of the SIP in their grammar cannot have been triggered by morphological evidence under the Bobaljik and Thráinsson account.

But to what extent do these speakers have V-to-T movement? And do the speakers of the morphologically richer dialects of Faroese uniformly have V-to-T movement? These questions will be answered in the next section and the answer will be considered in terms of the Bobaljik and Thráinsson account and from the point of view of the minimalist program in general.

4.3   Variation within individual languages

4.3.1   *Verb movement variation in Faroese*

4.3.1.1   **Some statements and claims**

As discussed in section 4.2.2 above, Vikner (1995a, 1995b, 1997–8) and Rohrbacher (1994, 1999) maintain that Modern Faroese does not have V-to-I movement of the appropriate kind, although they acknowledge that there may be some sort of "residual V-movement" in Faroese. Let us look at this "residue" in some detail.

Michael Barnes can be said to be a pioneer in modern syntactic research on Faroese. In an overview paper on Faroese syntax he states (1992, p. 27) that the "Icelandic" word order is "not common" in embedded clauses in Faroese, neither in the spoken nor the written language although both the Icelandic and Mainland Scandinavian orders can be found. Thus he gives examples like the following, for instance:

(30)a.   Hann spyr hví tað   **ikki eru** fleiri tílíkar samkomur.
 he   asks why there not are more such   meetings

   b.   Hann spyr hví tað   **eru ikki** fleiri tílíkar samkomur.
 he   asks why there are not more such   meetings
 "He asks why there aren't more meetings of that kind."

In (30a) the negation precedes the finite verb in the embedded clause (note that the embedded clause is an indirect question), as it would typically do in Mainland Scandinavian, but in (30b) we have the "Icelandic" order. Barnes obviously assumes that the "Icelandic" order is on the way out and states that his impression is that it is mainly used "in archaising style."

In their chapter on Faroese in a handbook on Germanic languages, Barnes and the Faroese linguist Weyhe say (1994, p. 215) that the order of the finite verb and the adverb in embedded clauses "may be reversed, as is normally always the case in Icelandic." Then they give the following example:

(31)a. . . . hóast   fólk   **ongantíð hevur** fingið fisk her
          although people never   have   caught fish here

    b.   . . . hóast   fólk   **hevur ongantíð** fingið fisk her
          although people have   never   caught fish here
      "although people never have caught fish here"

Here we find the Icelandic order in the embedded adverbial clause in (31a) and it seems that Barnes and Weyhe look at this as some sort of an exception, although they are not very specific about it.

In a recent grammar textbook, the Faroese teachers Andreasen and Dahl state that adverbs may either precede or follow the finite verb in embedded clauses in Faroese and give the following examples (1997, p. 184):

(32)a. Anna helt,   at   hann **var ikki** fittur.
          Anna believed that he   was not good

    b.   Anna helt,   at   hann **ikki var** fittur.
          Anna believed that he   not was good

It is interesting that they present the Icelandic order first, but the examples do show little, since the matrix verb is a "bridge verb" and it is well known that the complements of bridge verbs tend to have main-clause-like properties (cf. e.g. Vikner, 1995a, p. 70, passim, and references cited there; see also Petersen, 2000). We will return to this issue later in this section.

A similar comment can be found in a textbook on syntax by the Faroese teacher Henriksen. He also maintains that adverbs can either precede or follow the main verb in embedded clauses and then gives the following examples among others (Henriksen, 2000, p. 120):

(33)a. Hann spurdi hví hon **segði altíð**   tað sama.
          he   asked why she said   always the same

    b.   Hann spurdi hví hon **altíð   segði** tað sama.
          he   asked why she always said   the same
      "He asked why she always said the same thing."

Here the embedded clause is an indirect question and in such an example the Icelandic order would be ungrammatical in Danish, for instance. Yet Henriksen presents it first.

4.3.1.2   *Three acceptability studies*

In the research for her doctoral thesis, Jonas collected some data on the order of the finite verb and the adverb in Faroese embedded clauses. She found some variation and suggested that there was a dialectal difference in Faroese with respect to this. Her impression was that all speakers accepted the Mainland Scandinavian order whereas only a subset of them accepted the Icelandic order. She referred to the more liberal dialect as Fa1 but the more restrictive (the one only accepting the Mainland Scandinavian order) Fa2. Her examples include the following (Jonas, 1996b, ch. 4 – here Fa1: % means that the relevant example is acceptable in dialect 1 whereas Fa2: * indicates that the example is ungrammatical in dialect 2):

(34)a.   Tað er spell   at   tú   **kanst ikki**
          it   is bad-thing that you can   not
          vera her   longur. (Fa1: %, Fa2: *)
          be   here longer

   b.   Tað er spell   at   tú   **ikki kanst**
          it   is bad-thing that you not   can
          vera her   longur. (Fa1: %, Fa2: %)
          be   here longer
          "It is too bad that you cannot stay longer."

Jonas suggested that this dialectal difference was generational rather than geographic, that is that the younger generation was less likely to accept the Icelandic order.

   More recently, the Faroese linguist Petersen made a survey among 18 Faroese high school students (about 20 years of age). He used a grammaticality (or acceptability) questionnaire and compared the judgments for the Icelandic order and the Mainland Scandinavian order in the complements of bridge verbs and non-bridge verbs. His test sentences were of the following types (Petersen, 2000, p. 76):

(35)a.   Marjun sigur, at   Jóhan **drepur ikki** hundin.
          Marjun says   that Johan kills   not dog-the

   b.   Marjun sigur, at   Jóhan **ikki drepur** hundin.
          Marjun says   that Johan not kills   dog-the
          "Marjun says, that Johan doesn't kill the dog."

(36)a.   Marjun harmast um,   at   Jóhan **drepur ikki** hundin.
          Marjun regrets   about that Johan kills   not dog-the

   b.   Marjun harmast um,   at   Jóhan **ikki drepur** hundin.
          Marjun regrets   about that Johan not   kills   dog-the
          "Marjun regrets that Johan doesn't kill the dog."

In (35) the matrix verb is the bridge verb *say* and we have the Icelandic (V-to-I movement) order in (35a) and the Mainland Scandinavian (non-movement) order in (35b). In (36) the matrix verb is the non-bridge verb *regret* and again we have the Icelandic order in (36a) and the Mainland Scandinavian order in (36b). In Petersen's study the subjects were presented with 3–5 examples of each type and the main results can be tabulated as follows (where Vf–Adv indicates the Icelandic order with the finite verb preceding the adverb and Adv–Vf the Mainland Scandinavian order – see Petersen, 2000, p. 79–80):

(37) Judgments of the order of the finite verb and the adverb in the complements of bridge verbs and non-bridge verbs in Petersen's study (all 18 subjects):[12]

	Vf–Adv			Adv–Vf		
	✓	?	*	✓	?	*
bridge verb complem.:	83%	8%	9%	98%	0%	2%
non-bridge verb complem.:	31%	8%	61%	100%	0%	0%

As can be seen here, virtually everybody accepts the Mainland Scandinavian order in either type of complements. Equally importantly, there is a clear difference in the acceptability rate of the Icelandic order in bridge verb complements and non-bridge verb complements. A very high percentage of the bridge verb complements with the Icelandic order are accepted (83 percent of the total number were judged to be fine, only 9 percent rejected, the rest were judged questionable), whereas only one-third of the non-bridge verb complements with the Icelandic order were accepted (31 percent were judged to be fine, 61 percent were rejected and 8 percent found questionable). Based on this, Petersen concludes that "the generation under consideration has generally lost V-to-I movement in the complements of non-bridge verbs" (2000, p. 80).

While the picture is fairly clear, it is not obvious that Petersen's conclusion is entirely warranted. First, only five of the 18 subjects rejected all the non-bridge verb complements that had the Icelandic order. Second, almost a third of the non-bridge verb complements with the Icelandic order were judged fine by the subjects. That is presumably very different from what we would find, say, in a comparable survey among Danish high school students. At the same time it is important to note that those speakers who accept the Icelandic order in the complements of non-bridge verbs also accept the Mainland Scandinavian order in these complements. That is very different from the Icelandic situation (cf. the next subsection). But this also partly confirms Jonas' (1996b) finding, since her conclusion was that everybody accepted the Mainland Scandinavian order whereas only a subset of the population accepted the Icelandic one.[13]

My own findings in a comparable study are roughly similar to those of Petersen's, however. In this study I asked high school students in Tórshavn[14] to judge sentences that included various types of embedded clauses with the Icelandic and Mainland Scandinavian word order. These sentences were randomly distributed in two questionnaires that contained some 126 sentences in all. The questionnaires were presented to the students in two different sessions and the subjects received the following instructions (this is a translation of the Faroese instructions):

(38)   This is an investigation of Faroese usage. You are asked to mark the following sentences as shown here:
    ✓ = a natural sentence, a sentence I could very well use myself
    ? = a questionable sentence, a sentence I would hardly use
    * = an unnatural or wrong sentence

The bridge verb and non-bridge verb complements included the following:

(39)   *that*-complements of bridge verbs:
  a.   Hon sigur, at   hon **hevur ongantíð** verið í Koltri.
      she says that she has   never   been in Koltur

  b.   Hon sigur at   hon **ongantíð hevur** verið í Koltri.
      she says that she never   has   been in Koltur
      "She says that she has never been to Koltur."

(40)   *that*-complements of non-bridge verbs
  a.   Tað er spell, at   bókin   **kemur ikki** út   til jóla.
      it   is bad   that book-the comes not out by Christmas

  b.   Tað er spell at   bókin   **ikki kemur** út til jóla.
      it   is bad   that book-the not comes out by Christmas
      "It is bad that the book doesn't come out by Christmas."

We can now summarize the results the same way as we did for Petersen's study in (37):

(41)   Judgments by Faroese high school students of the order of the finite verb and the adverb in the complements of bridge verbs and non-bridge verbs (14 subjects – the figures from Petersen's study are given in parentheses below, for ease of comparison):[15]

	Vf–Adv			Adv–Vf		
	✓	?	*	✓	?	*
bridge verb	34%	33%	33%	75%	21%	4%
complem.:	(83%	8%	9%	98%	0%	2%)
non-bridge	14%	41%	45%	82%	14%	4%
verb complem.:	(31%	8%	61%	100%	0%	0%)

As is to be expected in studies of this kind, there is some difference between the two sets of figures. This may be partly due to different instructions, that is to say exactly how the students were using the acceptance markers. As can be seen here, the subjects of my study used the question mark more frequently than those in Petersen's study, for instance. This has greater effect on their judgment of the Icelancic order, especially in the bridge verb complements, where the judgments fall into three equally large groups. Still, one can argue that the general tendency is the same: the Mainland Scandinavian order (Adv–Vf) is preferred in both types of complements and the Vf–Adv order is more likely to be accepted in the bridge verb complements than in the non-bridge verb complements. As in Petersen's group, however, some subjects accept some of the examples with the Icelandic order in the non-bridge verb complements and here only less than half of these examples were found to be "unnatural or wrong." This suggests that the subjects are quite familiar with this order, although they are somewhat reluctant to claim that it is "natural" or something that they "could very well use" themselves (cf. the instructions). But as before, the general picture seems quite different from what one would expect to find in either Iceland or in Mainland Scandinavia.

I also included adverbial clauses, indirect questions, and relative clauses in my study. Representative examples are given in (42)–(44).

(42)   Adverbial clauses of various kinds:
   a.   Lat hana vera eftir um hon **vil**   **ikki** koma við.
        let her be   left if she wants not   come with

   b.   Lat hana vera eftir um hon **ikki vil**   koma við.
        let her be   left if she not   wants come with
        "Leave her behind if she doesn't want to come with us."

   c.   Vit fara hóast   veðrið   **er ikki** av tí besta.
        we go   although weather-the is not of the best

   d.   Vit fara hóast   veðrið   **ikki er** av tí besta.
        we go   although weather-the not is of the best
        "We go even if the weather isn't so good."

(43)   Indirect questions:
   a.   Eg spurdi hvønn hon **hevði ongantíð** tosað   við.
        I asked whom she had   never   spoken to

   b.   Eg spurdi hvønn hon **ongantíð hevði** tosað   við.
        I asked whom she never   had   spoken to
        "I asked whom she had never spoken to."

(44)   Relative clauses:
  a. Tað er hatta húsið sum eg **vildi**   **ikki** keypa.
      it   is this house that I   wanted not buy

  b. Tað er hatta húsið sum eg **ikki vildi**   keypa.
      it   is this house that I   not wanted buy
      "It is this house that I didn't want to buy."

A summary of the judgments for these sentences is given in (45) in a similar fashion to that employed above:

(45) Judgments by Faroese high school students of the order of the finite verb and the adverb in the complements of bridge verbs and non-bridge verbs (14 subjects):[16]

	Vf–Adv			Adv–Vf		
	✓	?	*	✓	?	*
adverbial clauses:	39%	37%	24%	51%	27%	22%
indirect questions:	5%	32%	63%	74%	21%	5%
relative clauses:	5%	31%	64%	81%	17%	2%

Here again we neither get the Icelandic nor the Mainland Scandinavian pattern. Again, the Mainland Scandinavian Adv–Vf order is preferred in all types of embedded clauses. Still, the picture is partly unexpected. First, the percentage of accepted instances of the Icelandic order in adverbial clauses is rather unexpected and even slightly higher than in the bridge verb complements. This is of some interest, although a part of the reason is undoubtedly the fact that some adverbial clauses are much more main-clause-like than others, as is well known from several languages,[17] and this was not sufficiently controlled for in the examples. Second, the acceptance rate for the Icelandic order is much lower in indirect questions and relative clauses than in any other type of embedded clauses. Even here, however, only about two-thirds of the examples are classified as ungrammatical.

   We can conclude, then, that the "Icelandic word order" in embedded clauses is in general not preferred by the younger speakers of Faroese. This is also what several linguists had suspected, including Barnes, Weyhe, Vikner, and Rohrbacher, as pointed out in sections 4.2.2 and 4.3.1 above. What is interesting, however, is that very few of the subjects tested reject all sentences with the Icelandic order, except in the case of indirect questions and relative clauses, where hardly any sentences were accepted without reservation and many of the subjects completely rejected all the examples. Now it would be interesting to test older generations of speakers in a similar fashion. While I have not done so yet, I should like to mention that two linguists who are native speakers of Faroese were asked to answer the same questionnaire as the high school students. Their judgments are summarized in (46) in the same way as before:

(46)

	Vf–Adv			Adv–Vf		
	✓	?	*	✓	?	*
bridge verb complem.:	67%	33%	0%	100%	0%	0%
non-bridge verb complem.:	50%	50%	0%	100%	0%	0%
adverbial clauses:	50%	50%	0%	84%	8%	8%
indirect questions:	37%	38%	25%	100%	0%	0%
relative clauses:	0%	50%	50%	100%	0%	0%

As expected, the lines are clearer here since the linguists are presumably more used to judging sentences. First, the Mainland Scandinavian Adv–Vf order was only found to be "unnatural or wrong" or "questionable" in one particular type of adverbial clause. Otherwise it was found to be natural. Second, the Icelandic Vf–Adv order was only found to be unnatural or wrong in indirect questions and relative clauses. Otherwise it was found to be natural or, at worst, only questionable. Here the bridge verb complements stand out as the environment where the highest percentage of Vf–Adv orders was accepted, with non-bridge verb complements and adverbial clauses being equal. As before, the Vf–Adv order was found to be worst in indirect questions and relative clauses. It was also interesting to see that one of the linguists was more tolerant towards the Icelandic order, finding it natural in many cases where the other found it questionable, and also calling it questionable when the other said it was unnatural or wrong.

While it would be interesting to look more closely into this to check for the robustness of the generational differences and look for geographic ones, the results of the preliminary surveys outlined in this subsection can be summarized as in (47):[18]

(47)a.   The Mainland Scandinavian order is preferred by all the speakers tested in all types of embedded clauses.

b.   The Icelandic word order is accepted by all the speakers tested in some types of embedded clauses, especially in bridge verb complements. Many speakers also accept it quite readily in the complements of non-bridge verbs and at least some types of adverbial clauses, but most speakers find it unnatural in indirect questions and (especially) relative clauses.

c.   Speakers seem to vary considerably in their acceptance of the Vf–Adv order.

d.   Although there are some indications that there is a generational difference in the acceptance of Vf–Adv order, with the younger speakers being less tolerant, it does not seem to be the case that the older generation has Icelandic verb movement grammar and the younger a Mainland Scandinavian non-movement grammar. The situation is more complex than that.

Now the conclusions in (47) are based on surveys of grammaticality judgments. Hence one might argue that they only reflect the "passive" knowledge of Faroese speakers, as it were. If the Icelandic Vf–Adv order is on the way out, one might imagine that nobody actually uses it although most speakers, especially the older ones, are familiar with it from texts or from the speech of older generations. Ideally, one would like to look into this by doing some sort of a survey of spoken Faroese. While I have not had the opportunity to do that, I have made a survey of Vf–Adv and Adv–Vf orders in embedded clauses in Faroese texts from the 19th and 20th centuries. This survey is discussed in the next subsection.

4.3.1.3   Word order in embedded clauses in Faroese texts

In this preliminary survey I have only looked at the position of the negation *ikki* "not," since this was the most common "sentence adverbial" in these texts and hence easiest to use for comparative purposes. The texts reported on here are written by 14 different authors born between 1819 and 1950. In the table in (48) I have grouped the authors according to age and the numbers in the table show the numbers of each order (Vf–Adv and Adv–Vf) found in each type of embedded clause.[19]

(48)   A table showing the frequency of Vf–Adv and Adv–Vf orders in embedded clauses of different kinds in some 19th and 20th century texts.

Number and generations of authors	Bridge verb complem.		Non-bridge verb complem.		Adverbial clauses		Indirect questions		Relative clauses	
	Vf–Adv	Adv–Vf	Vf–Adv	Adv–Vf	Vf–Adv	Adv–Vf	Vf–Adv	Adv–Vf	Vf–Adv	Adv–Vf
3 authors born before 1900	18	11	4	8	17	14	3	2	1	6
5 authors born 1900–39	29	1	10	12	36	25	3	5	5	6
3 authors born 1940–50	12	3	2	7	6	23	0	2	0	7
Total	59	15	16	27	59	62	6	9	6	19
% Vf–Adv order	80%		37%		49%		40%		24%	

This summary indicates that the Icelandic order is actually very common in the complements of bridge verbs, it also occurs about half the time in adverbial clauses, but in other types of embedded clauses it is not preferred, especially in relative clauses. But although the numbers are not very high, the table suggests that the Vf–Adv order may be on the way out in embedded clauses except for bridge verb complements, since the youngest generation of authors seems to use it much less frequently than the older generations in non-bridge verb complements, adverbial clauses, and, especially, indirect questions and relative clauses. Except for the adverbial clauses, this corresponds rather well with the judgments of the high school students reported on above.

Like all summaries and averages of linguistic usage, however, the table in (48) is rather misleading in several respects. The main reason is that it smooths out all individual variation, which is actually considerable. Thus one of the authors in the oldest group (Regin í Líð, born 1871) *never* uses the Icelandic order and one of the authors in the next group (Heðin Brú, born 1901) *always* uses the Icelandic order. In the youngest group, most of the examples (15 in all) of the Mainland Scandinavian Adv–Vf order in adverbial clauses come from one author (Bergtóra Hanusardóttir, born 1946), but she also uses the Vf–Adv order in adverbial clauses, although much more rarely, and I do not have any examples from her of Adv–Vf order in bridge verb complements.

We can now try to compare the results of this survey with the results of the acceptability judgments summarized in (47) above. Such a comparison could then read like this:

(49)a. Whereas the Mainland Scandinavian order was preferred to the Icelandic order in all embedded clause types in the acceptability test, most of the writers surveyed use the Icelandic Vf–Adv order more frequently than the Mainland Scandinavian order in complements of bridge verbs. In other types of embedded clauses, however, the Mainland Scandinavian order is more common, although there is virtually no difference in adverbial clauses.[20]

b. Most writers use the Icelandic order in some types of embedded clauses, especially in bridge verb complements. Many writers also make considerable use of it in the complements of non-bridge verbs and at least some types of adverbial clauses, but many writers use it very rarely if at all in indirect questions and relative clauses.

c. Speakers seem to vary considerably in their acceptance of the Vf–Adv order.

d. Although there are some indications that there is a generational difference in the use of the Vf–Adv order, with the younger writers using it less frequently in some types of embedded clauses (especially indirect questions and relative clauses), it does not seem to be the case that there is a clear generation break such that the older generation has Icelandic verb movement grammar and the younger a Mainland Scandinavian non-movement grammar. Both orders are used frequently in the 19th and 20th centuries, although one of the oldest authors appears to use the Mainland Scandinavian order exclusively while another author, some 30 years younger, only uses the Icelandic order. Most writers mix the orders, however.[21]

The general conclusion, then, is that the Icelandic Vf–Adv order is still used to a considerable extent in written Faroese, especially in bridge verb complements. Although writers vary considerably in their usage, most of them mix the orders. There are some indications, however, that the Icelandic order is on the way out in written Faroese in indirect questions and relative clauses.[22] That is also what we found in the survey of judgments reported on in the preceding subsection.

4.3.1.4   *Accounting for the variation in Faroese*

The survey of this variation in Faroese might appear to suggest that the facts are just a mess. What kind of a coherent account can be given of a situation of this sort?

It is clear that traditional grammar would be tempted to attribute this phenomenon to Danish influence. But that is not an adequate explanation since the situation is clearly different from what one would find in Mainland Scandinavia. As we have seen, it is not the case that the speakers of Faroese are simply adopting the Danish non-movement grammar. They may very well do that in the long run, possibly prompted by Danish influence, but they have not done so yet. Instead, they accept verb movement in some types of embedded clauses more readily than in others and they also move their verbs in some types of embedded clauses more readily than in others (at least in the written language).

Some historical linguists might want to refer to this kind of situation as a "change in progress." It is important, however, to try to work out what that could mean. It makes sense if one is looking at the history of the language from the outside, as it were, that is the history of the E-language (external language) in the sense of Chomsky (1986). But it is not so obvious what such a statement could mean if one is thinking of linguistic change as a change in the grammars acquired by speakers. What kind of grammars are reflected by the Faroese facts – and how are they different from a typical Icelandic and Danish grammar, for instance?

While one might be tempted to describe the Faroese facts in terms of an optional verb movement, we have seen above that this is not an option within the version of the MP assumed here. As explained above, the finite verb will have to move out of the VP in a split IP language but it does not have to move to I in a language with a non-split IP and hence it cannot under economy conditions. But how is that compatible with the observed Faroese facts?

Let us take the bridge verb complements first. It is well known that bridge verb complements have various main clause properties, one such property being that they allow Topicalization rather freely. Since it is usually assumed that Topicalization in Germanic verb-second (V2) languages moves the fronted element to SpecCP and forces the finite verb to move to the following C-position to license this fronted element, the standard account of this is to say that bridge verb complements can have a double CP ("CP-recursion") and the fronted element moves to the specifier position of the lower CP and the finite verb to the lower C-position. This can be illustrated as in (54) with Danish examples (see, e.g., Vikner, 1995a, pp. 65 ff. and references cited there):

(50)

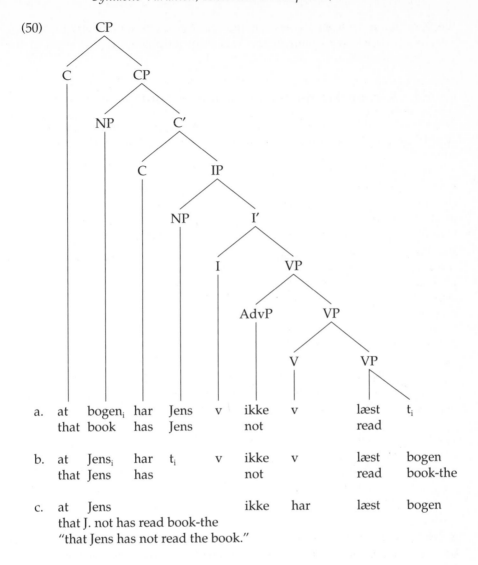

a. at   bogen; har   Jens   v   ikke   v   læst   t;
    that book   has   Jens   not   read

b. at   Jens;   har   t;   v   ikke   v   læst   bogen
    that Jens   has   not   read   book-the

c. at   Jens   ikke   har   læst   bogen
    that J. not has read book-the
    "that Jens has not read the book."

As shown here, the finite verb will precede a VP-adjoined adverb in bridge verb complements when an element is fronted to the (lower) SpecCP position. The object can only precede the finite verb when it has been fronted like that, whereas the subject will precede the finite verb whether or not it is in the canonical subject position SpecIP or fronted to SpecCP. Only in the latter case, however, will the finite verb move out of its VP in a non-split IP language like Danish. Hence the finite verb can either precede or follow a sentential adverb like the negation in subject-initial bridge verb complements but it will always precede such adverbs in object-initial bridge verb complements. This is illustrated in (50), whereas (51) is ungrammatical (with a fronted object and the finite verb in situ, following the negation):

(51) * . . . at   bogen   Jens ikke har læst
          that book-the Jens not   has read

This means that it is not the verb movement itself that is optional in bridge verb complements. What is "optional" is whether we have a topic or not. If we have a topic, it will have to be topicalized and then the finite verb has to move to the relevant C-position to "license" it.[23] In that sense the "extra structure" of embedded V2 is optional (in an embedded context you are not forced to have a topic although you can if you are in a bridge verb complement) but when it is present it forces verb movement.

Now although verb movement (i.e. V-to-C) is possible in Danish (and other Mainland Scandinavian) bridge verb complements, it is not the rule (see, e.g., Pedersen, 1996; Gregersen and Pedersen, 1997).

While one could technically account for the optionality of verb raising in Faroese bridge verb complements in a similar fashion, that does not seem satisfactory since for many speakers it is much more common than in verb raising in Danish bridge verb complements. Instead I want to argue for the following claim:

(52)   The data available to the child acquiring Faroese are ambiguous (or internally inconsistent) with respect to verb movement. The verbal morphology is in itself not rich enough to trigger a positive setting of the Split-IP Parameter (SIP). Yet the child will hear (and later read) a considerable number of sentences that can only be interpreted as involving V-to-T (finte verbs preceding sentential adverbs in non-V2 contexts). While these sentences will trigger a positive setting of the SIP, the child will also hear (and later read) a number of sentences where V-to-T should apply in a split IP language but does not. Hence (s)he will assume that two structures are possible in the language, namely a split IP and a non-split IP.

If this is the correct description of the scenario, the resulting grammar would be rather similar to the grammars described by proponents of the so-called Double Base Hypothesis. This hypothesis was originally proposed by Kroch (1989 – see also Kroch (2001) and references cited there) and first tried out by his students and colleagues in accounts of the historical development of Yiddish (Santorini, 1989) and Old English (e.g. Pintzuk, 1991). It has also been used to account for historical change in various languages, including the development from OV to VO orders in the history of Icelandic, for instance (see, e.g., Rögnvaldsson, 1994–95; and Hróarsdóttir, 1998). Furthermore, Rohrbacher (1999, p. 144) explicitly refers to it in his account of what he calls "residual V to I raising" in Faroese.

While the Double Base Hypothesis has mainly been used to account for historical changes that we cannot observe directly, as it were, I believe that the ongoing development in Faroese offers an interesting opportunity to see how changes of this kind actually occur. The reason is that here we can be sure who is the actual author of the various texts and we do not have to worry about the influence of scribes or earlier originals and the like. Even more importantly, of course, we can go and ask the relevant speakers about their judgments. The data surveyed in the preceding subsection suggest that this variation in verb movement has existed for at least two centuries. Furthermore, they indicate that the development may be coming to an end. The way this seems to be happening is that first the verb movement gets restricted to a subset of embedded clauses (cf. the reluctance of the youngest speakers/writers to use it in indirect questions and relative clauses). This indicates that the relevant speakers are not treating the two structures (the structures we have referred to as split and non-split IP) as functionally or semantically equivalent but they are re-interpreting them in some fashion. This is to be expected if "free variation" is an unnatural thing. But this will in turn mean that the children acquiring Faroese will get fewer and fewer examples suggesting that Faroese has a split IP and eventually verb raising will be lost since nothing indicates a split IP. The remaining examples of verb raising in embedded clauses will then be interpretable as instances of V-to-C in V2 contexts and then we will have the Mainland Scandinavian situation.

If this is the correct way of interpreting the development in Faroese, we might expect to find something similar in the development of the Mainland Scandinavian languages, namely that verb raising should not have disappeared at the same time as the verbal morphology was simplified. I will argue below that this seems indeed to be the case. Before we look into that, let us first look at apparent instances of verb-raising variation in Icelandic.

4.3.2   *Verb movement variation in Icelandic*

Although the Vf–Adv order is the general rule in all types of embedded clauses in Icelandic, it is possible to come up with examples of Adv–Vf in such clauses – and find them in texts. Thus, in the following examples, the b-versions are acceptable although the a-versions are the unmarked options (these examples are from a paper by Angantýsson (2001) or modeled on his examples):

(53)a.   Það   var   eitt   atriði   [sem hann **vissi ekki** á   prófinu]
 there was   one   item   that he   knew not   in exam-the

   b.   Það   var   eitt   atriði   [sem hann **ekki vissi** á   prófinu]
 there was   one   item   that he   not   knew in exam-the
 "There was one item that he did not know on the exam."

(54)a.   ... hið eina   [sem ég **hlaut aldrei**] var ...
 the only [thing] that I   got   never   was ...

b.   . . . hið eina   [sem ég **aldrei hlaut**] var . . .
     the only [thing]   that I   never got   was . . .
     ". . . the only thing that I never got was . . ."

(55)a.   . . . ef við **ljúkum ekki** verkinu í dag.
         if we finish   not job-the today

b.   . . . ef við **ekki ljúkum** verkinu í dag.
     if we not   finish   job-the today
     ". . . if we don't finish the job today."

(56)a.   Ég flyt   til Reykjavíkur [nema ég **geti ekki** selt jörðina]
         I   move to Reykjavík   unless I   can not   sell farm-the

b.   Ég flyt   til Reykjavíkur [nema ég **ekki geti** selt jörðina
     I   move to Reykjavík   unless I   not can sell farm-the
     "I move to Reykjavík unless I cannot sell the farm."

In a paper giving an overview of the possibilities of having an apparent Mainland Scandinavian word order in Icelandic embedded clauses, Angantýsson
(2001) shows that the Adv–Vf order is most easily acceptable in embedded
clauses of the type illustrated in the b-versions in (53)–(56). The optimal conditions can be characterized as follows:

(57)a.   The embedded clause exhibiting the Adv–Vf order is a relative clause,
         indirect question or an adverbial clause of some sort (e.g. temporal,
         conditional, or concessive).
     b.   The best examples typically have a stressed sentential adverb or an
         unstressed embedded subject (light or unstressed pronouns tend to
         be the best) or both.[24]

Now if the Bobaljik and Thráinsson account is correct, then the Icelandic
instances of the Adv–Vf order cannot be due to lack of verb movement out of
the VP: Icelandic has a rich verbal morphology that serves as an unambiguous
trigger for a positive setting of the SIP. Hence the finite verb is always forced
to move out of the VP. This means that it should always precede a sentential
adverb that is adjoined to the VP. Thus if the adverb is preceding the finite
verb in Icelandic it must be adjoined to a higher position. The TP is an obvious
choice if Bobaljik and Thráinsson are right in claiming that the finite verb does
not have to move higher than to T (except when it has some special business
higher up, like checking the features of a topic in a V2 environment). Thus the
relevant part of the structure of sentences like the ones in (53)–(56) could be
diagrammed as in (58):

(58)

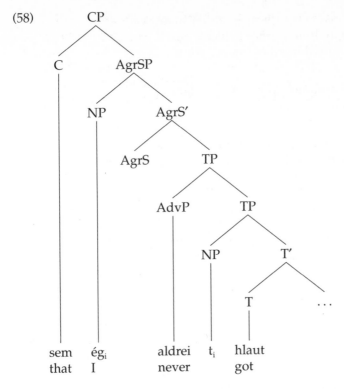

As explained in section 4.2.4 above, the AgrS could check necessary features with a verb that is (adjoined to) the head of its complement so no further raising is required. But since this adjunction site of the adverb is unusual or marked, it works best if the adverb is emphasized or focused in some sense (and/or the subject thus destressed).

Now it is not entirely clear why this positioning of sentential adverbs works best in this restricted set of embedded clauses, although it may have something to do with their role in discourse.[25] But as Angantýsson (2001) points out, this analysis makes an interesting prediction, if Bobaljik and Thráinsson (and Jonas, 1996b and others) are right in claiming that definite (or specific) subjects will typically move to SpecAgrSP whereas indefinite (or non-specific) subjects can stay in SpecTP. Thus there should be a contrast between the acceptability of sentences containing embedded clauses with the negation preceding the finite verb depending on the definiteness (or specificity) of the subject. This follows from the claim that in such sentences the negation preceding the finite verb is marking the left edge of the TP and thus a subject preceding it cannot be lower than in SpecAgrSP. This prediction seems to be borne out. Thus while all the versions of (59) are fine, (60c) is clearly worse than the others:

(59)a. Það var Hrafnkelssaga [sem hann **hafði ekki** lesið]
        it   was Hrafnkel's saga that he   not   had   read

   b. Það var Hrafnkelssaga [sem Haraldur **hafði ekki** lesið]
       it   was Hrafnkel's saga that Harold   had   not   read

   c. Það var Hrafnkelssaga [sem einhver   **hafði ekki** lesið]
       it   was Hrafnkel's saga that somebody had   not   read
       "It was the Saga of Hrafnkel that he/Harold/somebody had not
       read."

(60)a. Það var Hrafnkelssaga [sem hann **ekki hafði** lesið]
       it   was Hrafnkel's saga that he   not   had   read

   b. Það var Hrafnkelssaga [sem Haraldur **ekki hafði** lesið]
       it   was Hrafnkel's saga that Harold   not   had   read

   c. ?*Það var Hrafnkelssaga [sem einhver   **ekki hafði** lesið]
       it   was Hrafnkel's saga that somebody not   had   read

There would be no reason to expect this contrast if the finite verb was in situ in the sentences where it is preceded by the negation. Hence these facts support the analysis that Bobaljik and Thráinsson are forced to adopt here, namely that the verb must move out of the VP in all sentences in Icelandic and instances of Adv–Vf order are due to exceptional positioning of the adverb and not the verb.

4.4 The historical development reconsidered

As reviewed in section 4.2.1, it is typically assumed that the Mainland Scandinavian languages "lost" verb raising in embedded clauses roughly at the time when their verbal morphology was simplified. A closer look at the records indicates, however, that verb movement did not in fact disappear as soon as the verbal inflection was simplified. Thus Vikner (1997–8, p. 117) says, for instance, that according to his biconditional theory verb movement should have disappeared in Danish at least some 100–200 years earlier than it actually did. Besides, there are some indications that "residual verb movement" can still be found in Danish dialects (see Pedersen, 1996 and the example cited in (24) above; see also Gregersen and Pedersen, 1997).

    To the Tromsø-dialect examples of Vf–Adv order in embedded clauses cited above, one could add a couple of examples from Norwegian dialects given by Sandøy (2001, p. 139 – he only gives the Icelandic order since he is demonstrating its existence in Norwegian dialects "until our time" ("fram til vår tid") – I have added the Adv–Vf order for comparison and provided the translation):

(61)a. Dei måtte tilsetje ein fagmann [fordi   dei **kunne ikkje**
       they had-to hire   a   specialist because they could not
       greie   seg   åleine lenger]
       manage themselves alone anymore

b.   . . . [fordi   dei **ikkje kunne** greie   seg   åleine lenger]
. . . because they not   could manage themselves alone anymore
"They had to hire a specialist because they could not manage alone anymore."

(62)a.   Desse ungane i   klassen min [som **har**   **ikkje** lært   seg
these kids   in class-the my   that have not   taught themselves
gangetabellen   enno] . . .
multiplication-table-the yet

b.   . . . [som **ikkje har**   lært   seg
that not   have taught themselves
gangetabellen   enno]
multiplication-table-the yet
"These kids in my class, who haven't yet learned the multiplication table . . ."

Sandøy then remarks that the Adv–Vf order in sentences of this kind implies that the speaker is not presupposing the truth of the embedded clause. This suggests that the two different structures (a split IP and a non-split IP) may have survived side by side in these dialects because they acquired subtly different roles.

The development of subordinate clause word order has probably been studied even more in Swedish than the other Scandinavian languages (see e.g. Platzack, 1988a, 1988b; Falk, 1993). In Swedish the distinction between tense and agreement morphemes seems to be lost by the beginning of the 16th century (see, e.g., the overview in Vikner, 1997–8) and there are some indications that the frequency of verb raising in embedded clauses was declining already around 1500 (see, e.g., Platzack, 1988a, p. 232; Falk, 1993, p. 176). But this varies from author to authors. More importantly for our purposes, it seems that considerable evidence for verb raising in embedded clauses can still be found in the latter half of the 17th century. The following numbers from Platzack's papers indicate the average frequency of the "Icelandic" Vf–Adv order in embedded clauses in Swedish texts from three different periods:

(63)   authors born 1480–1530:   80%
authors born 1570–1600:   36%
authors born 1620–1665:   24%

These figures show that the verb raising order continued to be used in embedded clauses in written Swedish at least some 200 years after the verbal morphology was no longer an unambiguous trigger for a positive setting of the Split IP Parameter, although its frequency kept going down. That seems to be what we are now observing in Faroese. It is a development compatible with the Bobaljik and Thráinsson theorym as explained above, but very unexpected and hard to account for under any theory which predicts a direct biconditional relationship between rich verbal morphology and verb raising in embedded clauses.

4.5   Concluding remarks

In this paper I have tried to demonstrate how a fairly restrictive account in terms of the Minimalist Program rules out certain accounts of syntactic variation in the Scandinavian languages and forces a special kind of analysis of the obseved facts. I have then presented arguments for the correctness of this analysis – or rather for its superiority over previously proposed ones.

I would like to conclude by emphasizing that the analysis proposed here, and in the Bobaljik and Thráinsson paper that this chapter is based on to a large extent, only works because of its restrictiveness – and also because it is relatively old fashioned as minimalist analyses go. More specifically, it crucially has the following properties (as the observant reader has probably noticed already, although only some of these properties have been pointed out explicitly above):

(64)a.   The analysis only works because it assumes that functional categories do not come for free, as it were. Instead it maintains that the child acquiring language follows the Real Minimalist Principle (cf. Thráinsson, 1996, p. 261): Assume only those functional categories that you have evidence for.

    b.   The analysis only works because it assumes the economy principle that rules out optional movement: You don't move unless you have to (i.e. in order to check features).

    c.   The analysis only works because it assumes that (sentential) adverbs are adjuncts and do not head projections that form a part of the "spine" of the syntactic structure (contra Cinque, 1999, for instance).

    d.   The analysis only works because it accepts the (old) distinction between XP and X' and the restriction on adjunction which assumes that heads adjoin to heads and maximal categories to maximal projections and not to X'.

    e.   The analysis only works because it assumes that negation of the Scandinavian kind is adjoined like other adverbs and does not project a NegP (which forms a part of the spine of the syntactic structure).

The main reason for this restrictiveness, or "minimalistic minimalism," is the fact that while a more complex mechanism will obviously allow for a more detailed description of the observed facts, it makes the account less explanatory. It is the well-known conflict between description and explanation (see, e.g., the discussion in section 1 of Epstein et al., 1996).

Notes

1   I am indebted to Jonathan D. Bobaljik for joint work on some of the theoretical issues discussed here, to many linguists for laying out the crucial facts reported on

here and attempting to explain them, including Christer Platzack, Anders Holmberg, Sten Vikner, and Bernhard Rohrbacher, to Dianne Jonas for suggesting that Faroese was even more interesting than I had thought, to Hjalmar P. Petersen, Jógvan í Lon Jacobsen, and Zakaris Hansen for joint work on Faroese, and to the Icelandic Science Foundation for supporting my work on Faroese.

2 As the reader will see, the auxiliary verb *havde* "had" also follows the negation in these embedded clauses in Danish. In general, there is no difference between main verbs and auxiliary verbs in this respect in the Scandinavian languages: finite main verbs behave like finite auxiliaries and non-finite auxiliaries (e.g. auxiliaries preceded by other auxiliaries) behave like non-finite main verbs (see, e.g., the examples in Vikner, 1995a, 1995b). Hence examples with "moved" auxiliaries will sometimes be used as evidence for V-to-I movement below. In section 2 I will review the reasons why V-to-I movement has been assumed to be a plausible account of the position of the finite verb in Icelandic.

3 Exceptions to this last statement will be discussed in section 3 below.

4 The discussion here is restricted to V-to-I movement in embedded clauses since the so-called V2 ("verb second") phenomenon in main clauses makes it impossible to determine whether "independent" V-to-I takes place in these clauses. The V2 phenomenon is standardly believed to involve V-to-C (see e.g. Vikner, 1995a; Holmberg and Platzack, 1995, and the papers in Lightfoot and Hornstein, 1994).

5 Vikner restricts himself to (Germanic) SVO-languages since it is more difficult to determine the position of the finite verb in SOV-languages, like German and Dutch, for instance (see also Bobaljik and Thráinsson, 1998, p. 66). In addition, other aspects of word order are more controversial in these languages. I will follow Vikner's example and leave the SOV-languages out of the discussion for the most part here. In fact, I will almost only discuss data from the Scandinavian languages, my main excuse being limitations of space. More languages are discussed in Bobaljik and Thráinsson (1998). As explained there, the Bobaljik and Thráinsson account makes parallel predictions about SOV languages and SVO languages in principle.

6 They suggest such an analysis for English (Holmberg and Platzack, 1995, pp. 75–76), for instance, and they also mention this possibility for the Mainland Scandinavian languages (1995, p. 76), although these languages never have any kind of overt agreement.

7 I do not know anything about the relative frequency of V-to-I movement in embedded clauses in the Kronoby dialect of Finland Swedish, but it would be interesting to look into that.

8 Simplified, for instance, by omitting the commonly assumed AgrOP (between T and VP), since it is unimportant for the discussion below.

9 Note also that if languages with a split IP have an AgrOP as well as AgrSP, as assumed by Bobaljik and Thráinsson (e.g. 1998, p. 62), then that means that a verb in situ in a split IP language cannot even check features against T since the VP will not be a complement of T (although it is in the (simplified) diagram in (28) where the AgrOP is left out). In such a language, then, movement to T will be forced even if there is no agreement feature to check. This may explain the V-movement found in control infinitives in Icelandic (see Bobaljik and Thráinsson, 1998, p. 63). Note also that in V2-environments the finite verb will have to move higher than to T, presumably all the way to C (cf. Bobaljik and Thráinsson, 1998, p. 44; see also the discussion in section 3.1.4 below).

10 As Bobaljik and Thráinsson note (1998, p. 41), this concept of the relationship between verbal morphology and the corresponding functional projections is consistent with both a lexicalist approach and a distributed morphology.

11   According to Bobaljik (1995), Jonas (1996a, 1996b), Bobaljik and Jonas (1996), Thráinsson (1996), and Bobaljik and Thráinsson (1998), Transitive Expletive Constructions and full-NP Object Shift would also constitute relevant syntactic evidence here. Since these constructions are apparently quite rare (and Object Shift does not seem to occur at all in Modern Faroese) they can hardly be considered "salient syntactic evidence" and hence they will be ignored in the following discussion.

12   The percentages in this table are to be interpreted as follows: There were 54 "judgments" of sentences involving the Icelandic order (Vf–Adv) in bridge verb complements, that is 3 different sentences × 18 subjects; 83 percent of these judgments were positive. Similarly, there were 90 judgments of sentences involving the Icelandic order in non-bridge verb complements (5 different sentences × 18 subjects); 31 percent of these were positive.

13   The picture is obviously not as clear as Jonas had assumed since in Petersen's study most of the subjects accepted *some* examples of non-bridge verb complements with the Icelandic. But Petersen's conclusion (2000, p. 80) that there were "no dialect differences with regard to V-to-I movement" is nevertheless a bit misleading for two reasons. First, Petersen apparently means that there are no *geographic* dialects in Faroese w.r.t. verb movement. That may very well be true, although Petersen only had one or two speakers from some of the dialect areas, so statisticians are likely to find this conclusion unwarranted. Second, Petersen's results do indeed suggest that there *is* a dialectal (or at least idiolectal!) difference among speakers w.r.t. to the acceptance of the Icelandic order in the complements of non-bridge verbs. Third, Petersen's investigation does not rule out the possibility that there is a generational difference among speakers of Faroese with respect to verb movement since he only tested one age group. We will return to that question below.

14   Most of the students were about 20 years old at the time. The testing was administered by the Faroese linguist Zakaris Svabo Hansen and I thank him for his assistance.

15   Here I am only including the 14 students who judged two versions (Vf–Adv and Adv–Vf) of each embedded clause type, but the total number of participants was close to 80. The number of sentences of each type considered here ranged from two to four.

16   Here I am only including the 14 students who judged two versions (Vf–Adv and Adv–Vf) of all the relevant sentences testing word order in embedded clauses. The total number of participants in the survey was much higher, or close to 80. The number of sentences of each type considered here ranged from two to four.

17   Examples include German adverbial clauses introduced by *denn* vs. *weil* "because"; Danish *thi* vs. *fordi* "because," for instance.

18   This summary is mainly based on the results of my own survey but it is also compatible with the results reported by Jonas (1996b) and Petersen (2000).

19   For a more detailed presentation of the facts from this survey see, for example, Thráinsson (2001b, 2001c). Note, for instance, that translated texts are left out of the discussion here but some are included in the papers referred to.

20   As pointed out several times above, this is probably misleading since adverbial clauses are likely to differ in this respect.

21   It could also be mentioned here that the linguist Hjalmar P. Petersen (born 1962) has translated a novel from Icelandic. A survey of his use of the Icelandic and Mainland Scandinavian orders in this translation indicates that he uses the Mainland Scandinavian order almost exclusively (I found two examples of the Icelandic Vf–Adv order and they were both in bridge verb complements. Another translator, Martin Næs (born 1953) uses the Icelandic order most of the time in bridge verb

complements and also in the majority of cases in non-bridge verb complements less frequently in other types of embedded clauses in a translation from Icelandic (see, e.g., Thráinsson, 2001b, 2001c).

22   It could be mentioned here that a preliminary survey of the use of these two different word orders in the Faroese TV news indicated that there the Icelandic order is mainly used in adverbial clauses. No examples of the Icelandic order were found in complements of non-bridge verbs (10 of the Mainland Scandinavian one, on the other hand) and it also appeared to be very rare in bridge verb complements (one example of the Icelandic order vs. six of the Mainland Scandinavian one). This is rather suggestive, although the material was too limited (no examples of either order were found in indirect questions and relative clauses, for instance).

23   The exact nature of topic and Topicalization need not concern us here. What is clear is that it has to be licensed by the verb in the Germanic V2 languages, presumably by the checking of a feature in a spec-head relationship between the fronted element and the finite verb in C.

24   Actually, the requirement that the embedded subject be a light pronoun is not equally strong in all types of embedded clauses. Thus (ia) seems slightly better than (ib) (cf. (54) and (56):

  (i)a.   ... hið eina   [sem Haraldur **aldrei hlaut**] var ...
         the only [thing] that Harold   never got   was

   b.   Stína flytur til Reykjavíkur [nema Haraldur **ekki geti** selt jörðina]
        Stina moves to Reykjavik   unless Harold   not can sell farm-the

25   Interestingly, Angantýsson (2001) shows that the Adv–Vf order works best in those types of embedded clauses in Icelandic that are least likely to allow embedded Topicalization (Topicalization not being restricted to bridge verb complements in Icelandic, as has frequently been pointed out, see, e.g., Vikner (1995a, pp. 80 ff. and references cited there)).

References

Andreasen, P. and Dahl, Á. (1997). *Mállæra*. Tórshavn: Føroya Skúlabókagrunnur.

Angantýsson, Á. (2001). Skandinavísk orðaröð í íslenskum aukasetningum. *Íslenskt mál*, 23.

Bobaljik, J. D. (1995). *Morphosyntax: the syntax of verbal inflection*. Doctoral dissertation, MIT.

Bobaljik, J. D. and Jonas, D. (1996). Subject positions and the roles of TP. *Linguistic Inquiry*, 27, 195–236.

Bobaljik, J. and Thráinsson, H. (1998). Two heads aren't always better than one. *Syntax*, 1, 37–71.

Chomsky, N. (1981). *Lectures on Government and Binding*. Dordrecht: Foris.

Chomsky, N. (1986). *Knowledge of Language: Its nature, origin and use*. New York: Praeger.

Chomsky, N. (1991). Some notes on economy of derivation and representation. In Robert Freidin (ed.), *Principles and Parameters in Comparative Grammar* (pp. 417–54). Cambridge, MA: MIT Press. (Also published with slight revisions in Chomsky, 1995, pp. 129–66.)

Chomsky, N. (1993). A minimalist program for linguistic theory. In K. Hale and S. J. Keyser (eds.), *The View from Building 20: Essays in linguistics in honor of Sylvain Bromberger* (pp. 1–52). Cambridge, MA: MIT Press.

Chomsky, N. (1995). *The Minimalist Program*. Cambridge, MA: MIT Press.

Cinque, G. (1999). *Adverbs and Functional Heads: A cross-linguistic perspective*. Oxford: Oxford University Press.

Diesing, M. (1997). Yiddish VP order and the typology of NP movement in Germanic. *Natural Language and Linguistic Theory*, 15, pp. 369–427.

Epstein, S. D., Thráinsson, H., and Zwart, C. J.-W. (1996). Introduction. In W. Abraham, S. D. Epstein, H. Thráinsson, and C. J.-W. Zwart (eds.), *Minimal Ideas: Syntactic studies in the minimalist framework*. (pp. 1–66). Amsterdam: John Benjamins.

Falk, C. (1993). *Non-Referential Subjects in the History of Swedish*. Doctoral dissertation, University of Lund, Lund.

Gregersen, F. and Pedersen, I. L. (1997). Hovedsætningsordstilling i underordnede sætninger. *Dansk folkemål*, 39, 55–112.

Hagström, B. (1967). *Ändelsevokalerna i färöiskan. En fonetisk-fonologisk studie*. Stockholm Studies in Scandinavian Philology 6. Stockholm: Almqvist & Wiksell.

Henriksen, J. (2000). *Orðalagslæra*. Tórshavn: Sprotin.

Holmberg, A. and Platzack, C. (1990). On the role of Inflection in Scandinavian Syntax. In W. Abraham, W. Kosmeijer, and E. Reuland (eds.), *Issues in Germanic Syntax* (pp. 93–118). Berlin: Mouton de Gruyter.

Holmberg, A. and Platzack, C. (1995). *The Role of Inflection in Scandinavian Syntax*. Oxford: Oxford University Press.

Hróarsdóttir, T. (1998). *Setningafræðilegar breytingar á 19. öld. Þróun þriggja málbreytinga*. Málvísindastofnun Háskóla Íslands, Reykjavík.

Jonas, D. (1996a). Clause structure, expletives and verb movement. In W. Abraham, S. D. Epstein, H. Thráinsson, and C. J.-W. Zwart (eds.), *Minimalist Ideas* (pp. 168–88). Amsterdam: John Benjamins.

Jonas, D. (1996b). *Clause Structure and Verb Syntax in Scandinavian and English*. PhD dissertation, Harvard University, Cambridge, MA.

Kosmeijer, W. (1986). The status of the finite inflection in Icelandic and Swedish. *Working Papers in Scandinavian Syntax*, 26.

Kroch, A. S. (1989). Reflexes of grammar in patterns of language change. *Language Variation and Change*, 1, 199–244.

Kroch, A. S. (2001). Syntactic change. In M. Baltin and C. Collins (eds.), *The Handbook of Contemporary Syntactic Theory* (pp. 699–729). Oxford: Blackwell.

Lasnik, H. (1981). Restricting the theory of transformations: a case study. In N. Hornstein and D. Lightfoot (eds.), *Explanation in Linguistics: The Logical Problem of Language Acquisition* (pp. 152–73). London: Longman.

Lightfoot, David, and Hornstein, N. (eds.) (1994). *Verb Movement*. Cambridge: Cambridge University Press.

Pedersen, I. L. (1996). "Der kan jo være nogen der kan itte tåle det." Om hovedsætningsordstilling i bisætninger. In B. J. Nielsen and I. L. Pedersen (eds.), *Studier i talesprogsvariation og sprogkontakt*. Til Inger Eskjær på halvfjerdsårsdagen den 20 maj 1996. (pp. 242–51). Copenhagen: Reitzel.

Petersen, H. P. (2000). IP or TP in Moderne Faroese. *Working Papers in Scandinavian Syntax*, 66, 75–83.

Pintzuk, S. (1991). *Phrase structures in competition: variation and change in Old English word order*. Doktorsritgerð, University of Pennsylvania, Philadelphia.

Platzack, C. (1988a). The emergence of a word order difference in Scandinavian subordinate clauses. *McGill Working Papers in Linguistics*, Special Issue on Comparative Germanic Syntax, pp. 215–38.

Platzack, C. (1988b). Den centralskandinaviska bisatsordföljdens framväxt. *Studier i svensk språkhistoria*, pp. 241–55. Lundi.

Platzack, C. and A. Holmberg. (1989). The role of AGR and finiteness. *Working Papers in Scandinavian Syntax, 43*, 51–76.

Pollock, J.-Y. (1989). Verb movement, universal grammar, and the structure of IP. *Linguistic Inquiry, 20*, 365–424.

Roberts, I. (1985). Agreement parameters and the development of English modal auxiliaries. *Natural Language and Linguistic Theory, 3*, 21–58.

Roberts, I. (1993). *Verbs and Diachronic Syntax: A comparative history of English and French.* Dordrecht: Kluwer.

Rohrbacher, B. (1994). *The Germanic languages and the full paradigm: A theory of V to I raising.* Doctoral dissertation, University of Massachusetts, Amherst.

Rohrbacher, B. (1999). *Morphology-Driven Syntax: A theory of V to I raising and Pro-Drop.* Amsterdam: John Benjamins. (Revised version of Rohrbacher's (1994) dissertation.)

Rögnvaldsson, E. (1994–95). Breytileg orðaröð í sagnlið. *Íslenskt mál, 16–17*, 27–66.

Sandøy, H. (2001). Færøsk i vestnordisk språkhistorie. In K. Braunmüller and J. í L. Jacobsen (eds.), *Moderne lingvistiske teorier og færøsk* (pp. 125–54). Oslo: Novus.

Santorini, B. (1989). *Generalization of the verb-second constraint in the history of Yiddish.* Doctoral dissertation, University of Pennsylvania, Philadelphia.

Thráinsson, H. (1996). On the (Non-)Universality of Functional Categories. In W. Abraham, S. D. Epstein, H. Thráinsson and C. J.-W. Zwart (eds.), *Minimal Ideas. Syntactic Studies in the Minimalist Framework* (pp. 253–81). Amsterdam: John Benjamins.

Thráinsson, H. (1999). Um áhrif dönsku á íslensku og færeysku. In M. Snædal and T. Sigurðardóttir (eds.), *Frændafundur 3* (pp. 116–30). Reykjavík: Háskólaútgáfan.

Thráinsson, H. (2001a). Object Shift and Scrambling. In M. Baltin and C. Collins (eds.), *Handbook of Contemporary Syntactic Theory* (pp. 148–202). Oxford: Blackwell.

Thráinsson, H. (2001b). Syntactic Theory for Faroese and Faroese for Syntactic Theory. In Kurt Braunmüller and J. í L. Jacobsen (eds.), *Moderne lingvistiske teorier og færøsk* (pp. 89–124). Oslo: Novus.

Thráinsson, H. (2001c). Um sagnbeygingu, sagnfærslu og setningagerð í færeysku og fleiri málum. *Íslenskt mál, 23.*

Thráinsson, H., H. P. Petersen, J. í L. Jacobsen, and Z. Hansen (2002). *Faroese: An overview and reference grammar.* Linguistic Institute, University of Iceland, Reykjavík.

Trosterud, T. (1989). The null subject parameter and the new Mainland Scandinavian word order: a possible counterexample from a Norwegian dialect. In J. Niemi (ed.), *Papers from the 11th Scandinavian Conference of Linguistics, 1* (pp. 87–100). Joensuu: University of Joensuu.

Vikner, S. (1995a). *Verb Movement and Expletive Subjects in the Germanic Languages.* Oxford: Oxford University Press. (Revised version of Vikner's (1990) dissertation.)

Vikner, S. (1995b). V°-to-I° movement and inflection for person in all tenses. *Working Papers in Scandinavian Syntax, 55*, 1–27.

Vikner, S. (1997). The interpretation of object shift, optimality theory and minimalism. *Working Papers in Scandinavian Syntax, 60*, 1–24.

Vikner, S. (1997–98). V°-til-I° flytning og personfleksion i alle tempora. *Íslenskt mál, 19–20*, 85–132.

Weyhe, E. (1996). Bendingarmunur í føroyskum málførum. *Íslenskt mál, 18*, 71–118.

Chapter five

Phrase Structure

Robert A. Chametzky

You can't have everything. Where would you put it?
Steven Wright

5.1 About what we were talking

You might think that you are about to read a chapter about how, in the Minimalist Program, constituents are built up, X-Bar relations are derived, and heads, complements, and specifiers are ordered; in short, a chapter about phrase structure within minimalist syntax. Well, you are not. What with the respective titles of the chapter and of the book that contains it, you could be forgiven for having drawn such a conclusion. Nonetheless, this inference, no matter how defensible, is also defeasible. How and why such inferential processes do what they do (and don't) is also – though somewhat less surprisingly – not what the chapter is about. Instead of these – or infinitely many other – topics, the chapter considers phrase structure, minimalist syntax, and why you can have one or the other, but (probably) not both. So, while the "optimally relevant" conclusion is not right, it is not so far off afterall, and a slightly more cooperatively chosen chapter title (see below) might have avoided the whole inferential garden path. But that would have been a lot less fun.

The chapter has three (pretty obvious) parts: the first is on *phrase structure,* the second on *minimalist syntax,* and the third on why these two have something of the form of "thesis" and "antithesis" but notably fail to come together in a glorious, transcendent, "synthesis."[1] The idea is that the first two sections provide us with the "common ground" understandings with which we will work in the third section. We briefly preview each section below. I suppose that readers should also be forewarned that this is a *theoretical* chapter, and that when I use this term, I *really, really* mean it. So: no natural language data or analyses play any role in what follows. Chametzky (1994, 1995, 1996, 2000) provide exemplars of theoretical work of this sort.

5.1.1   *Bauplan*

In section 5.2, "Phrase structure theory," we discuss the concept "phrase structure." We discuss what this term means in the Principles and Parameters
(P&P) approach to syntax out of which minimalism has grown, and how it has
a somewhat different sense within at least some canonical minimalist work
(e.g. Chomsky, 1995) from that which it has in earlier P&P research (e.g. Speas,
1990). We also take note of some things which "phrase structure" in this tradition does not denote, but which it can or does denote elsewhere. Our goal,
immodestly enough, is to try and determine what is required of an approach
to syntax such that it should thereby be termed *phrase structural*. Here and
throughout, I will draw on, and refer to, Chametzky (2000).

In section 5.3, "Minimalist syntax," we consider what a "minimalist syntax"
is or might be. In addition to the obvious canonical statements of the Minimalist
Program (Chomsky, 1995, 2000, 2001), we will look at Martin and Uriagereka
(2000), Epstein, Groat, Kawashima, and Kitahara (1998), and Epstein and
Hornstein (1999). Taking off from Martin and Uriagereka's identification of a
"strong minimalist thesis" and a "weak minimalist thesis," we suggest a third
"empowered minimalist thesis," and this propels an extended analysis of some
current minimalist thinking; specifically, analyses are given of c-command
(from Chomsky, 2000), Merge, and Adjuncts (both from Chomsky, 2001). There
will not be anything as provocative, or probably pointless, as a definition of
"minimalist syntax," but some conceptual clarification can be claimed.

Section 5.4, "Not in my bare theory," makes an argument that *minimalist syntax
is not phrase structural* (there's the non-misleading, non-fun chapter title). In so
doing, it takes the conclusions of the previous two sections with respect to "phrase
structure" and "minimalist syntax" as its starting point. We begin with the conclusion of Chametzky (2000), wherein the non-phrase structural nature of minimalist syntax is (to my knowledge) first suggested. We add a new argument,
one I call, with startling straightforwardness, the modus tollens argument (1):

(1) I.   If there are Lexical Projections, then there are Functional Projections.
    II.   There are no Functional Projections.
    III.   Therefore, there are no Lexical Projections.

Premise I – the *Generalization Hypothesis* (GH) (see Chametzky, 2000, pp. 18 ff.
for discussion) – is introduced in Chomsky (1986a, p. 3), where it is suggested
that "the optimal hypothesis is that" the system regulating Lexical Categories
"extend[s] to the nonlexical categories as well." To my knowledge, this brief
statement comprises the entire theoretical defense of the GH in the literature.
Though brief, it is compelling, and only more so within the minimalist environment as we here understand this latter.

For Premise II we adopt the arguments and analyses, though not the conclusions, of Chametzky (2000, pp. 22–32). That work (correctly) accepts Grimshaw's
(1991, pp. 39–41) arguments which lead her to conclude that "[f]unctional
heads have no selectional powers at all," and then goes on to show that

Grimshaw's "projectionist" alternative "is unsound conceptually and technically flawed" (Chametzky, 2000, p. 29). At that point, instead of recognizing and accepting that this leaves us with no theory of Functional Projections (hence no Functional Projections), a "third way" based on earlier work by Lebeaux (1988) was sought. We now reject this suggestion; though rather too embryonic for detailed evaluation, like most "third ways" it appears a largely chimerical product of wishful thinking, and, insofar as it is evaluable, we argue that it does not comport with minimalist theorizing.

Having established (well, argued for) our premises, our conclusion follows immediately. And an immediate consequence of our modus tollens is that minimalist syntax is not phrase structural, as there are now no phrasal structures left in minimalist syntax.

We then turn to Collins (2001) and Collins and Ura (2001), works that independently come to the same conclusion we do vis-à-vis phrase structure in minimalist syntax (viz., there isn't any). These works are more concerned than we are with showing how one actually could do some non-phrase structural minimalist syntax, and rather less concerned than we are with arguing that one merely should do so.

We conclude by recognizing possible opposing conclusions to our story, including another modus tollens, no less, (2). *De gustibus non est disputandum?*

> (2)I.   If syntax is minimalist, then there is no phrase structure.
> II.   There *is* phrase structure.
> III.   Therefore, syntax is not minimalist.

5.2   Phrase structure theory

Everyone agrees that sentences are organized. "Phrase Structure" (PS) is one hypothesis about the nature of that organization. PS organizes sentences in terms of constituent hierarchies. PS derives from the American Structuralists' practice of immediate constituent (IC) analysis, the idea behind which was an iterative part/whole analysis of a linguistic string (see Chametzky, 2000, and references cited therein). Within generative grammar, including P&P work, the somewhat informal practice of IC analysis has generally been theoretically reconstructed in terms of (tree) *nodes* bearing (syntactic category) *labels*. This is neither entirely innocent nor inevitable, as, on the one hand, Chomsky (1995) eliminates (trees and) nodes[2] and, on the other, within IC analysis there was nothing that obviously corresponded to labels; we return to this later in section 5.3.3, when discussing Collins (2001).

5.2.1   *Alphabet soup 1: PS in P&P*

In P&P work, there is a further theoretical dimension to PS. PS is typically taken to be "lexical-entry-driven" (Borer, 1994), and PS is claimed to be "projected from the lexicon" (Speas, 1990). To explicate these somewhat gnomic bits of technicalese, I allow myself an extended quote from Chametzky:

> The guiding idea here is that there must be some systematic relation between individual lexical requirements (i.e., argument structure) and syntactic structure – lexical items cannot appear in arbitrary places in a well-formed sentence – and that characterizing this relation is to some degree what the theory of PS is about and for.... The reasoning behind this view is pretty familiar and clear. We are interested in what one knows when one knows a language. Part of that knowledge is knowledge of lexical items. Part of what it means to know a lexical item is to know the particular restrictions that item carries with it in terms of what it can or must cooccur with. This sort of lexical knowledge is not, strictly, grammatical knowledge, and has to be rendered in a format appropriate to (knowledge of) the grammar, given that grammar is the means by which lexical information is made recoverable for wider cognition (i.e., thought). In the P&P tradition, this systematic grammatical format is PS.   (Chametzky, 2000, p. 9)

So, within this P&P tradition, PS is both a strictly syntactic hypothesis postulating constituent structures and categories and also an *interface* hypothesis regulating the relation between the lexicon and the grammar proper. This, too, is neither entirely innocent nor inevitable, and we return to it below in discussing the Minimalist Program of Chomsky (1995).

The "lexical-entry-driven" approach to PS goes along with the program of "X-Bar reduction" which Stowell (1981) began and Speas (1990) essentially completed. Both of these were made possible by Chomsky's (1965) introduction of an independent lexicon. With this introduction, the grammar now contained a massive redundancy, as both phrase structure rules and subcategorization frames specified the same combinatoric information. In order to reduce the redundancy, one could try to eliminate either the phrase structure rules or the subcategorization frames. The "X-Bar reduction" program seeks to eliminate the rules,[3] arriving ultimately at "a theory of projection from the lexicon in which the only restriction imposed by X-Bar theory is the restriction that sentences have hierarchical structure, and that all structure is projected from a head. All other restrictions on domination relations are to be captured in other modules of grammar" (Speas, 1990, p. 55).

We can now see that the concept *head* is central to the P&P approach to PS; yet, oddly, *head* is a concept that is not native to PS. As to its centrality within P&P:

> A Head is generally taken to be the lexical item which determines the syntactic nature of a larger unit (a phrase) of which the Head is a part. Typically, a Head is taken to determine the syntactic category of the larger unit, to be a mandatory constituent of that phrase, and to determine to some degree what else, if anything, may or must also occur in the phrase.   (Chametzky, 2000, p. 15)

As to its non-native status, we need to analyze a little more fully and explicitly what a PS based approach to syntax is – and is not. As stated above, PS claims that sentences are organized in terms of constituent hierarchies, and P&P

reconstructs this idea in terms of nodes bearing labels, regulated by (the remnants of) X-Bar theory. Thus, the basic building blocks for syntax on this view are configurational position and word class membership, and all syntactically relevant concepts must be statable in a vocabulary built up from these basics. In particular, any *relational* concept must be so statable – thus the classic definitions of Subject and Direct Object as, respectively, NP immediately dominated by S and NP immediately dominated by VP (see Chametzky, 2000, p. 26).[4] Now, *head* is precisely a relational concept, one that is, moreover, imported from a relational theory, viz. Dependency Theory (see Chametzky, 2000, pp. 3–6, and references cited).[5] So, in order to coherently make use of such a concept, a PS analyst must provide (or have been provided with) a suitable reconstruction couched in the favored vocabulary.

We should take note of the fact that something like this idea was presented close to 40 years ago, by Postal (1964, p. 27) who argued that Harris (1946, 1951) attempted to reconstruct the notion *Head* in his substitutability equations by introducing "raised superscripts." More to the point, Postal argued that if Harris's move succeeded, then "we would be forced to reject a PSG [phrase structure grammar] interpretation for Harris equations involving superscripts and say that these involved some other type of . . . system." In other words, phrase structure grammars, by definition, cannot reconstruct the relational notion *head*. This is slightly different from our point in that Postal is discussing phrase structure grammars, that is systems of phrase structure rules; however, this leads nicely into our next brief topic, other uses of the term "phrase structure."

5.2.2   "Elsewhere"

Ever since its introduction by Chomsky in the 1950s, "phrase structure" has been a central part of ongoing mathematical work in formal language theory, work which explores rule systems of various types (i.e. with various restrictions on the form of rule allowed), the "languages" (generally, sets of symbol strings) which these systems generate/accept/enumerate, and relations between these rule systems and other formal devices (e.g. automata). This work is pursued today mainly by computer scientists and computational linguists. The central question of concern to (non-computational) linguists has been the (formal) (in)adequacy of phrase structure grammars for the description of natural language.

"Phrase structure" is also part of the name(s) of a family of current approaches to natural language syntax, viz. Generalized Phrase Structure Grammar; Head-driven Phrase Structure Grammar; Generalized Generalized Phrase Structure Grammar. These approaches eschew transformations (viz. a "movement rule" which maps one phrase structural object to another) while typically making use of explicit syntactic (phrase structure) rules and clinging to the labeled tree as the basic syntactic object. In this work there is also often some attention to mathematical dimensions of the inquiry, for example are the languages such grammars generate/accept/enumerate "context-free" or is there some ostensible "parsing" or "computability" advantage to the approach?

Other than the shared commitment to the labeled tree (as a theoretical descendent of IC analysis), neither of these sorts of (related) inquiries really has much to do with the P&P use of the term "phrase structure." This in itself is neither good nor bad, but probably needs to be made explicit, in order that confusions and pointless "debates" be avoided. We move now to another distinction between PS in P&P and PS elsewhere, this time in the Minimalist Program (MP) of Chomsky (1995).

5.2.3   *Alphabet soup 2: PS in MP*

As we have seen above, PS in P&P is both a "pure" syntactic proposal, hypothesizing labeled constituent hierarchies, and also an *interface* proposal, regulating the relation of the lexicon and the syntax, on account of being a "lexical-entry driven" proposal in which structure is "projected from the lexicon." In MP, the claims are put forward that "phrase structure theory is essentially 'given' on grounds of virtual conceptual necessity" (Chomsky, 1995, p. 249) and that "we may be able to eliminate the theory of phrase structure entirely, deriving its properties on principled grounds" (1995, p. 378). It seems, however, that MP is here referring only to the syntactic portion, and not the interface aspect, of what in earlier P&P work were together called "phrase structure theory." In Chametzky (2000), this interface aspect is called "structuralization/argument alignment" and it is observed that

> [w]hat is, perhaps, distinctive of MP is that it separates these two inquiries (syntactic objects and their construction and structuralization/argument alignment, respectively) and calls the first "phrase structure theory".... Whether this separation is a theoretical advance or not is unclear. That the terminological move may create confusion, and certainly changes the subject, is, once noticed, undoubtedly somewhat clearer.   (Chametzky, 2000, p. 133)

And again, this in itself is neither good nor bad, but probably needs to be made explicit, in order that confusions and pointless "debates" be avoided.

5.2.4   *What have we learned?*

Let us sum up. In order to be a PS theory, then, the one essential commitment has to be to organizing sentences in terms of constituent hierarchies. This typically takes the form of trees, constructed from nodes and labels, though this is not essential. Historically, and down to the present, this commitment has often been found with a reliance on and interest in rules of a certain form, but this is also non-essential. In P&P, the commitment has been part of a theory of the lexicon/syntax interface, but this, too, seems inessential. As in any theoretical inquiry, the analyst is limited to the basic vocabulary for the essentials and what can be constructed from that basic vocabulary. We move on now to minimalist syntax.[6]

5.3   Minimalist syntax

What makes a syntactic proposal/analysis/theory "minimalist" in the favored sense? Well, for one thing, "[i]t is a misunderstanding to contrast 'minimalism and X' where X is some theoretical conception (Optimality Theory, Lexicalism, etc.). X may be pursued with minimalist goals, or not" (Chomsky, 2000, p. 141, n. 13). And, for another, "[t]here are minimalist questions, but no minimalist answers, apart from those found in pursuing the program: perhaps that it makes no sense, or that it makes sense, but is premature" (Chomsky, 2000, p. 92). So, minimalism perhaps might be better thought of as a Koan or a Way rather than as a Twelve-Step Program. Be that as it may, we can get somewhat more concrete and positive. Chomsky writes of minimalism that:

> [i]ts task is to examine every device (principle/idea, ...) that is employed in characterizing languages to determine to what extent it can be eliminated in favor of a principled account in terms of general conditions of computational efficiency and the interface condition that the [language] organ must satisfy for it to function at all. Put differently, the goal is to determine just what aspects of the structure and use of language are specific to the language faculty, hence lacking principled explanation at this level.   (Chomsky, 2001, p. 3)

Minimalist syntax, then, seeks to invoke elements and operations only to the extent that such elements and operations are made necessary either by the interface of language with external systems (e.g. sensorimoter and conceptual-intentional) or by general design considerations (e.g. concerning complexity; see Chomsky, 2000, pp. 99–100). Minimalist syntax requires radical rethinking. But how should we approach this? We shall examine some ideas about how.

5.3.1   *Two theses of minimalism: Martin and Uriagereka*

Martin and Uriagereka (2000, p. 1) propose two minimalist theses, a *methodological minimalism* or "weak minimalist thesis" and an *ontological minimalism* or "strong minimalist thesis." I think this bifurcation, while insightful and useful, is not complete. I suggest in addition that there is something we might call (so that Martin and Uriagereka do not have all the good names) a *deontological minimalism* or "empowered minimalist thesis." The problem with Martin and Uriagereka's division is that the weak version – "[t]he drive for simple and nonredundant theories of the world" – is, they say, "business as usual," while their approach to the strong thesis – the hypothesis that language shows "optimal design ([in] meeting the demands of interface specifications) ..." – is "the idea that a good research strategy in our early exploration ... is ... to seek answers and to ground 'economy' explanations in the hard sciences," which they then pitch at a level that leads them to ask "[b]ut what difference does any of this make to the working linguist?" And yet, minimalist thinking really is different in ways that really do matter for what most linguists really do most of the time. The empowered version highlights this difference by providing explicit guidance for what is right and good in syntactic decision making, viz. conceptual arguments have pride of place, followed closely by purely theoretical considerations, with empirical analysis a laggard third. Indeed, empirical analyses on this view serve to provide "input grist" for the theoretical and conceptual mills; insofar as the goal is to show that what is possible is also necessary, empirical "arguments" are always just starting points. It might be held that this just is (a version of) weak/methodological minimalism; perhaps so, but calling it also "business as usual" is wishful thinking. Although both are "subservient to the strong thesis" (Martin and Uriagereka, 2000, p. 11), the crucial difference between the weak and the empowered theses is perhaps this: the weak thesis is a general methodological precept, while the empowered thesis directs us to examine our specific linguistic concepts and theories.

Before turning to examine a few examples of minimalist thinking wherein I think the third thesis is useful, there is a further conceptual clarification needed with respect to Martin and Uriagereka's two theses.

5.3.1.1   *A fine old conflict*

Martin and Uriagereka locate a conflict between their two theses – a conflict that I think is actually spurious. Martin and Uriagereka (2000, p. 11) write that "[w]hen the best theory happens not to match the best design, so much the worse for the best theory." This is the sort of surprising observation and turn of phrase that one could wish to have made oneself; having not done so, the only alternative is to impugn it. Martin and Uriagereka here are examining Chomsky's consistent rejection of the analysis of movement put forward by Lasnik and Saito (1984), "a grammar that allows back-and-forth movement" (Martin and Uriagereka, 2000, p. 10). They argue (2000, p. 10) that Chomsky's preferred alternatives are methodologically "costly" in that his "theory needs a new set of axioms," that empirically his proposals "have in fact been considerably less adequate," and that there is no clear and usable sense of *naturalness* which one can invoke to choose between the proposals. Instead, they conclude (2000, p. 11) that Chomsky has taken his position due to the strong thesis, which asks *"why language is that way,"* and that the Lasnik and Saito theory fails to address this issue in that it does not provide "a motivation for movement." This leads them to their admirably provocative slogan quoted directly above.

However, as noted, I do not think that there really is such a clash between their theses. Indeed, I think that there cannot be such a clash. It seems to me that the best way to understand the strong thesis is as an adequacy condition on *linguistic* theories; that is, as a piece of *specific* (linguistic) metatheory, while the weak thesis is a piece of *general* metatheory.[7] Understood this way, then, it simply is not possible in minimalist theorizing for the best theory not to match the best design, as being the best *linguistic* theory means (in part) adhering to the strong thesis. So, while it is true that a theory that is better in terms of general adequacy conditions may not be the better theory in terms of domain specific adequacy conditions, this should not cause surprise, alarm, or, sadly, memorable phrases. As one is pretty much free to choose such specific conditions as one's investigatory intuitions and hunches lead one to, in linguistics various specific metatheoretical conditions (e.g. explanatory adequacy, degree-of learnability, direct semantic interpretability, efficient parsability, etc.) have been used in just such a way.

All this may seem merely an instance of terminological quibbling. Martin and Uriagereka (and perhaps Chomsky before them) have chosen to apply "best theory" only in terms of general adequacy conditions on theory construction, while I have chosen to apply it in terms of domain specific adequacy conditions as well. I would claim, however, that once the distinctions and clarifications I urge are recognized, their choice appears both arbitrary and needlessly paradoxical.

5.3.2   *Empowered minimalist thinking*

Just before our little metatheory interregnum, I said we would examine some examples of minimalist thinking. It might be a friendly gesture to do so at this point. We shall look at *c-command* from Chomsky (2000, p. 116), *internal and external Merge* and *Adjuncts*, both from Chomsky (2001, pp. 7–8, 14–18). These even have phrase structural significance.

5.3.2.1   *C-command*

Chomsky (2001, p. 116) derives the crucial syntactic relation *c-command* from two more basic relations, *sisterhood* and *immediately contain*, by means of "the elementary operation of composition of relations." The basic relations themselves are direct results of the fundamental operation *Merge*, where Merge returns a new syntactic object $K(a,b)$ given input syntactic objects a and b. *Sisterhood* holds between a and b, while *immediately contains* holds of K and a, K and b, and K and K. Given these and the relation composing operation, "[a]pplying it in all possible ways, we derive three new relations: the transitive closure *contain* of *immediately contain*, *identity* (= sister(sister)), and *c-command* (= sister(contain))." Well, yes and no; we do get these derived relations, no doubt. But what about immediate contain(sister)=?, sister(immediate contain)=?, and contain(sister)=?; if we are indeed "applying it in all possible ways" then surely composition of relations gives us these derived relations, whatever they are, as well. And why should it stop there? Why not contain(sister(c-command(immediately contain(sister)))) and so forth? If these are not useful syntactic relations, we need to know why. The strong thesis, recall, requires us to ask "*why language is that way.*" Until and unless good minimalist reasons are given for why *just these* derived relations are syntactically potent, we have got, at best, nowhere in our minimalist inquiry into c-command.[8]

We will allow ourselves to get a little ahead of our otherwise severely linear presentation, and point out how this result is particularly significant in the unfolding argument that minimalist syntax is not phrase structural. C-command is arguably the central hierarchically (i.e. phrase structurally) defined predicate in syntax. It has been invoked in mediating a wide range of substantive syntactic relations, most notably those of anaphora. A failure to be straightforwardly and insightfully derived through minimalist thinking is precisely what we should expect were minimalist syntax not phrase structural, and it is a substantial failure, given c-command's presumed role in syntactic theory and analysis.[9]

I think this is an instance of how deontological minimalism helps us. We have been offered an appealingly simple and straightforward analysis of c-command that appears to flow smoothly from the bases of the approach. But, when we ask where the theoretical and conceptual sorters are for culling our specific relational wheat from the (possibly infinite) pile of relational chaff, we realize that we have none at all. And, indeed, even that such tools are required seems not to have been recognized. Now it is true that it is the strong thesis's *"why language is that way"* question that gives our objection its bite; but that is to be expected, as both the empowered and weak theses are "subservient" to the strong thesis, as noted above. Maybe the weak thesis would also lead to our questions; perhaps applying Ockham's Razor would require us to denounce relation composing as far too promiscuous an operation, allowing for unconstrained and unlimited couplings. But objecting to relation composing on account of its apparent libertinism seems to me to somewhat overshoot the mark, pushing theoretical abstemiousness from the prudent to the prudish. It is not that there is something somehow in principle wrong with all those (potential) relations; it is that we have not been given (the right sort of) reasons for picking out just those that we do in fact want and need. Such reasons are precisely what the empowered thesis, unlike the weak thesis, directs us to demand, which is why it is deontological, and not merely methodological.

5.3.2.2   *Merge*

In his analysis of *external* and *internal Merge* (e-Merge and i-Merge), Chomsky (2001, pp. 7–8) has put forward one of the most remarkable potential advances yet derived from minimalist thinking. He argues that given i-Merge, "displacement is not an 'imperfection' of language; its absence would be an imperfection" (2001, p. 8). This would answer one of the deeper conceptual objections that have been raised with respect to minimalism,[10] viz. why should such a theoretical architecture have any movement – more generally, any displacement – let alone show it in all languages?

The argument itself is stunning both in its conclusion and its brevity – this last not taking away from its force, while allowing us to repeat it in full.

> SMT [Chomsky's strong minimalist thesis – no aspects of the initial state of the language faculty are unexplained] entails that Merge of *a,b* is unconstrained, therefore either *external* or *internal*. Under external Merge, *a* and *b* are separate objects; under internal Merge, one is part of the other, and Merge yields the

property of "displacement," which is ubiquitous in language and must be captured in some manner in any theory. It is hard to think of a simpler approach
than allowing internal Merge (a "grammatical transformation"), an operation
that is freely available. Accordingly, displacement is not an "imperfection" of
language; its absence would be an imperfection.   (Chomsky, 2001, p. 8, emphasis
in original)

That an argument promises an unprecedented advance does not mean that it
can be afforded an uncritical acceptance. There are two interrelated questions
to be raised. The first, narrower, question has to do with the pair e-Merge and
i-Merge. The more general second question is about the necessity of any Merge.

   Chomsky (2001, p. 8) writes that "[t]here are two kinds of Merge (external
and internal) . . ." with different constraints on their respective operations, which
he goes on to investigate in hopes of showing "that the constraints are principled. . . ." Our first question is whether these two, e-Merge and i-Merge, are
on a par with one another. That is, can we determine that one of the pair has
some sort of priority, and, if so, what might this entail? Chomsky (2001, p. 5)
also assumes that lexical items "are 'atoms' . . . undergoing no internal tam-
pering in NS [narrow syntax] . . . understanding this to mean that there is no
feature movement and hence no 'modified lexical items' . . ." Given this, we
can see that e-Merge does have a kind of priority: with respect to lexical items,
i-Merge cannot apply. It follows, then, that i-Merge can only apply after e-
Merge has, e-Merge having created at least one (complex) syntactic object,
minimally from two (syntactified) lexical items. But so what? Well, we can
now see that e-Merge is *required* in a way that i-Merge is not: there would be
no derivations at all without e-Merge, but this is not true of i-Merge. And if e-
Merge is *necessary* for derivations, we can ask if it is also *sufficient* for (any)
derivations.

   Notice where either answer to this last question leads. If e-Merge is both
necessary and sufficient for *any* derivations, then we need to ask why it is
not sufficient for *all* derivations; that is, why is there also i-Merge? Suppose
instead that e-Merge is necessary for all derivations but not sufficient for any
derivations. Again, we need to ask why this should be so: why should the
minimally necessary operation not also be the *only* necessary operation – again,
why is there also i-Merge? That what we discover to be necessary should also
prove to be sufficient is one of the core tenets of minimalism. It tells us *"why
language is that way."*

   Chomsky (2001) has suggested a rationale for i-Merge in the displayed quote
above. I-Merge exists because we would have to limit Merge's domain in
order for there to be no i-Merge, and any such limitation would, presumably,
be an arbitrary stipulation. While not implausible, this is also unexamined.
This leads us directly to our second, more general, question about the necessity of any Merge at all.

   Merge exists in order that separate syntactic objects should become a single
syntactic object. But why should this be necessary? An odd question; but odd,
perhaps, in just the right way: it seems so obvious. Epstein et al. have help-
fully examined this obvious topic:

> Consider what we shall call the First Law: the largest syntactic object is the single phrase-structure tree. Interestingly, this hypothesis is so fundamental, it is usually left entirely implicit. . . . Informally, by the most fundamental definition of "syntax," there are no syntactic relations from one tree to another distinct tree; that is, the laws of syntax are "intra-tree" laws: X and Y can enter into syntactic relations only if they are in the same tree. (Epstein et al., 1998, p. 39)

So, Merge exists to create new, complex syntactic objects, the domain of "intra-tree" syntactic relations. Without Merge, distinct syntactic objects could not enter into syntactic relations. More bluntly: no Merge, no syntax. Or, more precisely: no *e-Merge*, no syntax. From the point of view of the First Law, which explains the need for (e-)Merge, i-Merge looks increasingly strange. Recall that "under external Merge, [*a*] and [*b*] [the Merged objects] are separate objects; under internal Merge, one is part of the other." But this fact about i-Merge means that its *a* and *b* are *already* parts of the same tree, they can (and do) already stand in syntactic relations to one another. So, the justification for Merge – the First Law – holds only for e-Merge, not for i-Merge; indeed, i-Merge now appears not merely unmotivated, but also redundant.

There is an evident reply to be made. Let us, at least for the sake of the argument, grant all the preceding objections. It is nonetheless still the case that i-Merge comes for free. Indeed, the case for it may even have been strengthened. We have seen that (e-)Merge is inevitable in minimalist syntax. Given that some kind of Merge is necessary, not to (also) have i-Merge would, as noted above, require adding stipulated limits on the operation's domain, apparently just to debar i-Merge. Moreover, if i-Merge, unlike e-Merge, is "unmotivated" with respect to the First Law – well, so what? Merge is "motivated," and i-Merge is just the further application of Merge to an output of e-Merge. And e-Merge, recall, has "priority." Why, then, should i-Merge need this – or any – further "motivation" of its own? As for i-Merge seeming "increasingly strange" and "redundant" when viewed from the First Law – well, why not? It is, let us not forget, *displacement* that i-Merge analyzes, and displacement is, despite its ubiquity, nonetheless an *odd* fact about human language:

> The "deep" (LF) properties [quasi-logical properties such as entailment and theta-structure] are of the general kind found in language-like systems; the "surface" properties [topic–comment, presupposition, focus, specificity, new/old information, agentive force, and others] appear to be specific to human language. If the distinction is real, we would expect to find that language design marks it in some systematic way – perhaps by the dislocation property, at least in part. (Chomsky, 2000, p. 121)

On this view, "[a]rgument structure is associated with external Merge (base structure); everything else [semantic] with internal Merge (derived structure)" (Chomsky, 2001, p. 8). That is, e-Merge, an operation that is necessary if there is going to be a single syntactic thing (the First Law), is how human language constructs objects to represent meaning relations common to various symbolic systems, while i-Merge, a free-rider on the required (e-)Merge, is how human language constructs objects to represent meaning relations specific to itself.

These correlations now seem less mysterious and arbitrary. I-merge is "internal": it is parasitic on e-Merge because it operates only on complex, purely syntactic objects, and the objects it builds represent meaning relations peculiar to human language. E-Merge, conversely, is "external": it has priority over i-Merge precisely because it necessarily operates on atomic, "interface" objects – lexical items – and the objects it builds represent meaning relations that other symbol systems also use.

Let us sum up. Chomsky's (2001) radical recasting of displacement from its usual role as spoiler to that of favorite son stands up very well under scrutiny. The scrutiny itself is motivated, once more, by our deontological minimalism. Guided, as always, by the strong thesis's question *"why language is that way,"* we sought conceptual and theoretical clarifications of and motivations for the choices made – and we found them. Again, it seems highly unlikely that something as general as Martin and Uriagereka's methodological minimalism would have rubbed our faces so directly and forcefully in such linguistics specific questions and answers. Our empowered minimalist thesis thus receives some further support; and, more importantly, so does what we might call the biggest minimalist result yet.

5.3.2.3   *Adjuncts*

Chomsky (2001, p. 15) suggests that there are two basic questions to ask about the phenomenon of Adjuncts (non-argument modifiers of a head):[11] "(1) Why does it exist?[12] (2) How does it work?" and observes that "[t]here has never, to my knowledge, been a really satisfactory theory of adjunction, and to construct one is no slight task."[13] He sets out to construct such a theory "starting from first principles."

The "central property of adjunction is that adjunction of [a] to [b] does not change the properties of [b]" (Chomsky, 2001, p. 16). Elaborating slightly, "[t]he construction is crucially asymmetric: if [a] is adjoined to [b], the construction behaves as if [a] isn't there apart from semantic interpretation . . . [b] retains all its properties, including its role in selection" (Chomsky, 2001, p. 15). Before examining Chomsky's answers to questions (1) and (2) about adjuncts, we might briefly look at a quirk in his general framing of the problem.

He writes (Chomsky, 2001, p. 15) that "it is an empirical fact that there is also an asymmetric operation of adjunction, which takes two objects [b] and [a] and forms the ordered pair [<a, b>], [a] adjoined to [b]." Now, if it is a fact that this is the correct way to characterize adjuncts, it is nonetheless still not a straightforwardly *empirical* fact. That there exist an *asymmetric operation* and an *ordered pair* are analytic claims made in a specific theoretical vocabulary. If it turns out that this is the best theoretical vocabulary and that these are correct analytic claims, then we would be justified in concluding that they are also facts, and we could call them "empirical facts." But we should be clear that they are highly theoretically mediated facts, unlike, say, "adjuncts iterate" which, while requiring commitment to "adjuncts," requires fewer and less specific theoretical commitments. So, while the claim put forward might turn out to be true, it is probably premature and needlessly tendentious.

Returning to question (1) about adjuncts, Chomsky (2001, pp. 15–16) speculates that they exist due to requirements of the conceptual–intentional interface, specifically that "an operation of predicate composition" may be required
by this interface, and that this is what adjunct structure, as opposed to either
of the sorts of structures built by e-Merge or by i-Merge, represents. This
answer to (1) is "a promissory note, given the limitations of understanding of
C-I [the conceptional–intentional interface], but not unreasonable."[14] At this
stage, there is not much more to be said about question (1) or this gesture at
answering it. So, we turn to question (2).

As pointed out directly above, Chomsky (2001) analyses adjuncts by means
of an asymmetric operation forming ordered pairs. This contrasts with Merge,
which is symmetric and forms binary sets. These sets are called *simple* syntactic
objects, and the respective operations are called pair-Merge and set-Merge;
"like other operations," pair-Merge applies cyclically (Chomsky, 2001, p. 15).
When pair-Merge applies to a and b, $<a,b>$ replaces the set-Merged b (2001,
p. 16). There is a further operation, SIMPL, which "converts [$<a,b>$] to [$\{a,b\}$]"
(2001, p. 17) – that is, into a simple syntactic object – and "is part of the
operation TRANSFER . . . , which transfers the NS [narrow syntax] derivation
(specifically, its last line) to both [PHI, the phonological component] and
[SIGMA, the semantic component]" (Chomsky, 2001, p. 16). After considering
some details of SIMPL, TRANSFER, and SPELL-OUT, and how Move might
apply to adjuncts, Chomsky (2001, p. 18) concludes, "we have the basic outlines of a theory of adjunction that satisfies SMT [his strong minimalist thesis
– no aspects of the initial state of the language faculty are unexplained]."
Perhaps so; but doubts, both specific and general, obtrude.

Let us begin with something specific. It is a basic fact about adjuncts that
they iterate. How is this to be accommodated? Where a is the adjunct and b is
the "host" (Chametzky, 1996, p. 87), we are to take b "to be in fact set-merged
in the standard way; adjunction then applies" and replaces b with $<a,b>$
(Chomsky, 2001, p. 16). But now, if there is c, also an adjunct with b the host,
how does the structure compose, given that b has been *replaced* by $<a,b>$? We
might suppose that $<a,b>$ functions as b, and c as a, but recall that b is "set-
merged in the standard way," and it is precisely the point of $<a,b>$ that it is *not*
set-Merged. So this fails. Presumably, then, c must pair-Merge directly with b.
But how can this be, given that b has been *replaced* by $<a,b>$ and that pair-
Merge applies cyclically? It seems that the available object $<a,b>$ is the incorrect sort, while the correct object b is unavailable.[15]

A possible route out is waved at by Chomsky:

> Given the basic properties of adjunction, we might intuitively think of [a] as
> attached to [b] on a separate plane, with [b] retaining all its properties on the
> "primary plane," the simple structure.   (Chomsky, 2001, p. 15)

This could afford the means of integrating multiple adjuncts with a single
host. The problem, evidently, is that replacing b with $<a,b>$ does not seem to
reconstruct the intuition that there are "separate planes," and we have been
given nothing else. Without something more to go on, it is quite difficult to

evaluate – or even really understand – what Chomsky is suggesting.[16] Despite this tantalizing aside, then, we still have to conclude that one of the basic facts about Adjuncts seems not merely unaccounted for, but positively precluded.

A second specific concerns c-command relations. Chomsky (2001, p. 16) asks "[w]hen X c-commands [<a,b>], does it also c-command [a] and [b]?" He says "no" for a and "yes" for b. His reasoning for b is that "[b] was introduced by set-Merge, and before [a] was adjoined to it, X c-commanded [b]." And as b does not in general lose any properties on account of serving as host to an adjunct a, so in particular it does not lose the property of being c-commanded by X. But wait: how could it be that X c-commanded b *before* the adjunct a was added, if pair-Merge applies cyclically? When X c-commands b, X and b must both be parts of a single syntactic object and X must be the sister of something which contains b.[17] And this entails that for a to be cyclically pair-Merged to b, it must be that a is pair-Merged before X is Merged – if X c-commands b, b is not available to serve as host for cyclic pair-Merge. Therefore, it is false that X c-commanded b before a was pair-Merged with b, and Chomsky's argument, which depends on this as a premise, fails. We now step back from these specific puzzles and problems to a more general concern, noting that such specific, technical failures are exactly what we should expect if there are also more general, theoretical/conceptual flaws as well (I am fond of this point; see Chametzky, 2000, pp. 29, 64, 128).

The most general concern is simply this. What is going on here anyway? We have a new, special purpose operation, pair-Merge, which creates a new sort of object, <a,b>, with purely stipulated properties (including the fact that <a,b> and not <b,a> is the new object – what possible difference could this make, given that the specific ordering plays no role?). Finally, we are given another *sui generis* operation, SIMPL, which *undoes* the results of pair-Merge.

If this is what a theory of adjuncts "that satisfies SMT" looks like, then it seems reasonable to conclude that there is no such thing. Given that "the construction behaves as if [a] isn't there apart from semantic interpretation" (Chomsky, 2001, p. 15) – that is, that *adjuncts have no syntax* – this is not such a far-fetched conclusion.

Indeed, I have reached it before (Chametzky, 2000, p. 141–5). I point out there that adjuncts are optional and argue that:

> Minimalist theorizing is about trying to discover and use only that which is necessary. There might be, then, a principled tension between the phenomenon of Adjuncts and minimalist theorizing. Adjuncts might be simply the wrong sort of things for there to be a minimalist theory of. Minimalist theorizing aims to employ only operations that cannot be avoided, operating on objects that are mandatory. Adjuncts are not mandatory, and the operation Merge simply assimilated them to the form of mandatory objects . . . , and the special nature of Adjuncts entirely disappeared.   (Chametzky, 2000, p. 142)

After briefly speculating about what a putatively minimalist theory of adjuncts might look like, I concede that what it does not look like is particularly minimalist (Chametzky, 2000, p. 142). I then conclude that "[t]he presupposition is that even if there is no direct minimalist theory of adjuncts, nevertheless Adjuncts should, somehow, be a part of the syntax. This might well be incorrect . . ." and that "[t]he issue . . . comes down, ultimately, to how and to what degree adjuncts need to be incorporated into the computational component (the syntax)" (Chametzky, 2000, pp. 142, 144). At present, there seems not to be any principled "how" and this correlates nicely with there not being any perceptible "degree."

I think that Chomsky's (2001) approach to Adjuncts leaves us pretty much where Chametzky (2000) did. What with its theoretical contortions and analytical arabesques, calling this a strongly minimalist theory of Adjuncts seems akin to suggesting that Procrustes had a strongly minimalist approach to a good night's sleep.

As in section 5.2.2.1 with c-command, so too here with Adjuncts: the lack of a satisfactory minimalist account suggests that minimalist syntax is not phrase structural. In this case, we have a case nearly complementary to that of c-command. "Adjunct," unlike "c-command," is not a structural predicate, but rather is a relational concept, one that comes from dependency syntax. Where with c-command the attempt was to extract something purely structural from a system that (we will claim) is not naturally structural, here the attempt is to reconstruct structurally something inherently relational in that same system. It might be a concern that we are trying to have it all ways: how can it be that failure with both structural and relational predicates supports the anti-PS argument? Who is playing Procrustes here anyway? But there need not be any concern. Our argument will be that the deep problem, the one from which both the c-command and adjunct failures stem, is trying to maintain syntax as phrase structural when minimalist thinking leads away from this conception. If this truly is the problem, then we cannot expect to discover either satisfactory minimalist reconstructions of relational concepts or satisfactory minimalist derivations of structural predicates within the preferred PS vocabulary.

As always in these investigations, our inquiry has been guided by our deontological minimalism. Once more, we have searched through specific conceptual and theoretical proposals, seeking to unearth justifications for and implications of these choices. What empowers the empowered minimalist thesis is, again, precisely its particularity in directing us to scrutinize specifically linguistic conceptual and theoretical arguments in light of the strong thesis's question as to *"why language is that way."*

We return now to some ideas on what minimalist syntax is, and how to do it.

5.3.3 *Derivation without representation: Epstein et al.*

Epstein et al. (1998) engage in the radical rethinking that minimalism expects. They propose that the only syntactically potent object is the *derivation*, "a partly ordered list (a 'quasi order') of successive application of the rules Merge and Move" (Epstein et al., pp. 13–14). Thus, there are no syntactic representations that play any role in syntax: no relations are defined on representations (e.g. c-command, government), no representations serve as input for post-syntactic interpretation or computation, and both semantic and phonological interpretation are "invasive to the syntax" – they proceed concurrently with each step in the syntactic derivation (Epstein et al., pp. 13–14). We shall not be concerned with what Epstein et al. do with these ideas, nor whether or to what degree they succeed.[18] Instead, we shall simply highlight a conceptual justification they offer for moving from the usual P&P approach to their rule-based, derivational approach. We do this because their conceptual move is such a beautiful example of the radical rethinking minimalism requires that anyone whom it does not excite, or at least impress, probably should not bother with minimalism at all.

> While the abandonment of rule systems and the adoption of principles . . . was an entirely natural development, there is an alternative . . . given that it was the language-specificity and construction-specificity of rules, and not the fact that they were rules *per se* that apparently threatened explanatory adequacy, an alternative to the postulation of principle-based theories of syntax is to retain a rule-based framework but to eliminate from the rules their language-particular and construction-particular formal properties. That is, instead of universal principles . . . , an alternative is to postulate universal rules. . . . Rules are then purged of all language-particular or construction-specific properties: apparent cross-linguistic differences are attributed, by hypothesis, to morphological variation that affects the possible application of those rules.   (Epstein et al., 1998, p. 20)

Epstein et al. here return to the most basic premise of P&P syntax, viz. that *principles* which apply to representations, not *rules*, are the best basis for theory construction in syntax. They then ask whether, despite its naturalness, this choice was the only possible one consistent with the metatheoretical condition of explanatory adequacy. They answer "no," and sketch out an alternative basis: "universal rules . . . purged of all language-particular or construction-specific properties." Now, this does not offer any reasons that one *should* do what they suggest, only that one *could* do so. While Epstein et al. (1998, pp. 11–12) do also offer such reasons, if, as it is said, *should* implies *can*, then the enabling argument has a conceptual priority. Until it can be shown that one can do X, there is not much point in wondering whether one ought to do X.

This is, I think, exemplary minimalist syntax. Holding fast to a domain specific metatheoretical condition (explanatory adequacy), Epstein et al. (re)examine a fundamental theoretical choice, and reject the received view – a fine example of the work the empowered minimalist thesis exhorts us to do. The specific choice Epstein et al. make entails eliminating enormous amounts of what had been standard issue P&P syntax (viz. representations and principles or filters defined on them), a bracing application of the weak minimalist thesis. Finally, their new architecture can claim to answer the strong thesis's question of *"why language is that way"* as well or better than anything else currently on offer.

Epstein et al. have provided one answer to the question of the relation of standard P&P syntax to minimalist syntax. We turn to more general reflection on this question in examining our last minimalist thinkers.

5.3.4   Guide for the perplexed: Epstein and Hornstein

Epstein and Hornstein (1999) provide some cogent, at times aphoristic, insights into the what and how of minimalist syntax. "Minimalism," they observe (Epstein and Hornstein, 1999, p. ix), "is anchored in the suspicion that at certain times and for certain purposes less can be more."[19] They argue that minimalist syntax "grows out of the perceived successes of the principles-and-parameters approach to explaining human grammatical competence" (1999, p. ix).

To put matters more tendentiously than is warranted:

> given that principles-and-parameters models "solve" Plato's problem, the paramount research issue becomes which of the conceivable principles-and-parameters models is best, and this issue is (in part) addressed using conventional (not uniquely linguistic) criteria for theory evaluation. (Epstein and Hornstein, 1999, p. xi)

This is particularly salutory for the following reason. Successful practitioners of P&P syntax might well be frustrated by minimalism: not only because "the distance between minimalist concerns and concrete analyses often [is] substantial" (Epstein and Hornstein, 1999, p. ix) – no small thing for the great run of analytically minded linguists – but also because it has been hard to discern the relation between the familiar P&P work they are accustomed to doing and the obscure minimalist work they are exhorted to do. Epstein and Hornstein here exhibit a missing link, and what they provide suggests that the route from P&P to minimalist work might be more akin to punctuated equilibrium than to evolutionary gradualism, hence the difficulties a successful P&P researcher might encounter.

Epstein and Hornstein, however, do not solely want to explain why minimalism might be so impracticable, they also want to suggest how minimalism might become more "do-able." So, they continue, while "[g]eneral precepts are all well and good" (1999, p. xi), rather more specific guidance is required from a research program in any particular domain. Epstein and Hornstein (1999, p. xi) then locate "two types of economy considerations" in minimalist syntax: "*methodological economy* . . . standard Occam's razor sorts of considerations" and "*linguistic economy* . . . [t]he idea is that locality conditions and well-formedness conditions reflect the fact that grammars are organized frugally to maximize resources." These economy considerations "promote a specific research strategy: look for the simplest theory whose structure-building operations and representations have a least effort flavor" (Epstein and Hornstein, 1999, p. xii). We can feel pretty comfortable with this, as it tracks our own discussion of Martin and Uriagereka's weak minimalist thesis and the proposed empowered minimalist thesis, though their *linguistic economy* is more specific in content than the latter, and so encourages a more focused, if narrower, range of inquiry.

Their overall evaluation of minimalism is that it "is especially exciting [in] that it brings new and seemingly fundamental questions to the fore . . . [while] . . . [i]t also allows old quesions to be reexamined in a new light" (Esptein and Hornstein, 1999, p. xviii). This seems just about right as a characterization of minimalist syntax, and so just about right as a moment to leave minimalist syntax as such.

We now have what was promised at the start: tolerably, and usably, clear shared understandings of *phrase structure* and of *minimalist syntax*. These allow us to go forward and, in Yogi Berra's formulation, take the fork in our particular road.

5.4   Not in my bare theory

It is a standard bit of beginning dramaturgical advice that you do not introduce a gun in Act One if it will not go off in or by Act Three. Well, we are at Act Three, so it is time to fire away. We begin by recapping the arguments from the Conclusion of Chametzky (2000). We move on to the new modus tollens argument, followed by a look at the work of Collins (2001) and Collins and Ura (2001). The Coda, section 5, suggests avenues the faithful might try for resurrecting PS in minimalism.

5.4.1   *It ain't necessarily PS: Chametzky (2000)*

There are two, brief, interrelated arguments in Chametzky (2000, pp. 158–60) that minimalist syntax is not phrase structural. One is directly about minimalism, and involves Merge. The other is somewhat indirect, and involves phrase structure rules. We begin with the first argument.

5.4.1.1   *It sure* looks *flat*

Chametzky (2000, pp. 127–9) contrasts Merge with *concatenation*.[20] A pair of seemingly oxymoronic, and antithetical, claims are made about concatenation: first, that it is "more minimal" than Merge, so that it ought to be preferred on conceptual grounds; second, that it is "too minimal" and so ought to be rejected on theoretical grounds. The crucial issue over which the battle is joined is whether or not sentences are hierarchically structured objects. If they are, "sticking strings next to one another to make a new, bigger string does not provide the means for analyzing sentences as hierarchicially structured objects" (Chametzky, 2000, p. 158). That is, if syntax is phrase structural, then concatenate cannot be the basic operation. In minimalist syntax, sentences are generally *assumed* to be phrase structural (or at least hierarchically organized).

Chametzky (2000, pp. 158–9) then makes the following argument. Suppose sentences are hierarchically structured objects. Suppose, too, (1) that minimalism is basically the right way to think about syntax, and (2) that we had always been thinking *minimalistically*, as it were. That is, suppose that we did not arrive at minimalist thinking after doing lots of the other kind, but had been doing it in syntax from whenever it is we declare syntactic thought to have begun. Now we have a problem. The analysis of sentences as hierarchically structured objects is not one that is, so to say, endogenous to minimalist syntax; rather, minimalist syntax inherits it from previous, wrong-headed ways to think about syntax. But we are now supposing that we never did syntax other than minimalistically, so there is no such inheritance to draw on. Without that bit of accumulated, but unearned, analytic capital, minimalist thinking will settle on concatenate as the basic syntactic operation, and so will get the nature of sentence structure irremediably wrong.

The problem here is really a rather deep one. The right sort of way to think about syntax *necessarily* gets wrong something absolutely fundamental, unless it is preceded by some thinking that is not of the right sort. That is, as minimalistically thinking analysts, in this case we *must* get off on the wrong foot and proceed down the garden path into a blind alley. "This strikes me, at least, as a singularly terrible thing for the right kind of theory to do" (Chametzky, 2000, p. 159).

Things are actually even worse than this. We do have the inherited finding that sentences are phrase structurally organized. Why, however, should we accept this result into our minimalistically constructed view? Well, because it is empirically (very) well motivated. Yes, but: such motivation is entirely *internal* to the old, wrong way of thinking about syntax. In general, why should we accept *any* result from the wrong sort of thinking that is not naturally derivable using the right sort of thinking? It is, afterall, part of what it is to be a *new* way of thinking that at least some of what went on before will not be carried over into the new regime. In our case, we can build in the result by stipulating that *Noahistic* (two-at-a-time) Merge (Chametzky, 2000, p. 129) is the basic operation, but this does not answer the strong thesis's question as to *"why language is that way."* "In other words, within [minimalism] the right conclusion might be that the assumption that sentences are hierarchically structured objects is not merely corrigible, but 'corriged'" (Chametzky, 2000, p. 159).[21]

5.4.1.2 *Rules, schmules?*

Standard P&P syntax has grievances with phrase structure rules (PSR) and seeks (with success) to eliminate them. The specific grievances are: PSR are (1) stipulative and (2) redundant. As to (1): "[s]tipulative: they simply *say* that this or that is the mother of these or those; they do not provide insight into or explanation of the mother/daughter relations they encode" (Chametzky, 2000, p. 159, emphasis in original). And as if that were not bad enough, they are also unnecessary, because of (2): "[r]edundant: combinatoric information they encode is already available in the lexical entries of lexical items" (Chametzky, 2000, p. 159). As stipulation and redundancy are "prime demons in the P&P anti-pantheon" (Chametzky, 2000, p. 159), PSR were exorcised.

But were PSR such completely maculate entities that nothing of value was lost with them? Despite their real and (eventually) evident blemishes, PSR did provide "a specific place/module/component of the grammar where generalizations about phrase structure could be *explicitly stated*" (Chametzky, 2000,

p. 159, emphasis in original). There are evidently two alternatives here. Either there are such generalizations, or there are not. If there are, then we seem to have lost something of significance. But now suppose that there are no true, significant generalizations of this sort.

> if there really are no such generalizations, what, exactly, is the point of phrase structure? . . . Consider: if there are no significant statements to be made in terms of phrasal categories and their constructional occurrences, why should we want our syntax to be built up and out of *precisely* these? Phrase structure theories are about the part/whole relation of constituency. Phrase structure rules allow for explicit statements about these relations, and the extraction and encoding of generalizations pertaining thereto. Getting rid of the phrase structure rules (for independent reasons) leads to the conclusion that there are no (worthwhile) such generalizations. And, as suggested, once you arrive here, the (not so?) obvious next step is to ask why think in terms of phrase structure at all, since the grammar does not let you talk about it.   (Chametzky, 2000, p. 160, emphasis in original)

The argument, then, is this. If P&P research is correct in demotivating PSR, then P&P also demotivated phrase structure itself, though this was not noticed. If P&P is wrong in demotivating PSR, then we might conclude that P&P in general was on very much the wrong path, as central aspects of the P&P research program are here implicated (viz. eschewing stipulation and redundancy). And here is where things get even more interesting, leading us back to the previous, minimalist argument against syntax being phrase structural.

We argued there that minimalist syntax inherits phrase structure, but does not give rise to it endogenously. The general problem is why and how something from the old, wrong way of thinking gets incorporated into the new, right way of thinking.[22] In this particular case, there did not seem to be any good reason or way. Now, however, "it seems that the old, wrong [way of thinking], properly understood, also demotivates phrase structure. Moreover, it is precisely those aspects of earlier P&P work that most create the lineage with [minimalist syntax] (viz. abhorrence of redundancy and stipulation) that provide the grounds for eliminating [PSR], and thus questioning phrase structure itself" (Chametzky, 2000, p. 160). So, it turns out that minimalist syntax need not inherit phrase structure from earlier P&P work: that work had its own, internal reasons to doubt that syntax was phrase structural. Moreover, those reasons are of precisely the sort that best carry over from earlier work into minimalist thinking, so our worry about how and why to naturalize old concepts into the new approach is largely allayed. Thus, our two arguments mutually support one another, each gaining plausibility in the context of the other.

We move now to the new modus tollens argument against PS.

5.4.2   *The modus tollens argument*

The argument has been outlined as (1) (repeated here) and previewed in section 5.1 above. We devote a subsection to discussing and motivating each of the two premises.

(1)I.   If there are Lexical Projections, then there are Functional Projections.

    II.   There are no Functional Projections.

    III.   Therefore, there are no Lexical Projections.

5.4.2.1 *From Wibbleton to Wobbleton: the Generalization Hypothesis*

The only conceptual or theoretical argument I am aware of for Premise I of (1) – what Chametzky (2000) ingeniously dubs the *Generalization Hypothesis* (GH) – comes from Chomsky (1986a, p. 3). Chomsky asks whether the system of categorial projection which regulates Lexical Categories, and its structural concomitants, "extend[s] to the nonlexical categories as well."[23] The answer he gives is "[e]vidently, the optimal hypothesis is that it does."

> The argument is familiar and not uncompelling: if there is a set of clear cases (in this instance, the Lexical Categories) for which we have a theoretical proposal, then the null hypothesis is that this carries over to less clear or central cases (Functional Categories), until and unless there develops strong evidence to the contrary. (Chametzky, 2000, p. 18)

There are a couple of points to discuss here. The first is why and in what sense lexical categories are the clear and central cases and functional categories the less clear and central cases. The second is the status of "the optimal hypothesis" in minimalist syntax.

The lexical versus functional distinction is a theoretical reconstruction of a more traditional distinction between "content words" – Nouns, Verbs, Adjectives, and (some) Prepositions – and "function words" – every/anything else. The problem which this reconstruction addresses is the following. Syntactic structure is not arbitrary – lexical items do not appear just anywhere – but "content words" can be idiosyncratic in their individual selectional requirements. P&P uses PS to solve this problem, because PS is "projected from the lexicon"; that is, PS is "a means of representing information carried by lexical items in their lexical entries, where this information is both the category of the lexical item itself and restrictions on its cooccurrence with other items or phrases" (Chametzky, 2000, p. 17). So, if the need is "to tame the (selectional) idiosyncrasies of individual lexical items" (Chametzky, 2000, p. 29), then it is no doubt necessary to begin with items which actually show such idiosyncrasies, viz. the "content words," theoretically reconstructed as the lexical categories. Thus, functional categories are less central because they do not carry in their lexical entries the sort of idiosyncratic cooccurrence information that creates the original problem which P&P addresses with PS.[24]

Now, what about GH, "the optimal hypothesis"? It seems pretty clear that it carries even more force within minimalist syntax. Minimalist thinking very strongly favors alternatives that are better on general methodological grounds (recall Martin and Uriagereka and Epstein and Hornstein). To reject GH, we would need to explain both why and how the optimal hypothesis did not answer the strong thesis's question *"why language is that way"* and why and how something less than optimal did. Put differently, we would need to explain why and how the optimal hypothesis was not really optimal afterall. This is an instance of Martin and Uriagereka's "best theory versus best design" conflict. While I have argued that there cannot be this sort of conflict, there nonetheless remains a (really hard) problem: answering the strong thesis's question with a theory/hypothesis that is less good on general methodological grounds. While surely not impossible, it is not what minimalist thinking expects.

It is probably a good idea to be very clear about what will not tell against GH: an argument that the theory elaborated for lexical categories does not carry over to functional categories. This is because GH is not an hypothesis about what *is*, but one about what *should be* – discovery that what should be in fact is not does not change the "normative" claim (no deriving *ought* from *is*). This is crucial to the modus tollens argument, because in the next section it is claimed that the lexical category theory does not carry over to functional categories. That finding, in combination with GH, is the modus tollens argument. We turn now to developing that claim.

5.4.2.2   *Yes, we have no functional projections*

In this subsection we first discuss Grimshaw (1991). This discussion (almost) gets us to our desired goal, Premise II of (1), the modus tollens argument. "(Almost)" because we first have to consider – and reject – the alternative theoretical architecture proposed by Lebeaux (1988) and taken up by Chametzky (2000), an architecture which suggests a possible way to side step the dilemma and conclusion reached in the Grimshaw discussion. With good minimalist reasons to refuse this wholly original and otherwise captivating proposal, we have our needed Premise.

ONLY PROJECT: GRIMSHAW (1991)

The fundamental relation which GH extends from lexical categories to functional categories is the *selection* relation. As we have hinted at above, there is something a bit odd about this extension: functional categories do not seem to have the sort of selectional powers and possibilities of lexical categories. Grimshaw (1991) develops these hints into a devastating critique of the generalization of selection from lexical to functional categories. Her conclusion is that "there is nothing substantive to the claim that the relationship between an F-head [functional category] and its complement is one of selection" (Grimshaw, 1991, p. 40). And that "[t]he character of the relationship between a functional head and its complement is quite dissimilar from that between a lexical head and its complement" (Grimshaw, 1991, p. 41). Viewing it as selection

> takes the combinatoric (im)possibility facts . . . [concerning Functional Categories] . . . as arbitrary facts. And it ignores the salient dissimilarities between the two cases; Grimshaw (1991, p. 40) cites the familiar facts that Functional Heads take only one category as a complement and that, as a result, there is little or no

lexical variation within Functional Categories with respect to complement categories. Further, it ignores what Grimshaw (1991, p. 40) calls the "stability" of the relations between Functional Heads and their complements "both within a language and cross-linguistically." Grimshaw cites as an example the fact that "C is always on top of I rather than vice versa . . ." Again, this is unexpected if the mechanisms in play are "isolated stipulations about what goes with what." (Chametzky, 2000, pp. 24–5)

Having successfully consigned selection by functional categories to the rubbish-bin of history, Grimshaw elaborates her alternative: *(extended) projection*. On her view, the respective complement relations between lexical categories and functional categories are regulated by disjoint systems: lexical categories by selection and functional categories by (extended) projection. Before we say anything about extended projection, we should pause and take note that we have moved about as far from the "optimal hypothesis" as possible. It is not that the system regulating lexical categories fails to completely carry over to functional categories, it is that it completely fails to carry over. Instead, we have two types of categories and two entirely distinct regulating systems; we might ask *"why language is that way."* Among other problems, extended projection does not answer this question. We have the makings of a dilemma here. On the one horn, we accept extended projection and find ourselves unable to address the fundamental minimalist question. Or, on the other, given its other problems, we reject extended projection and find ourselves without a theory of functional categories.

The other problems are detailed in Chametzky (2000, pp. 25–9), and are both conceptual/theoretical and technical. We will deal here with the former. The first problem is that Grimshaw incorporates non-categorial, relational information into syntactic categories. In addition to category features +/–N and +/–V and bar-level features, Grimshaw (1991, p. 3) introduces into syntactic categories a new feature, the ternary valued {F}(=Functional). Difference in {F} value does not make for a difference in syntactic category; only differences in the +/–N and +/–V features do that. It is, on the face of it, puzzling to include non-categorial information in syntactic category specification. Moving from the face to a full-body search, puzzlement gives way to enlightenment, of a sort, as we locate a disabling error. Grimshaw herself articulates {F}'s fatal flaw; naturally, she does not see it that way.

> The categorial theory which is the basis for extended projection makes explicit the hypothesis that a functional category is a relational entity. It is a functional category by virtue of its relationsip to a lexical category. Thus DP is not just a functional category, it is the functional category *for N*, as IP is *for V*.   (Grimshaw, 1991, p. 3, emphasis in orginal)

The problem with this is that Grimshaw is working with a PS based theory, and, as we have pointed out already in our brief discussion of *head* in Section 5.2 above, such a theory "can refer to a 'relational entity' only if it is definable in PS terms" (Chametzky, 2000, p. 26). Recall again, in this regard, the PS definitions of Subject and Object. Moreover, in PS syntax

to claim that syntactic entities are of identical syntactic category is to be committed to their having identical syntactic behavior. . . . There just is no other sort
of information in such an approach other than the syntactic category labels, based
in word classes, and the constituent structure positions of such category labels
. . . either the feature makes a categorial contribution, distinguishing subcategories,
or it is syntactically invisible and inert.   (Chametzky, 2000, p. 26)[25]

This does not mean that Grimshaw's observation about the relational nature
of functional categories is necessarily wrong. Who knows? – she might be
right. But a PS theory cannot accommodate the observation in the way she has
encoded it. Moreover, notice where this would leave us in our examination of
PS and minimalism. If Grimshaw's observation is correct, then syntax is not
(strictly) PS: it requires concepts that are apparently not reconstructable in the
vocabulary of PS syntax.[26] So, we have, potentially, another argument against
the phrase structural nature of syntax. However this may turn out, our point
here is that Grimshaw's own proposal is untenable, and we return to this
argument.

Grimshaw has proposed a theoretical change that is, I think, both unwit-
tingly enormous and enormously obscure, or, where not obscure, entirely
incoherent. Given this overall conceptual unsoundness, it is unsurprising
that there are also more technical problems as well. Chametzky (2000, pp. 27–
8) examines two, but we shall look at only one, the less purely technical of
them.[27]

The {F} feature is ternary vauled. However, it is not merely ternary valued.
It is notated with 0, 1, and 2, and this notation itself is crucial to Grimshaw's
proposal. Specifically, it is crucial for defining an extended projection that one {F}
value can be higher or lower than another {F} value (Grimshaw, 1991, pp. 3, 4).
But this is surely absurd. It cannot be right that "apparently deep linguistic
properties hinge on the vagaries of notation" (Chametzky, 2000, p. 27). Afterall,
one could easily enough notate a ternary feature with symbols on which no
ordering is defined (Chametzky, 2000, p. 27 offers "#, @, and $"). This is not a
merely technical issue, as it indicates seriously confused thinking: this is a
profound misclassification of the sort of problem that is being examined, and
thus of the sort of solution that is required.

We are now at the promised point of reckoning for GH. Grimshaw (1991)
dismantled any claim to plausibility that generalizing *selection* from lexical
to functional categories might have had. Chametzky (2000) undermined
Grimshaw's *projectionist* alternative. "As these approaches – one based in
selection, the other in projection – would seem to partition the ways in which
to carry out the generalization of structuralization from Lexical to Functional
Categories, the prospects for a theoretically contentful 'generalization' do not
look promising" (Chametzky, 2000, p. 29). This is where I would like to stop:
we have no possible theory of functional projections, hence no functional
projections,[28] which result combines with GH, Premise I, to entail that we have
no lexical projections, either. No lexical projections + no functional projections
= no phrasal projections = no phrase structure. However, as pointed out above

and in Section 5.1, Chametzky (2000, pp. 29–32) suggests that there may be a usable theory lurking in the work of Lebeaux (1988). So we have to go on a bit more, but I will try to make it brief.

(OPEN AND CLOSED) CLASS COLLABORATION: LEBEAUX (1988)

Lebeaux (1988) suggests building a syntactic theory and architecture on the basis of the distinction in the lexicon between lexical and functional categories.[29] Theory construction in sytnax is to be constrained by (3), the *General Congruence Principle* (Lebeaux, 1988, p. 65, his (37)).

(3)   General Congruence Principle:
      Levels of grammatical representation correspond to (the output of) acquisitional stages.

One such stage is that of "telegraphic speech" in which closed class items (functional categories) are absent, so given (3), there are separate representations comprising open class (lexical categories) and closed class (functional categories), respectively. Further, Theta relations are represented by the open class object and case relations are represented by the closed class object; that is, open class items license semantically and closed class items license syntactically. These distinct objects, with their distinct vocabularies and categories (Lebeaux, 1988, p. 242), are then composed into the single phrase marker for the entire sentence (Lebeaux, 1988, pp. 243–4), which allows for both the semantic (theta) and syntactic (case) licensing of all (meaningful) elements. Lebeaux (1988, p. 245) says that closed class items create "the frame into which the theta representation is projected." The difference between Lebeaux's approach and that represented by the GH, Grimshaw, and just about everyone else who has written on the subject is close to total.

> [Everyone else] takes Functional Elements to be part of the problem, when in fact they are a part of the solution. The problem, recall, is the systematic structuralization of the idiosyncratic (selectional) properties of Lexical (Open Class) items. Having made headway on this issue, the tradition extends – generalizes – its findings to Functional elements, despite the fact that there is no corresponding problem. (Chametzky, 2000, p. 32)

Putting aside questions of likeliness, attractiveness, and correctness, we can ask what to make of the ideas just sketched from within minimalist thinking. We can contrast Lebeaux's position on the relation between acquisition theory and data and more "internal" syntactic theory and data, viz. he does "not really differentiate between" them (Lebeaux, 1988, p. 6), and the position on this relation adumbrated in Chomsky (2000, p. 96). There is a very basic, very substantial conflict here. Chomsky proposes "the strongest minimalist thesis" (his (2)):

(4)   Language is an optimal solution to legibility conditions.

As explication of (4), Chomsky suggests that we

> [s]uppose that FL [faculty of language] satisfying legibility conditions in an optimal way satisfies all other empirical conditions too: acquisition, processing, neurology, language change, and so on. Then the language organ is a perfect solution to minimal design specifications. That is, a system that satisfies a very narrow subset of empirical conditions in an optimal way – those it must satisfy to be usable at all – turns out to satisfy all empirical conditions. Whatever is learned about other matters will not change the conclusions about FL. . . . information about other matters (sound-meaning connections, neurophysiology, etc.) may be helpful in practice – even indispensable – for discovering the nature of FL and its states. But it is irrelevant in principle.   (Chomsky, 2000, p. 96)

Much – perhaps most – of the distinctiveness of Lebeaux's proposal is found precisely in its interweaving of acquisitional and "purely syntactic" data in constructing and justifying a theoretical architecture. And as this is a matter of theoretical principle, not merely analytic practice, it directly contradicts the minimalist position delineated by Chomsky above. Adopting Lebeaux's theoretical architecture would then foreclose the possibility of discovering whether or not (4) is true. Lebeaux's position tacitly presupposes that anything like (4) is false, and goes on from there.

Presumably, this is enough to dissuade a committed minimalist from pursuing this avenue of inquiry. Nonetheless, it may be worth noting as well that Lebeaux's approach denies Chomsky's "optimal hypothesis" with respect to GH, and does so without providing insight into *"why language is that way."*[30] Further, Chametzky (2000, pp. 104–5) hazards the suggestion that Lebeaux's work might be combined with Kayne's (1994, p. 30) distinction between "intrinsically contentful" Heads and Heads "lacking intrinsic content" where this latter division cross-cuts the Lexical versus Functional Category taxonomy (Kayne proposes Functional Heads of both sorts). The idea is to identify, more or less, Lebeaux's Closed Class items with Kayne's "abstract functional heads" (those "lacking intrinsic content"). We thereby dissolve *Functional Category* as a theoretical kind. From the minimalist's vantage, the crucial point is that "[o]n this view . . . one of the principal properties of syntax is to introduce material [abstract functional heads, with no interface roles] that, from all other perspectives, is irrelevant and invisible. All this material does is support a purely phrase structural object in terms of purely phrase structural relations" (Chametzky, 2000, p. 105). Postulation of such "purely phrase structural" material is evidently out of step with "legibility driven" minimalist syntax. Granting that this speculation is not Lebeaux's (nor Kayne's), it nevertheless does grow out of a sympathetic, contemporary reading of Lebeaux (1988).[31] As noted, it is quite egregiously unminimalist in its postulation of "purely phrase structural" elements, and in this it adds to our mounting pile of disparately arrived at cases in which minimalist syntax and phrase structure do not well comport.[32]

SEZ YOU

I think we have fairly well accomplished our goal of motivating the premises, and therefore also the conclusion, of the modus tollens argument. The major problem with this sort of an argument, as I see it, is that it probably convinces no one. Bertrand Russell, I believe, said about philosophy something like: one starts with statements no one doubts, proceeds by means of reasoning no one questions, and arrives at conclusions no one accepts. As we are here doing theoretical linguistics, not philosophy, we cannot claim such strict apodicticity, but the overall sentiment seems apropos. We will move on now to another sort of argument that might be somewhat more convincing to linguists.

5.4.3   *Eliminative minimalism: Collins (2001) and Collins and Ura (2001)*

Collins (2001) and Collins and Ura (2001) arrive at our conclusion of non PS syntax quite independently of our investigations. What is in some ways most striking about these papers is their attempt to work within the general P&P-to-minimalism lineage while at the same time rejecting basic building blocks for P&P/minimalist analyses. The papers are, in fact, largely devoted not to theoretical/conceptual arguments for eliminating these basics, but rather, having done so, to sketching ways in which to deal with some central and obvious analytic problems that immediately arise. It is these demonstrations that relatively familiar sorts of analytic work are still possible which might seem more convincing to many linguists, but we will not here give much space to reviewing them, as our concerns are, as ever, conceptual/theoretical.

Collins (2001) represents a sort of half-way house on the road to PS-free living. It is useful for us to stop and look around, in part because what we see is that theoretically reconstructing the American Structuralists' IC analysis does not require (phrase level) labels – objects that were notably missing from the IC work itself.[33] Collins offers two arguments against labels. One is related to our PSR argument in section 5.4.1.2 above. He points out (2001, p. 2) that once PSR were eliminated for independent reasons, one of the core uses of labels had also vanished. The second argument is a minimalist one, in two steps.

The first step justifies forming constituents by means of Merge. "This operation is a necessary part of any theory of human grammar. It allows us to explain how grammar makes 'infinite use of finite means'" (Collins, 2001, p. 4). The second step argues that this is *all* that the need to make "infinite use of finite means" requires: "[t]he assumption that {V,{V,X}} is formed rather than {V,X} (that a label is chosen), goes way beyond what is necessary" (Collins, 2001, p. 4). As he notes (Collins, 2001, p. 6), a label-free syntax is "highly derivational" because "[l]abels are a part of a representation." And without the labels, there is less syntactic information in the representation and so correspondingly less syntactic work the representation can do. The resulting syntactic slack has to be taken up by "the interaction of economy conditions, the properties of individual lexical items . . . , and interface conditions" (Collins, 2001, p. 6).

The bulk of the paper outlines how to do labelless work in four areas: X-Bar theory, selection, Minimal Link Condition phenomena, and the PF interface. In working with such a theory, emphasis shifts from syntactic categories (and configurations) to syntactic relations: "In a theory without labels, it is necessary to be very specific about the elementary syntactic relations given below" (Collins, 2001, p. 40, his (45))

(5)a. Theta(X,ZP)   X assigns a theta-role to ZP
   b. EPP(X,ZP)   YP satisfies the EPP feature of X
   c. Agree(X,Y)   X matches Y, and Y values X
   d. Subcat (X,Y)   X subcategorizes for a feature

The need for this shift points to the instability of the label-free but constituent-bound theory. Once it is "the elementary syntactic relations" that are the motors for actual analyses, then it is probably only a matter of time before questions about the efficacy of constituent structure arise. And, indeed, following quickly after Collins (2001) came Collins and Ura (2001).

Collins and Ura (2001, p. 1, their (2)) propose (6) as their bases. Of (6a) they say it "is not controversial, and is shared by all theories of syntax, so the novelty evidently inheres to (6b). And, indeed, (6b) proscribes relata larger than the lexical item – most notably for us, the phrasal category.

(6)a. Syntactic operations create syntactic relations.
   b. Syntactic relations hold between X and Y where X and Y are either feature or lexical items.

In fact, we can get rather more basic than Collins and Ura do in explicating (6). We can note that minimalist thinking generally (1) takes lexical items composed of features to be what is given to syntax from the lexicon; and (2) that syntax works only with these. So far, nothing new. But if what syntax does is *exhausted* by (6a) – the creation of syntactic relations – then, in particular, what syntax cannot do is build new objects. Therefore, if syntax is limited to what it gets from the lexicon and to doing only what it must do if it is to do anything, then (6b) follows. This seems about as minimalist as one could hope for.

Collins and Ura (2001, p. 1) propose, accordingly, that the general syntactic operation is not Merge(X,Y) but Establish Rel(X,Y), where the establishable relations are those in (5) above.[34] "On this conception, a representation is a set of lexical items, and the relations between them" (Collins and Ura, 2001, p. 2). As they note (2001, p. 2), this view "is closely related to that of dependency-based grammars." They also claim (2001, p. 2) that "[t]he differences between our theory and Hudson's [Word Grammar – a dependency theory] far outweigh the similarities." Why or that this is so is unclear, and Collins and Ura point only to the "highly derivational" nature of their approach (Hudson's is not), leaving "to future work" further comparison. Whatever way this might finally turn out, Collins and Ura are clearly committed to seeing their work as part of the P&P-to-Minimalist Program lineage, and much of their project is to retain and reconstruct concepts and analyses from this lineage in their non PS based minimalism. In this, at least, they are surely very different from Hudson or other dependency theorists, who evidently have no such commitments.

Collins and Ura look at three presumably problematic areas for their PS-less syntax. One is "accessibility" – what lexical items are available to be "searched" for establishing/satisfying a syntactic relation; specifically, how to limit such search to something reasonable in some minimalist way. A second is linearization, viz. "Spell-Out" and the Linear Correspondence Axiom of Kayne (1994). Finally, they propose a search algorithm substitute for the structural predicate c-command (Collins and Ura, 2001, p. 13). They suggest "that the empirical effects of c-command can be derived from a search algorithm which is defined over syntactic relations."[35]

We will not look further at the details of these demonstration cases. This despite the already remarked on likelihood that many linguists doubtless find this amplifying analytic work more convincing (or at least more reassuring) than our constricted (some might say constipated) theoretical work. Instead, we shall simply emphasize that Collins and Ura outline a *postive program* for PS-free minimalist syntax, something we have not attempted to do. Their work and ours are then both convergent and complementary, with a conspicuous lack of overlap on other than their fundamental conclusion/hypothesis. I think these works provide substantial independent support and confirmation both of each other and of that fundamental conclusion/hypothesis, viz. that *minimalist syntax is not phrase structural*.

5.5   PS, I love you

Some may still not be totally convinced. They may firmly believe that syntax is phrase structural. They may strongly believe that there is too much empirical evidence in favor of PS for it to be jettisoned. They may actually believe that they *know* these things. They may even be right. To them, therefore, I offer two somewhat conciliatory, if not wildly attractive, options. One is that what we have argued above to the contrary notwithstanding, minimalist thinking can somehow accommodate and motivate phrase structural syntax. Plainly, I don't think this has much going for it, but that need not stop someone else from devoting some portion of their waking life to it. Second, and more confrontationally, is the alternative modus tollens (2) (repeated here), from section 5.1.[36]

(2)I.   If syntax is minimalist, then there is no phrase structure.
   II.   There *is* phrase structure.
   III.   Therefore, syntax is not minimalist.

Bon chance.

Notes

1   There is also a brief "concluding unscientific postscript," Section 5.
2   Chomsky argues that there are only basic syntactic objects translated from the lexicon, complex syntactic objects built from these by set-Merge (see below,

sections 3.2.2 and 3.2.3), and labels. All other "additional elements such as nodes, bars, primes, XP, subscripts and other indices, and so on" (Chomsky, 1995, p. 244) are such that "empirical evidence would be required to postulate [them]" (Chomsky, 1995, p. 245). See Chametzky (2000, pp. 150–1) for some discussion.

3   Gazdar and Pullum (1981), also observing this redundancy, go via the other route, getting rid of the subcategorization frames in their GPSG approach.

4   This requirement looms large in our discussion of Grimshaw (1991) in section 4.2.2.1 below.

5   This is also true of the the concept *adjunct*.

6   There are two books which ought to be discussed in this section, but, due to derelictions of duty on my part, they are not. The first is Uriagereka (1998). The second is Hornstein (2001).

I do not discuss Uriagereka (1998) because I had not read it before writing this chapter. It elaborates and extends, in spirited and quotable prose, the ideas adumbrated in Epstein and Hornstein (1999) (section 3.4 below). It consistently adverts to conceptual, theoretical, and methodological arguments in favor of its general project of eliminating rules of construal, making it an exemplar of minimalism in action. It shows, to paraphrase Levi-Strauss, that "minimali(ism)s are not good to eat, they are good to think."

7   See Chametzky (1996, pp. xvii–iii) on the distinctions among (general and specific) metatheoretical, theoretical, and analytic work.

8   Chomsky (2000, p. 146, fn. 67) refers to the derivational approach to c-command of Epstein et al. (1998). He notes that "[t]he derivational definition also raises some questions: in particular, why does 'containment' enter (i.e. why does X merged with Y c-command terms of Y)?" The same can now be asked of Chomsky (2000). I might also point out that this view of c-command is basically that of Richardson and Chametzky (1985) and Chametzky (1996). I discuss all this, and why the derivational approach fails, in Chametzky (in preparation).

9   Collins and Ura (2001) provide a minimalist, non-structural reconstruction of c-command. See below, section 4.3.

10 In, for example Chametzky (1996, pp. 158–60), Chametzky (2000, pp. 115–19).

11 Chomsky (2001) alternates between "adjunct" and "adjunction," but it is clear that throughout he is only discussing the former, never the latter, in the sense of the structure-building movement rule. I have flagged – and flogged – this distinction enough elsewhere (Chametzky, 1994; 1996; 2000).

12 To my knowledge, this is first asked in Chametzky (2000, p. 37, fn. 34; 65).

13 We might wonder which syntactic phenomenon does have "a really satisfactory theory"; regardless, I think Chametzky (1996, ch. 4; recapped in Chametzky, 2000, pp. 55–65) does pretty well at constructing a genuine and explanatory theory of adjunct(ion)s, from within pre-minimalist P&P assumptions.

14 See Chametzky (2000, p. 65) for similar speculation as well as argument that central properties of the syntax of adjuncts follow directly within the theory adumbrated there.

15 Or perhaps not: as noted above in the text, Chomsky (2001, p. 15) writes, "if [*a*] is adjoined to [*b*], the construction behaves as if [*a*] isn't there apart from semantic interpretation." So perhaps *b* remains available. But how? And what then is the point of constructing <*a*,*b*>? See the text below.

16 It has been proposed that coordination could be analyzed in something like what Chomsky seems to be indicating here, under the so-called "union-of-phrase-markers" or "three-dimensional" approach (Goodall, 1987). Now, it happens that Chametzky (1987) is by far the most exhaustive – at times exhausting – working

out of this idea, and Chametzky (1996) investigates its relation to adjuncts as well. So, if I do not know where to go with Chomsky's intuition, it's pretty hard to say who would.

17 In the old terminology, X is a sister of something which dominates *b* (dominance reflexive) (Chametzky, 1996).

18 As noted in note 3, I do not think they fully succeed; I give my reasons in Chametzky (in preparation).

19 Chametzky (2000, ch. 4) agrees.

20 Epstein et al. also talk about *concatenation*, but they do not use it "in the mathematical sense of the term as an operation on strings" (Epstein et al., 1998, p. 45, fn. 1) This is precisely how I use the term.

21 A minimalist thinker inclined to resist this line of argument would need a principled explanation for sentences being hierarchically structured. It seems this reason would likely be external to the syntax. Such a thinker might start with a look at Chametzky (1995, p. 175, 1996, pp. 16–17).

22 See Chametzky (2000, p. 145) on *naturalization*.

23 Chomsky (1986a) uses *nonlexical* for what have come to be called *functional* categories (Chametzky, 2000, p. 38, fn. 47).

24 More on this in Section 4.2.2.1, in the discussion of Grimshaw (1991).

25 Anyone worried about "bar-levels" need not be. Either they do not exist or they serve to distinguish subcategories (Chametzky, 2000, pp. 25–6).

26 Recall Postal's (1964) comments on Harris (1946, 1951) from Section 2.1 above.

27 The second involves the definitions of *perfect projections* and *extended projections*, and the work these do or do not do in accounting for the combinatoric (im)possibilities of Functional Categories. The details take us too far into Grimshaw (1991) and out of our own inquiries.

28 This might seem enthymematic, or at least a *little* fast – isn't there a difference between our not having any *theory of* X and there not *being any* X? Yes, certainly, in principle. But here (1) the text claims there is no *possible* theory of functional projections and (2) functional projections are surely theoretical entitites, so there being no theory of them really does seem to mean there is no *Dasein* there.

29 Lebeaux actually uses the terms *open class* and *closed class*.

30 It might be objected that all this is unfair to Lebeaux (1988), as it was written well before the advent of minimalism. True enough, and it is certainly open to any such objector to try and reformulate the insights of Lebeaux in ways consistent with minimalist strictures. I wish anyone well who tries.

31 See immediately previous note.

32 We might, probably should, take note here of Cann (2000). Cann outlines a view of the functional/lexical distinction that is so novel as to be difficult to adequately summarize or to fully grasp. On the one hand, Cann reviews purely linguistic evidence for the functional/lexical distinction, and finds that while there is strong evidence for it, "none of these linguistic characteristics is individually sufficient or uniquely necessary to determine whether a particular expression in some language is functional or lexical" (Cann, 2000, p. 50). On the other hand, Cann then turns to psycholinguistic evidence of three types that bears on the distinction: "language processing, patterns of aphasic breakdown, and language acquisition" (Cann, 2000, p. 51). He locates "an apparent contradiction between the categorial nature of the functional–lexical distinction implied by the psycholinguistic evidence and the noncategorial nature of the distinction implied by lack of definitional linguistic properties" (Cann, 2000, p. 57). Cann's resolution of this contradiction is to invoke (a version of) Chomsky's (1986b) *I-language* versus *E-language* distinction: "at the

level of E-language (the set of expressions, particularly basic experessions, that extensionally define a language), the [functional–lexical] distinction is categorial" (Cann, 2000, p. 58). Psycholinguistic investigation and evidence is, Cann says (2000, p. 58), "principally concerned with" E-language. Contrary to Chomsky and those who follow him, Cann (2000, p. 59) proposes that "[a]spects of E-language may determine certain aspects of grammaticality and interact with I-linguistic properties in interesting ways." The overall goal is a model that can "reconcile the apparently conflicting hypotheses about linguistic structure" that one gets "from psycholinguistic investigation and from the arguments of theoretical syntacticians" (Cann, 2000, p. 71). It is unclear whether this is at all compatible with minimalist syntax (Cann, 2000, pp. 70–1 believes it is), but it couldn't be further from Chomsky's (1986a) "optimal hypothesis" on GH. However, it does seem to have some conceptual connection with Lebeaux's views, in that it seeks to bring psycholinguistic evidence directly into "purely linguistic" research, and finds the means for doing so in the lexical versus functional category distinction. I forbear attempting further analysis or comment, as that would take us beyond my current understanding of Cann's program.

We should also mention Hudson (2000). Hudson, in part drawing on and converging with Cann, argues (2000, p. 9) that "the construct Functional Word Category (FWC) . . . is not justified." While Hudson is clear that "even if this conclusion is correct, it will still remain possible that some subword and position categories are functional [e.g. "the position category C"] . . . FWCs are part of the evidence that is normally adduced in support of the more abstract categories, so anything that casts doubt on the former must affect the credibility of the latter." For the minimalist champion of Functional Categories, then, there is no good news here, only the prospect of mitigating some bad news.

33   See McCawley (1982, pp. 1–3) on "linguistic package deals."
34   *Pace*, Collins (2001, p. 4), who, as noted above, holds that Merge "is a necessary part of any theory of human language."
35   In a brief comparision with Epstein et al. (1998), they note that the otherwise highly derivational approach of the latter nonetheless contains "a representational redundancy: there is a syntactic relation (EPP, Subcat, Theta, Agree) and in addition a constituent created by Merge" (Collins and Ura, 2001, p. 18). This is a telling point. See Chametzky (in preparation).
36   Paraphrasing Lady Bracknell, someone might suggest that while putting forward one such argument is a miscalculation, putting forward two looks like compulsiveness.

References

Borer, H. (1994). The projection of arguments. In E. Benedicto and J. Runner (eds.), *University of Massachusetts Occasional Papers 17* (pp. 19–48). Amherst: GLSA.

Cann, R. (2000). Functional versus lexical: a cognitive dichotomy. In R. Borsely (ed.), *Syntax and Semantics 32: The nature and function of syntactic categories* (pp. 37–78). San Diego: Academic Press.

Chametzky, R. (1987). *Coordination and the organization of a grammar*. PhD dissertation, University of Chicago.

Chametzky, R. (1994). Chomsky-adjunction. *Lingua*, 93(2), 245–64.

Chametzky, R. (1995). Dominance, precedence, and parameterization. *Lingua*, 96(2–3), 163–78.

Chametzky, R. (1996). *A Theory of Phrase Markers and the Extended Base*. Albany, NY: SUNY Press.

Chametzky, R. (2000). *Phrase Structure: From GB to Minimalism*. Oxford and Malden, MA: Blackwell.

Chametzky, R. (in preparation). If you build it, will they C-command? or, No derivation without representation: Comments on Epstein et al.'s *A Derivational Approach to Syntactic Relations*.

Chomsky, N. (1965). *Aspects of the Theory of Syntax*. Cambridge, MA: MIT Press.

Chomsky, N. (1986a). *Barriers*. Cambridge, MA: MIT Press.

Chomsky, N. (1986b). *Knowledge of Language*. New York: Praeger.

Chomsky, N. (1995). *The Minimalist Program*. Cambridge, MA: MIT Press.

Chomsky, N. (2000). Minimalist inquiries: the framework. In R. Martin, D. Michaels, and J. Uriagereka (eds.), *Step by Step* (pp. 89–155). Cambridge, MA: MIT Press.

Chomsky, N. (2001). *Beyond explanatory adequacy*. Unpublished manuscript, MIT.

Collins, C. (2001). *Eliminating labels*. Unpublished manuscript, Cornell.

Collins, C. and Ura, H. (2001). *Eliminating phrase structure*. Unpublished manuscript, Cornell & Kwansei Gakuin University.

Epstein, S. and Hornstein, N. (1999). Introduction. In S. Epstein and N. Hornstein (eds.), *Working Minimalism* (pp. ix–xvii). Cambridge, MA: MIT Press.

Epstein, S., Groat, E., Kawashima, R., and Kitahara, H. (1998). *A Derivational Approach to Syntactic Relations*. New York & Oxford: Oxford University Press.

Gazdar, G. and Pullum, G. (1981). Subcategorization, constituent order, and the notion Head. In M. Moortgat, H. v. D. Hulst, and T. Hoekstra (eds.), *The Scope of Lexical Rules* (pp. 107–23). Dordrecht: Foris.

Goodall, G. (1987). *Parallel Structures in Syntax*. Cambridge: Cambridge University Press.

Grimshaw, J. (1991). *Extended projection*. Unpublished manuscript, Rutgers University.

Harris, Z. (1946). From morpheme to utterance. Reprinted in M. Joos (ed.) (1957). *Readings in Linguistics* (pp. 142–53). New York: ACLS.

Harris, Z. (1951). *Methods in Structural Linguistics*. Chicago: University of Chicago Press.

Hornstein, N. (2001). *Move! A Minimalist Theory of Construal*. Oxford and Malden, MA: Blackwell.

Hudson, R. (2000). Grammar without functional categories. In R. Borsely (ed.), *Syntax & Semantics 32: The nature and function of syntactic categories* (pp. 7–35). San Diego, CA: Academic Press.

Kayne, R. (1994). *The Antisymmetry of Syntax*. Cambridge, MA: MIT Press.

Lasnik, H. and Saito, M. (1984). On the nature of proper government. *Linguistic Inquiry*, 15, 235–89.

Lebeaux, D. (1988). *Language acquisition and the form of the grammar*. PhD dissertation, University of Massachusetts, Amherst. Amherst: GLSA.

Martin, R. and Uriagereka, J. (2000). Introduction: Some possible foundations of the Minimalist Program. In R. Martin, D. Michaels, and J. Uriagereka (eds.), *Step by Step* (pp. 1–29). Cambridge, MA: MIT Press.

McCawley, J. (1982). *Thirty Million Theories of Grammar*. Chicago: University of Chicago Press.

Postal, P. (1964). *Constituent Structure*. Bloomington: Indiana University Research Center in Anthropology, Folklore, and Linguistics.

Richardson, J. and Chametzky, R. (1985). A string based reformulation of C-command. *NELS*, 15, 332–61.

Speas, M. (1990). *Phrase Structure in Natural Language*. Dordrecht: Kluwer Academic.

Stowell, T. (1981). *Origins of phrase structure*. PhD dissertation, MIT.

Uriagereka, J. (1998). *Rhyme & Reason*. Cambridge, MA: MIT Press.

Index

Brugger, G., 66n
Burzio, L., 67n

Cagri, I., 74n
Cann, R., 223n
case, 6, 14, 15, 18, 20, 21, 24, 41, 53, 68n,
    69n, 127, 135, 136, 148n, 217, 220
Castillo, J. C., 68n, 72n
c-command, 13, 27, 28, 30, 31, 40, 51, 52,
    58, 60, 96, 101, 107, 125–7, 134, 137,
    139, 146, 157, 193, 200, 201, 206–8,
    222n, 223n, 101
CED effects, 69n
chain, 29, 40, 69n, 104, 143–7
Chametzky, R., 192, 193, 194, 195, 197,
    200, 205, 206, 207, 210–16, 222n, 223n,
    224n
checking, 20, 31, 39, 71n, 161, 163, 164,
    165, 166, 183, 186, 189n
Chomsky, C., 70n
Chomsky, N., 2, 20, 23, 26, 38–40, 59,
    65n, 67n, 68n, 69n, 70n, 97, 101, 107,
    109, 113n, 116n, 117n, 118n, 125–8, 131,
    132, 135–40, 145, 147, 148n, 155, 163,
    178, 193, 195, 197, 199, 200–2, 204–7,
    213, 217, 218, 221n, 222n
Choueri, L., 76n
Cinque, G., 112, 186
clausemate, 132, 137, 147, 148n
clitic, 69n
closed class, 217
collective predicates, 71n
Collins, C., 194, 210, 219–21, 224n
commitative, 73n
comparative, 118n
complement, 108, 192
computability, 196
Comrie, B., 70n
concatenation, 210, 223n
concessive, 182
Condition A, 97
conditional, 182
conjunct, 90, 91
construal, 11, 52
constructions, 208
content words, 213
context free, 196
contraction, 20–2
control, 3, 6, 129–31, 143, 145, 148n, 149n
control shift, 36, 37, 70n, 71n
Cooper, R., 114n

coordinate structure constraint, 115n, 116n
coordinate structure constraint, 90–2
copy theory of movement, 4, 31, 64n,
    66n, 100–3, 108–10, 113, 117n, 140, 144,
    146, 147
copying, 39
coreference, 72n
corpus analysis, 176
covert movement, 2, 87, 89, 92, 103, 109,
    118n, 127
CP recursion, 178
Cresti, D., 112
crossover, 61–3, 115n, 125
Culicover, P., 73n
cycle, 101, 115n, 118n, 205, 206

Dahl, O., 169
Danish, 153–6, 169, 171, 178–80, 184, 187n
dative, 100
daughter, 211
de se interpretation 14, 27, 28, 32, 36, 44,
    58, 62, 63, 68n
deep structure, 23
definite description, 111
definiteness, 183
deictic, 75n, 76n
deleted VP, 93
deletion, 66n
den Dikken, M., 127–9
deontological minimalism, 198, 201
dependency theory, 220
derivation, 3, 29, 31, 69n, 70n, 104, 112,
    134, 136, 139, 149n, 207, 219
derivational theory of complexity, 2
determiner replacement, 144
dialects, 188n
Diesing, M., 116n, 149n, 164
direct object, 196
distributed morphology, 187n
do support, 86
dominance, 223n
double base hypothesis, 180
Drury, J. E., 68n, 72n
d-structure, 3, 6, 7, 9, 10, 22, 64n, 67n,
    125, 126, 133, 135, 139
Dummett, M., 114n
Dutch, 164, 187n

eclectic interpretation of PRO, 26
economy, 4, 52, 69n, 152, 154, 164, 186,
    198, 209

Weinberg, A., 139
Weyhe, E., 167, 169, 174
wh movement, 24, 103, 104, 107, 117n, 118n, 127, 138, 140
wh-phrase, 96, 139
Wilder, C., 92, 119n
Williams, E., 45, 46, 65n, 68n, 74n, 101, 106, 115n, 118n
Williams' generalization, 106, 107, 118n

Witkós, J., 70n
Wurmbrand, S., 66n

X' theory, 164, 186, 192, 195, 196, 198, 223n

Yiddish, 180

Zwart, C. J. W., 115n